All the Pretty Things is a transparent journey into the heart of a little girl whose broken father is her hero. I haven't read a memoir like this since *The Glass Castle*. It takes you to the hard places, and those places bring you home. Highly recommended.

EMILY T. WIERENGA
Founder of The Lulu Tree and author of *Atlas Girl* and *Making It Home*

A bittersweet mix of crushing heartbreak and wry humor, Edie's story captured me the very first page and didn't let go. An honest and unapologetic look at the reality of growing up amidst poverty and alcoholism in East Tennessee, *All the Pretty Things* is ultimately a story of redemption we can all relate to—and one we all need to read. I literally couldn't put it down. If you only read one book this year, let this be it!

RUTH SOUKUP
New York Times bestselling author of *Living Well, Spending Less* and *Unstuffed*

Edie Wadsworth is an observer of people, a lover of words, and a masterful storyteller. All those qualities converge to make *All the Pretty Things* one of the best memoirs I've ever read. I sat down with the intention of reading the first few chapters and looked up hours later to realize I'd finished the entire thing. And her story, her people, and her heart stayed with me for days afterward. You will find yourself alternately cheering, laughing out loud, and crying, but I guarantee you won't be able to walk away unmoved.

MELANIE SHANKLE
New York Times bestselling author of *Nobody's Cuter Than You*

Part Southern gothic, Part C. S. Lewis, part pure poetry, *All the Pretty Things* is one of those books that will stay with me for a long time. Beautiful, heartbreaking, redemptive. I knew going into it that I'd be captivated by Edie's story, but what I didn't expect is how much I'd fall in love with her people. Her affection for those people, in the midst of heartache and hardship and hilarity and everything in between, makes the already vivid images in this book just flat-out leap off the page. Now that I've finished reading it, I'm more awed by the author—and the Author of it all—than ever before. You will be too. Don't miss it.

SOPHIE HUDSON
Author of *Giddy Up, Eunice* and *Home Is Where My People Are*

The most beautiful things are born in pressure and birthed through pain. Pain is the silent author behind thousands of great stories and songs. Edie's story is born of pain and rejection—it is raw-throated and broken open; it is fragile and strong and bright. It is ten thousand fireflies dancing over a Tennessee field. And Edie is masterful in the telling. Read this book—but more than that, open your soul and let this book read you.

JOHN SOWERS
Author of *Heroic Path*

Edie's memoir is a rare gem in this world of books, one where I actually felt like I was growing up right alongside her. You will laugh and cry and cheer and be dismayed. Her storytelling is gripping, and it is easy to find ourselves in her shoes, looking for all the pretty things in this harsh world as we live each day, putting one foot in front of the other. The pinnacle of this piece of art are her encounters with the fiery pursuit of God—the same relentless pursuit He uses to come after you and me, no matter how we try to burn it all down.

BRI McKOY
Writer at OurSavoryLife.com, speaker, leader of Compassion Bloggers

Through Edie's blog we've come to know her as a gracious, joyful soul with a passion for loving and serving others. Now within these pages we meet the innocent little girl who loved with a brave fierceness, and we champion her on as she gracefully walks through fire time and time again. We cheer alongside the perpetual cheerleader as she dusts off the ashes and holds forth with an open, hospitable hand a crown of beauty adorned with all the pretty things.

PAIGE KNUDSEN
Lifestyle and portrait photographer and blogger

Edie Wadsworth drops the needle on her life's record and lets it play. The result is a vernacular collection of moments both beautiful and terrible; in other words, intensely human. Each reader will hear it a bit differently, but I was struck by two constant refrains: The Father will never forsake us, and there's something hauntingly precious about a daddy. Thanks, Edie.

JOHN D. BLASÉ
Poet and author

I looked forward to reading Edie's memoir from the day I learned she was writing it. In *All the Pretty Things*, she shares the story of her impoverished childhood in the Appalachian foothills of Tennessee with truth and vulnerability, weaving together feelings common to childhood with experiences unique to her situation. You'll ache for Edie as a little girl, starved both for food and the time and attention of the daddy she adores. The desire for a father's love and approval doesn't decrease with time and age, as Edie learns through the struggle and striving of her teen and adult years.

All the Pretty Things is a reflection on the importance of family and the sacred duty of parent to child; the hunger for an earthly father that sometimes only our heavenly Father can fulfill; and the truth that earthly riches are no guarantee of happiness—and how easily they can all go up in smoke.

DAWN CAMP
Editor and photographer of *The Gift of Friendship*

Within twenty-four hours of receiving Edie's book, I had read it from cover to cover. She warmly drew me into her story with her Southern charm and wit, and yet pierced my heart with the painful childhood memories of personal wounds left on her by her father. I was in awe of her strength throughout her struggles that would have left most of us in a crumpled up mess. Her story is one of enduring, hopeful love of a little girl for her earthly father, and the relentless, redemptive love of a heavenly Father for his beloved daughter.

TRACI HUTCHERSON
CEO and Founder, Beneath My Heart

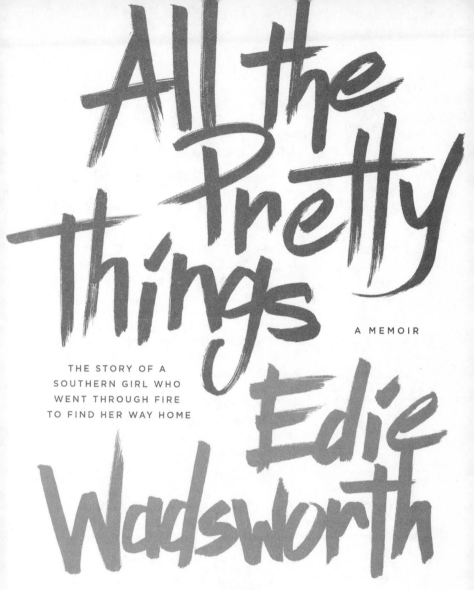

All the Pretty Things

A MEMOIR

THE STORY OF A
SOUTHERN GIRL WHO
WENT THROUGH FIRE
TO FIND HER WAY HOME

Edie Wadsworth

TYNDALE®
MOMENTUM

An Imprint of
Tyndale House Publishers, Inc.

Visit Tyndale online at www.tyndale.com.

Visit Tyndale Momentum online at www.tyndalemomentum.com.

Tyndale Momentum and the Tyndale Momentum logo are registered trademarks of Tyndale House Publishers, Inc. Tyndale Momentum is an imprint of Tyndale House Publishers, Inc.

All the Pretty Things: The Story of a Southern Girl Who Went through Fire to Find Her Way Home

Designed by Jennifer Phelps

Edited by Bonne Steffen

Published in association with the literary agency of The Blythe Daniel Agency, P.O. Box 64197, Colorado Springs, CO 80962-4197.

The stories in this book are about real people and real events, but some names have been omitted or changed for the privacy of the individuals involved. Dialogue has been recreated to the author's best recollection.

Library of Congress Cataloging-in-Publication Data

Names: Wadsworth, Edie, author.
Title: All the pretty things : the story of a southern girl who went through fire to find her way home / Edie Wadsworth.
Description: Carol Stream, IL : Tyndale House Publishers, Inc., 2016. | Includes bibliographical references.
Identifiers: LCCN 2016020194 | ISBN 9781496403384 (sc)
Subjects: LCSH: Wadsworth, Edie. | Christian converts—United States—Biography. | Fathers and daughters—United States—Biography. | Children of alcoholics—United States—Biography.
Classification: LCC BV4935.W23 A3 2016 | DDC 277.3/083092 [B] —dc23 LC record available at https://lccn.loc.gov/2016020194

Printed in the United States of America

22   21   20   19   18   17   16
7   6   5   4   3   2

This book is for Daddy, my first love,
and for Mama, my first light.
Being your daughter has been God's grace to me.

And for my children—
Taylor, Caiti, Emme, Elea, Malachi, Savannah,
Marcus, Nick, and Thomas.
You have been my miracle, my life's richest blessing.

Daddy and me

All things of grace and beauty such that one holds them
to one's heart have a common provenance in pain.
Their birth in grief and ashes.

CORMAC MCCARTHY, *THE ROAD*

CONTENTS

ON JANUARY 4, 2016, my forty-sixth birthday, I am standing on the precipice of Cherokee Bluff, staring down into the cold waters of the Tennessee River. My sister, my cousin, and I, accompanied by our girls, have hiked (in not-so-appropriate shoes) a mile out to see the bluff, as a sort of memorial to Daddy, the man who gave us a life of equal parts blessing and curse.

With the winter wind howling, we cinch up our coats, laughing most of the way, and keep climbing until we reach the infamous spot a relative recently told us about—the place where Daddy pushed a blue Malibu right off the cliff nearly forty years ago. It says so much about our family that this story has just surfaced, not considered even remotely bizarre enough to count of as one of the "greatest hits" we've been recounting to each other over the years.

While the bare branches of the dogwoods flail in the frigid gust, I sit down on a rock and dangle my feet over the edge, imagining all the stories that lay cold and swallowed up by the river below, all the pretty things that lay rusted and buried beneath silt and debris.

I think about the book I am writing, the book about Daddy and me.

It's the story I never wanted to tell.

It's the story I've been trying to run from for forty years and the story I've been skirting around for nearly three as I wrote. The words in these pages are all raw and fresh and hard-fought. What I don't want to write about is the thing that scares me to death. What I don't want you to know is that fatherlessness is my deepest ache, and being untethered and unspoken for is my suffocating fear. These are the memories that have wrecked me for far too long.

Above all, this is the story of my homecoming; the demons that are always holding me back and the legions of angels that keep me safe along the way; the way everything was always falling apart and the beautiful ways God has been piecing it back together; the dark and lonely parts and the parts where God dazzled me with His light shining deep into my heart; the way I was always trying to hide and the way He never stopped finding me.

A sliver of sun is now warming the edge of my face. I stand back up, peering down over the edge of the rocky outcroppings. The view is stunningly beautiful, but fierce and dangerous, too, as the wind whips the river into swirling motion. Standing there, at the top of that drop-off, I think of you, my reader. I imagine that you and I and a multitude of our sisters are huddled together at the edge of the bluff, wondering what it'd be like to jump, to live our lives from the deep end, unafraid to be jolted awake from the sleepy lies we've believed about who we are and what we were created to do. I look around and see courage on your face, bravery in your eyes.

In my mind, I take a running start and leap wild off the edge, arms and legs flailing against the free fall, splashing into the deep blue river. For what seems like a long time, I am underwater and everything is in slow motion. But then I spring up toward the light—that same light that is always calling me home. Breaking the surface, I gasp and choke, and then I cry—sob, even—surprised and thankful that I am still alive, that I have breath. Tears turn to laughter as I yell back up to you who are still poised on the edge of the precipice, "Come on, my sister. Don't wait until you're not afraid—jump scared."

This book is my cliff jump.

I pray it will lead you to your deepest bravery, your most vulnerable self, knowing that your Father who has baptized you with water and blood and fire will turn your sorrow to joy, your suffering to gifts of grace, your terrifying deep waters into soul-quenching cisterns that refresh us all as we walk through fire, together toward home.

See you soon, dear sister.

I'll be waiting for you in the deep end.

XOXO,
edie

P.S. I changed a few names and left out portions of my life that were not pertinent to this story. I also left out a few tender memories, sometimes to protect others and sometimes to protect myself. Some wounds take their slow time healing, so I chose to hold them close to my heart. I know you'll understand.

P.P.S. Sometimes the only tangible thing I had of Daddy's was the music he played when we were together, music from a different time, almost a different world. So I've used his favorite country songs—along with some favorites of my own—as chapter titles. I hope they'll make you smile. Maybe you'll find yourself humming a few notes as you go along.

RING OF FIRE

I DON'T KNOW HOW OLD I was the night the trailer burned down—or if the rumor was true that Daddy was the one who set it on fire.

What I do remember is cracking open the back bedroom door of the single-wide trailer just the tiniest sliver and poking my nose through to see why everything had gone so quiet inside. I could see beyond the living room to the yellow porch light that was swarming with moths. And I could see the outline of Daddy's face.

I nudged my head out farther but still couldn't tell what he was doing, maybe just fumbling for another bottle of beer in the Styrofoam cooler set by the front door. Out of the corner of my eye, I spotted the needle lowering on the record player to start another twangy country song.

I shrugged my shoulders and shut the door with a thud.

"I don't know what they're doin', but they went outside on the porch for something," I said to Sister and Jamie.

I hadn't started school yet, and my sister, Gina, was sixteen months younger. Our cousin Jamie was four years older than me, and it was always a treat when Daddy brought us to visit her on a Saturday night.

Jamie lived in Rockford, a little town south of Knoxville, Tennessee, with her mother and stepdad—my aunt Glenda, who was Daddy's closest sister, and her husband, George. They lived in a trailer park called Rocky Branch, just down the road a piece from Aunt Glenda and Daddy's mother, Mamaw.

We'd paused our game so I could check on Daddy, like I always did. When my mama was working nights at Genie's Bar, Daddy had a tendency to get himself into trouble, so from as early as I can remember, I put myself in charge of making sure he was okay. He rarely was.

His presence usually meant there'd be drinking and loud music, since Daddy's inclination was to turn every kitchen into a certifiable honky-tonk. Through the wall, I heard the raspy voice of Tammy Wynette, so all seemed right with the world again. I knew that the adults would soon begin dancing around the kitchen or out on the front porch, smoking Winston cigarettes and clanking their bottles of beer while they jigged.

Daddy was always shirtless and half-lit, leading the drunken parade and hollering "Woo, doggies!" whenever the pure joy of it all hit him just right.

"Okay, let's start over then," Jamie said to my sister and me, always keeping us on track with our games. She had us corralled in the back bedroom to play *Bonanza*, our version of house inspired by the Cartwright family in the popular seventies television show.

"Gina, you play like Hoss is just coming home," Jamie said, ushering Sister over to the corner of the room that we designated the kitchen.

"I'll be married to Little Joe again, and Edie, you'll be married to Adam. Gina, you're living with Hoss, and we'll play like he's just come home drunk, wanting you to fix him some breakfast."

"Why do I always have to be married to Hoss?" Sister complained. "He's mean, and I don't like fixing breakfast."

"You're the youngest and you have to do what we say, and besides, fixing breakfast ain't that hard and he ain't that mean," Jamie declared.

Being the oldest, Jamie always got to be Little Joe's wife, he being the most handsome and respectable of the Cartwright brothers. As Adam's wife, I was treated well too. Although I didn't think he was as handsome as Little Joe, he never came home drunk trying to pick a fight.

In our game, Hoss seemed to be a composite character of all the worst men in our lives, a character who pretty much embodied some of Daddy's kinfolks. He was always pushing Sister down on the bed, cussing her out, busting out the windows, or making her cook scrambled eggs for him in the middle of the night—like we'd seen some of the men in our family do.

"Play like Hoss is throwing his work boots at you, Sister."

"I don't want him to throw his work boots," Sister said, sitting down on the bed with her arms folded in rebellion.

Just as Jamie picked up Uncle George's boots to throw them across the room, we heard Daddy yelling.

"Girls, hurry up and get in the car! We gotta blow this joint!"

I grabbed Sister's hand as the three of us bolted from the back room out the front door. We dodged empty beer bottles on the floor and ran by the record player, which was still blaring. The next thing I remember, I was standing outside, staring at the other end of the trailer, trying to figure out why everybody was leaving so quick.

Daddy herded us into the backseat of his white Plymouth, us girls still wondering what was causing the commotion. It was a crisp spring night, and we watched the tree swallows swarming around the power lines looking for a place to land. With the windows down, I could hear Tammy still twanging out her last song as Daddy shifted the car into drive and we began to move. Through the back window, it looked like flames were shooting out of the other end of the trailer, and I began to worry over what was going on.

"Daddy, what's wrong? Did something happen to the trailer?" I said, on the verge of tears as I always was when things went south, which they had a way of doing when he was around. Jamie went quiet, like she usually did when things got crazy, and Sister was oblivious, leaning her head on my shoulder.

"Nothin'. We're going up to your mamaw's," he said, wiping from his forehead the sweat that was rolling toward his eyes.

Mamaw's trailer sat on the side of Brown's Mountain and was the official gathering place in good times and bad for the clan— a group of un- and underemployed relatives, subsisting largely on government checks, government peanut butter, and huge yellow blocks of government cheese.

All the way to Mamaw's I worried about the trailer and especially about the Tammy Wynette album that I loved more than anything. Jamie and Sister remained silent beside me, staring out the window.

I was sniveling when Daddy turned onto Mamaw's steep dirt driveway, careening over the washed-out ruts and bringing us in on two wheels, with us kids bouncing up and down in the backseat like whack-a-moles.

At the top of the hill, Daddy hit the brakes, put his arm over the seat, and looked back at me. "Listen here, Nise. Don't start squawlin'; there ain't nothin' to cry over. Bad things happen and there ain't no way you can make it better by going on about it." Daddy nearly always called me by a shortened version of my middle name, Denise.

Daddy was right—bad things did happen—and I tried my best not to get worked up over it. But all the country records I loved were in the trailer, along with all the pretty things Jamie's daddy bought her when he won a card game, which would eventually make it to Sister and me as hand-me-downs.

And why were all the grownups acting so funny? Daddy was wrong when he said there was nothing to cry over.

I rubbed my eyes and dried my hands on my dirty navy turtleneck and plaid polyester pants that were two inches too short, quietly asking Daddy, "Can we call Mama and tell her?"

Mama and Daddy were divorced, and Mama didn't like it when Daddy took us places he shouldn't or when bad things happened because he was drinking.

"Listen, Nise, ain't nobody hurt and ain't nobody crying but you," Daddy said as we walked up to the porch, his gait not quite as steady as it ought to have been.

Daddy didn't call Mama. He marched us up the porch steps in single file like soldiers going to war and pushed through the screen door to a trailer full of relatives. Papaw was in the corner strumming some Hank Williams song on his flat top guitar with his head down and his eyes closed. Uncle Gene, Daddy's brother, was nearly passed out over the arm of the couch. Daddy's sisters were there, too, as well as the fire victims, Aunt Glenda and Uncle George. Before long it felt like a regular old family reunion. Daddy told Mamaw to make a pot of coffee, which was always the answer to a family crisis.

Within a half hour, most of the clan was crowded around a table in the tiny kitchen and the adults were telling stories, like they always did when they gathered, Daddy's version, of course, being the most interesting and the most likely to be embellished. I glanced up at the wall where the oversized wooden fork and spoon hung slightly crooked, which reminded me I was hungry.

"Daddy, I'm starving," I said, peering around the television. I was trying not to listen too closely to what was being said, afraid I might hear things I shouldn't. I let it all become a jumble of noise.

"Daddy, did you hear me?" I said, walking up to tap him on the shoulder.

He gave a sort of nod, but after a few more futile attempts to get his attention, I gave up and crawled up on the couch in the living room. It felt like something heavy was crushing me as I agonized over things too complicated for a child to process. A strange sensation came over me and my eyes began to water.

It was as if I were floating above the room looking down on everyone. I could see their mouths moving amid the cacophony of voices, but the sound seemed to come from a million miles away.

Mama's finishing her shift at Genie's Bar right about now, I thought. *I wish she was here with me.* Daddy said nobody was hurt and there was nothing to tell her, and maybe he was right. But everything seemed better when she was around.

Sister and Jamie disappeared into the bedroom, but I stayed on the couch, hoping someone would fix something to eat. My stomach gnawed like it might bite a hole in my shirt—hunger mixed with sadness pulled by a strong longing for something I couldn't define.

The women stayed up most of the night rolling homemade cigarettes and drinking black coffee, while the men eventually passed out drunk from whatever was being sloshed around the room in a mason jar.

The sensation of being in another world eventually left me, and I was just a little girl again with dirt under her fingernails and cold, clammy hands. Before too long I fell asleep on the couch in my clothes, using Papaw's scratchy plaid wool coat as a blanket.

I woke up before dawn to the sizzle of fried potatoes cooking in lard, with the smell of liquor still floating around the room like a kite.

Daddy stood shirtless at the stove, waiting for the coffee grounds to boil. I watched him hitch up his faded blue jeans that always hung loose below the waist of his Fruit of the Looms.

"Well, if it ain't ole Edie Nise, up like her daddy before the crack o' dawn," he said, pouring coffee into his cup, grounds and all.

He grinned from ear to ear, whistling snatches of "Dixie" like everything was right in the world. I threw off Papaw's coat and rubbed my eyes to get the sleep out, then moved a chair over to the stove to help Daddy cook. Climbing up on the seat and leaning my head on his shoulder, I wished the potatoes in the iron skillet would hurry up so they could ease the ache that was burning in my stomach.

I had a feeling like something wrong had happened the night before, but there was no sign of it on Daddy's face so I tried not to show it on mine either. Besides, could anything really be wrong when Daddy was grinning and whistling, with dawn spilling like watercolors in the eastern sky?

The two of us sat at the table and ate a heaping plateful of fried potatoes apiece while the sun came up, taking turns sipping his black coffee, the bitter hot numbing my tongue.

We didn't talk; we just let the early morning wrap around us, somehow making everything all right again.

Later that afternoon, we went to the trailer site and dug through the ash heap with Aunt Glenda, looking for anything that could be salvaged. There was no sign of Jamie's canopy bed or any of her clothes or furniture. All we took away were two eight-track tapes and a smell so fierce it took up permanent residence in my memory.

A few weeks later, Jamie moved to a new trailer and Daddy never mentioned the night again.

No matter what the circumstances, the time Daddy and I spent together felt like time that stood still.

Mama said I was the apple of his eye from the minute he laid eyes on me.

2

HELLO DARLIN'

I CAME INTO THIS WORLD during a blustery January ice storm that was beating the tin roof of the lowbrow beer joint where Mama was working nights.

She was a pregnant, barely married mother of a seven-year-old boy named Todd. That night as she was refilling a pitcher of beer from the tap, she felt the first labor pains. It was the coldest winter Mama could remember in this part of Tennessee, and the looks of it made her shiver as she glanced through the dirty bar windows toward her car.

She knew it was time, so she wiped her hands on the bar towel and slung the cloth with the fury of a woman who'd had just about enough of life with my daddy—the handsome fedora-wearing man who drank too much and wouldn't keep a job long enough to pay the rent like he promised he would. It must have been Daddy's charm and blue eyes that hooked her, but I suspect she was already regretting their shotgun nuptials. She hung her apron on the nail by the door, wrapped herself up in an oversized coat, and cranked up the rusted-out Oldsmobile on the first try to drive herself to the hospital.

Mama was approaching her twenty-fifth birthday and was exhausted at the thought of trying to raise another baby on her own.

My half brother, Todd, was staying with his daddy for the weekend, and I'm sure at this point, Mama was even regretting their split up. They had married in high school when Mama got pregnant with Todd, just two kids themselves. But he had a job, a good running car, and churchgoing parents who helped make sure that Todd was raised right. This further highlighted the problem with my daddy, who Mama said was too busy raising hell to raise babies.

She didn't even bother to call Daddy when she left for the hospital, but that didn't stop him from eventually finding out where she was and waltzing into the maternity ward hours later, half-tipsy and promising the moon for his first child.

"You have no business walking into this hospital dog drunk," Mama said as she sat up in her hospital bed. Mama held me tight against her chest to delay for just a moment longer my introduction to Daddy.

"Oh, Sharon Kay, quit your squawlin'. I'm finally a daddy. Let me hold that little punkin head."

Mama handed me to Daddy with hesitation, scolding him for not being more careful to hold my head up, then took the opportunity to go to the bathroom while Daddy was there to help.

"I ain't gonna hurt this baby. Not ever," Daddy said when she opened the bathroom door. "Now, what are we going to name her? I told you I want to name her Edie, after my brother Ed. Is that what you told them nurses?"

"You really want to name this child after your brother who spent most of his life in prison and is now dead?" Mama said with some dismay, splashing water on her face to tidy herself up a little.

"What, you think that's some kind of a curse? I don't believe in things like that. And old Ed was a pretty good feller when he wasn't drinking and never shoulda spent his life in prison nohow," Daddy said.

"Well, fine then. As long as we don't call her Edith, I'm okay with it. I guess we'll call her Edie Denise, after my brother Dennis."

"Edie Denise. Sounds like a winner to me," Daddy said as he handed me to Mama, who was back in bed, arranging the blankets for the two of us.

"And another thing, Jim Rudder. Don't you come back up here until you sober up."

Mama recuperated a week in the hospital, visited only by her mother and my unpredictable daddy. When she was released, her mom wheeled Mama out the double doors to her car in the bitter cold, with me in Mama's arms and the weight of the world on her shoulders.

When we arrived at the apartment building, Mama trudged up to the second floor with me swaddled in hospital blankets and balanced on her hip. At the door, she fumbled with her keys, trying to jiggle the lock on the loose doorknob. As we crossed the threshold of their sparsely furnished, dimly lit apartment, the sour smell of spilled beer was rancid. Looking around, she must have thought that there wasn't one thing about this place worth all the misery she'd been enduring . . . except me. It was no place to bring a newborn baby, let alone raise a family, this building where misfits rented rooms by the week. Probably most people mistook it for a rundown brothel, the way the tenants came and went at all hours of the night.

Daddy had promised Mama on the phone that he'd meet her at home, but he was nowhere to be seen. She knew he'd been hanging wallpaper with his brother that week, getting paid by the day, but he would drag himself to the hospital after Mama was asleep, avoiding questions about his intention to pay the rent, much less pay his dues as a father.

Mama got to work making a pillow fort in her bed for me to

safely sleep in. Making her way around the empty beer bottles strewn all over the floor, she opened the kitchen cupboards one after another. There were two cans of pork and beans and an empty can of JFG coffee.

Maybe there's something in the refrigerator to eat.

A half-used bottle of ketchup and a small box of leaf lard stood side by side on a shelf like two vagabonds stranded on the side of the road. Mama crawled into bed next to me and drifted off to sleep, hoping tomorrow would come with answers, or food, or maybe somebody to pay the electric bill before everything was disconnected.

What Mama didn't know was that Daddy had a surprise for her.

Daddy showed up just like he said he would, but it was 3:00 a.m. and he wasn't alone. He had the honky-tonk band from Genie's Bar with him and two quarts of Pabst Blue Ribbon to make sure the good times rolled.

I'm sure it had sounded like a fine-and-dandy idea as Daddy's friend Speck and the other bandmates clanked their last round of shots at the bar, toasting Daddy and his brand-new baby.

I can imagine what Daddy might have said next.

"Speck, you've always been a feller with your head screwed on right. Why don't you go tell them pickers that they ort to come over to the house and give that baby o' mine a proper homecomin'? It ain't ever' day that Jim Rudder can say he's become a daddy. I told her mama that I'd be there tonight, and I aim to keep my word."

Less than an hour later, the band had loaded all their makeshift equipment into the back of a worn-out Chevy pickup, hauled everything up to our second-floor apartment, and set up shop in the kitchen, a tiny U-shaped room just to the left as you walked through the door. Back in 1970, it probably didn't take much to convince a third-rate honky-tonk band in South Knoxville that this gig was worth doing. They fired up their instruments just two paper-thin walls away from where Mama and I slept.

Mama woke up with a start. It sounded like a gang of wild toddlers had opened up the cabinets and were repeatedly throwing all the pots and pans down on the floor.

Within minutes, she was standing at the edge of the kitchen with her hands set on her hips. She didn't even care that she was in her nightgown in front of the band members.

"Jim, what in the name of heaven are you doing? You brought a pack of guitar-playing drunk men into this house with a brand-new baby trying to sleep in the next room?"

Pulling out his full charm, Daddy whisked Mama into his arms. "She don't need to be in the next room. Brang her in here; this is all for her!"

"What on earth are you thinking, Jim?"

"Sharon, the fact that you're askin' me that tells me that you don't know what kind of man Jim Rudder is. There ain't nothin' I wouldn't do for that girl o' mine, and I aim to show her what kind of daddy she's got."

The band was getting all twitchy about this time, looking around the room and wondering what to do next.

"You're showing her, all right," Mama said, trying to keep from exploding. "She's got a drunk for a daddy who ain't got enough good sense to know that newborn babies need somewhere decent to live, and electricity that don't get turned off every other week, and maybe some food in the cabinets. They don't need honky-tonk bands to keep them awake at night when they're trying to sleep."

About that time I woke up and started crying. Daddy nodded to Speck and consoled me with a gift that sealed my musical tastes—to this day, old country-and-western music still sounds like home to me.

Daddy took me in his arms and twirled me around the room while the band played and Speck danced one off. The percussion man banged a solitary bass drum while he smoked his Marlboro cigarette, the long ash falling in one piece onto the linoleum.

Every few minutes, Daddy would elbow the banjo player, who was always on the verge of lapsing into a beer coma.

According to Mama's slightly bitter recollection, they drummed and clanged like a pack of drunken hillbillies while Daddy jigged around the kitchen singing loudly, occasionally letting out his exuberance with, "Whoa, daddy. Jim Rudder's got him a baby girl!"

I've begged my dear mother to remember what songs they played for me that night. I mean, any girl with this kind of homecoming would be curious to know the country-and-western tunes that ushered her into this world. I can only guess that they lit into a rousing rendition of "Ring of Fire" by Johnny Cash. Or maybe Merle Haggard's "Mama Tried." Whatever the playlist, I've lived with plenty of regret that I was too fresh into the world to enjoy any of it. And had Mama known what lay in store for her with my daddy, I probably wouldn't be here.

Eventually the homecoming serenade woke up the entire building, and one thing Mama remembers with clarity is that the musicians didn't finish their set. Because it's all fun and games until the baby starts crying.

My mama might have been alone in the world, but she was a spitfire of epic proportions when she needed to be. The band was ordered to pack up (I'm sure the language was colorful) and get out. Daddy was ordered to sober up on the couch right after he handed over the leftovers of his scrawny wages so there'd be money left for diapers, baby formula, and the electric bill. However much he had to pay the bar band, the gesture is not lost on me. It's one of those odd things I tell people with a hint of pride in my voice.

With a homecoming fit for a queen, I was officially welcomed into the Rudder clan.

And so began my life with the most wonderful and heartbreaking man I would ever know.

3

THEY DON'T MAKE 'EM
LIKE MY DADDY

I WONDER WHAT SMOKY'S so riled up about?

I cupped my hands around the edges of my eyes and pressed my nose to the clammy window of Mamaw's trailer, trying to block the glare so I could see why the dog was barking so loud. Smoky was tied up beside the driveway, and I could see him yanking his neck against the chain so hard I was afraid he might break it. The window was filmy and smelled like smoke, but I could see the insurance man in his shiny car slowly trying to navigate the driveway, then struggling to make the narrow turnaround.

The steep gravel drive to Mamaw's trailer ought to have had a warning sign: *Herein lies rough terrain. Enter at your own risk. And leaving won't be easy either.*

I don't know why more people didn't just park at the bottom of the driveway near the road, though walking up was no picnic either. Rainwater had worn gullies and ruts so big on one side that my mama drove up with two tires on the grass, trying to avoid getting stuck in the trenches. She had to give it all the gas to clear the bottom half, and by the time we were near the top we were in a cloud of dust so thick she had to stop and let it settle before driving around back to park.

Funny thing is, nobody ever talked about how hostile an entry-way it was. Maybe in comparison, it wasn't any more difficult than anything else in their lives.

After finally making it up the driveway, he got out of the car and rounded the corner with his big black binder in one hand and a bag of Dum Dum suckers swinging in the other. I jumped down off the couch, hitched up my shorts, and ran barefooted to the door.

"Mamaw, the insurance man is here," I said, pushing the screen door open so fast it hardly creaked, saying hi to the man in the suit and pretending I wasn't interested in the suckers.

"Well, let him on in," Mamaw said from the kitchen table, where she was finishing a cup of coffee and taking a long draw on her cigarette.

The insurance man patted my head as he lumbered through the front door, his weighty girth making the soft linoleum floor sink with every step, like any minute he might fall right through the floorboards.

It was the year before I started kindergarten. We were at Mamaw's most weekends now because Daddy was drinking a lot and Mama didn't trust him with us alone at our place. So we stayed with Daddy's family at the trailer while Mama worked at Genie's, struggling every weekend to make enough money to feed her three kids, after having my baby sister, Gina.

The insurance man was like a permanent fixture. He came every Friday afternoon to collect on the plethora of life insurance policies that Mamaw had taken out on her most worried-over children and grandchildren. I loved to see him coming; he was one of the few outside visitors and the only one who consistently brought treats. I liked him on those grounds alone.

He grabbed a chair beside her and said hello to my aunt

Darlene, who was also at the table, trying to drink her coffee from a saucer. Darlene was Mamaw's youngest daughter, and she had cerebral palsy, which made her movements stiff and spastic, so Mamaw kept a threadbare kitchen towel handy to dab up the spills. Once Darlene got the saucer to her mouth, though, she had the precision of a surgeon.

"Do you wont some coffee?" Mamaw said to him as he took a pen from his suit coat pocket and opened up his black binder.

"No, I'm okay, Miz Jessie, thank you. It sure is good to see you again. Hope you're doing all right. It looks like you've got a houseful here for the weekend," he said, wiping sweat off his forehead and trying not to look as out of place as he probably felt.

"I ain't doin' suh good. Since Earn died I don't care about nothin'. I'd ruther just go on than have to live in the misery I live in," Mamaw said, tapping her cigarette repeatedly on the side of a green glass ashtray, tears collecting at the edges of her lifeless eyes.

Aunt Johnny, Mamaw's oldest daughter, was sitting at the table, too, and interjected, "Yeah, I've been worried about Mama; she ain't eatin' nothin' since Daddy died and ain't sleepin' good neither."

"I know it must have been hard for the family and especially for you, Miz Jessie, but at least you had peace of mind with that policy on him to pay for a good burial and all." Once again the insurance man took out his handkerchief to wipe the sweat that was already beading under his eyes.

Papaw hadn't been gone long, but everybody said he was better off. He'd spent the last few years mostly in a vegetative state—propped up in a hospital bed in the living room while various relatives took turns feeding him, changing his diapers, and suctioning the mucus out of his throat when he launched into a coughing fit and didn't have the strength to clear it. I missed Papaw, but I didn't miss the gurgling sound of that suction machine.

"I wish't I'd just go on; my life ain't nothin' but pure hell anyhow," Mamaw said, reiterating the phrase she constantly repeated like some might recite a psalm or a prayer.

Her version of "pure hell" could apparently be assuaged by a multitude of life insurance policies. The insurance man was all too willing to oblige.

He came every Friday like clockwork because that's the way Mamaw preferred to pay her debts—by the week and in person. He was a jolly man with red cheeks, always ripe with sweat and brimming with friendliness. He ledgered the payments like a dutiful marketeer, making his living off the fears of backwoods country people who probably ought to have been spending their money on food for their families instead of planning for the untimely death of any number of their kinfolks.

"Let me ast you something," Mamaw interrupted. "Are them policies I took out on Edie and Gina still good?" She strained to read our names in the black binder. The insurance man pulled our policies out of the binder and plopped them onto the wobbly veneered table.

"Those are James's daughters, right?" he said, clearly not knowing the family well enough to know that everybody called my daddy Jim, not James.

"Yes, they are," she said patting the papers with the pride of a woman who was doing her best to provide for her children and grandchildren despite life's uncertainties.

"Well, everything's paid up and in order."

I was leaning on the edge of Mamaw's chair back when he finally got to the Dum Dums. He held the bag out to me and Sister, and I shuffled around in the bag looking for the cream soda–flavored one. I handed a fruit punch sucker to Sister.

A few minutes later, when all the important business was taken care of, the insurance man got up to leave. Aunt Johnny followed him out the door with a basket of clothes to hang on the line, and me on her heels carrying the bucket of clothespins. I stopped for a moment and admired his shiny car before it disappeared in a cloud of dust. Then I walked around the side of the trailer to help Aunt Johnny hang the clothes.

Uncle Gene drove up just as we crossed the driveway, his car appearing through the dust cloud. He was Daddy's oldest brother and had never been married. He lived with Mamaw and Aunt Darlene and was an intolerable drunk in his own right, though he would eventually become an irritable teetotaler.

The clothesline on the edge of the property marked an imaginary barrier between us and the kudzu-covered cliff that dropped a hundred feet straight down just to the right of the driveway. The clothes hung off that line in defeat as if they themselves had lost the will to live.

More than once, I lay on my belly to rescue pairs of Uncle Gene's white Fruit of the Looms that had blown off the line and were teetering on the edge of the cliff. *I wonder what it would be like to be blown off the cliff, to drift in the wind like a parachute, to keep going until I was somewhere too far away to be found.* Or maybe I'd just land in the backyard of the house at the bottom, where I knew there was a swimming pool that sat right on top of the ground. When Mamaw made us scale down that ridge to pick pokeweed for poke salad, I could hear kids laughing and playing and splashing around in the water. It was the first time I remember feeling sorry for myself and wishing that I had been born into a different family. The taste of pokeweed gave me the dry heaves, though it was only supposed to be poisonous if you ate the roots and berries.

With the Dum Dum dissolving in my mouth, I handed Aunt Johnny the clothespins to secure the thin and fraying towels to the line. Smoky was growling himself into a bark at the tree nearby, with the look of an animal that leaned toward meanness if for no other reasons than constant hunger and general abandonment. He might have been a fine dog under different circumstances. Maybe he wished he'd been born to a different family too.

I turned toward the trailer, which looked faded and weary from the weather, weighed down from bearing years of stored misery too difficult to account for.

Wiping the sweat that was beading around my hairline, I walked behind the doghouse and sat under a row of shade trees, a respite from the unforgiving summer heat. Under that shade tree, it was easier to breathe and think, not crowded in the stifling trailer with jobless relatives who congregated around pots of coffee and the most recent tragedy. It would be several years before we got air-conditioning.

Even at my tender age, I was well aware that there was always too little of everything.

The money pooled from the government checks meant that once a month for a span of a whole weekend there was ample food at Mamaw's if we were lucky. But most of the time there was a palpable scarcity that covered the place like the kudzu slowly obliterating the mountainside.

The afternoon fell into a dark Appalachian night—the kind of night that carried with it a strange sort of loneliness that mountain people knew all too well. Alone with the night. Alone with the poverty. Alone with a low-grade hunger that was impossible to fill.

I went inside to wait for Daddy, but I didn't have to wait long.

His car's tires stirring up the gravel was a welcome sound, so Sister and I met him at the screen door. He was carrying his little brown bag of beer, a loaf of bread, and a gallon of buttermilk. He slung the milk into the refrigerator, dropped the bread on the counter, and opened the first quart of beer.

"Girls, your daddy's been painting an old car all day, and I'll tell you what I'm gonna do now. I'm gonna play y'uns some good old country music."

Gina was too little to care about Daddy's music so she joined Uncle Gene on the couch to watch the dancers on *The Lawrence Welk Show.*

Daddy held my hand while he sauntered me out to the front

porch, like he was leading me onto a dance floor. I knew just where to sit and just what to do. Before I could squirm around enough to steady the aluminum lawn chair that always sat crooked by the door, the music started playing on the record player inside and Daddy sloshed his beer right out of the bottle as he tried to keep time with Johnny Cash.

"Turn that music down, Jim. I'm tryin' to watch this ole television," Uncle Gene said, irritated enough to turn the TV up louder.

"I will, brother Gene, as soon as me and this girl o' mine sang this song," Daddy slurred.

My feet didn't reach the ground, but I tapped them to the beat anyway, pushing down the thick humid July air and swatting at the cloud of gnats gathering above my head.

Daddy held the brown quart glass bottle up close to his mouth and sang the words straight into his makeshift microphone, like a man trying his best to tell the truth, with the kind of passion and conviction that was missing when he was sober.

By the second quart there was no doubt in his mind that he was Johnny Cash. He had the tattoos and the hard living to prove it. He taught me the lyrics to "Folsom Prison Blues" before I learned my multiplication tables. I didn't mind a bit when he insisted that I sit right down and pay attention to the words.

I was president of Daddy's fan club and his most attentive audience, so when he finished the first stanza, he was generous with the microphone. I sang the next verse, about shooting a man in Reno, with all the gusto I could muster, while Daddy, off balance, two-stepped all around me.

The twanging, wavy sound of the steel guitar made me happy. When Daddy turned that amber bottle straight up to finish it off, the yellow porch light seemed to dance off him like he was a star in a movie.

"Get in there and make us some bologna sandwiches, Nise. I've been paintin' that old car and ain't eat a bite all day."

Daddy had a thing for rusted-out cars and for calling me Nise.

He was forever making up lyrics to funny little tunes and adding my name to it like it was supposed to be there. That man could get me to do just about anything by finishing his request with *Nise*.

I opened the screen door and pulled it fast behind me, hoping nobody would holler about the gnats getting in.

Mamaw was in deep concentration at the kitchen table, filling up the last of her S&H Green Stamp books, a Pall Mall perpetually dangling from the right side of her mouth. She was too busy with her project to notice what quick work I had made of shutting the door without making a peep. Nothing could bring the wrath of an Appalachian woman like a screen door slamming.

I dragged the wooden chair over to the counter and gathered all my supplies—the two-pounder loaf of Kern's bread, the thick, precut bologna with the red plastic casing, and a big jar of JFG mayonnaise.

I plated the sandwiches up on Mamaw's gold-rimmed Corelle dishes and poured Daddy a glass of buttermilk to go with his supper. He once made me taste the thick, sour milk just like he made me taste his Budweiser, and as much as I wanted to love everything he did, I never learned to like either one.

We ate our fill on the front porch while the cicadas clicked their loud applause for his faithful performance. Soon Daddy was splayed out limp over the lawn chair, his head too heavy to hold upright and drool pooling on one side of his mouth. I tried to wake him up enough to get him to bed, but Mamaw looked up from the rickety kitchen table to say her piece through the screen door.

"You just let him lay right there. If he's too no account to quit drankin' before he passes out sloppy drunk, then he can sleep right out there on the porch. Now, get on in yonder and lay down with your sister."

I took the quart bottle from Daddy's hand before it fell to the ground and wiped the drool off his mouth with the end of my shirt sleeve before I made my way to the back bedroom where Sister was already sleeping.

I climbed in bed beside her, both of us sleeping in the same clothes we had been wearing all day. "I miss you, Mama," I whispered in the darkness as I closed my eyes. *Sister must miss her too,* I thought. After all, she was only three or so, and not yet old enough to sing with Daddy or make him bologna sandwiches. It was hard to sleep with the cicadas' deafening love song from outside filling the room. But eventually I was lulled by the whirring insects' calls.

Way before sunrise I could hear Daddy whistling and singing, rustling a pot onto the old gas stove. I left Sister sleeping and snuck into the kitchen.

"Well, Nise, if you ain't the ugliest thang I ever seen. Me and you's gonna make us some breakfast, ain't we?"

"Yeah, Daddy, I'm hungry," I said, staring with him at the contents of the mostly empty refrigerator.

For all the world, I wanted to think that Daddy loved our mornings together and those nights on the porch as much as I did, but I had a sneaking suspicion that Daddy loved something more than all of us, even more than he loved himself.

4

D-I-V-O-R-C-E

"HOLD STILL, HONEY, AND quit kicking your legs, while I try to even up this side of your bangs. You look just like your daddy, with that wide forehead and the same stubborn cowlick. That's why I'm going to have to hide my scissors from you too," Mama said, smiling, patting me on the head as she carefully evened up my bangs. I was only five but loved nabbing Mama's new scissors when I could to fix my hair like hers.

I tried to sit perfectly still and not swing my legs back and forth, kicking into the cabinets.

"Mama, why does Daddy drink so much?" I asked, almost wishing I hadn't said it, the words betraying me faster than I could stop them.

"I don't know, honey—sure wish I did. Guess I should have paid more attention to the fact that I met him at a bar," she said, standing back to admire the evenness of her trim.

"Do you think he'll ever stop?"

I took her hand to help me down off the counter.

"I'm beginnin' to think he couldn't stop if he wanted to," she said with a sound in her voice that made me think she knew something that was too complicated to explain.

Mama was the proud graduate of beauty school when she and Daddy moved us into a new mobile home park where the single-wide trailers were stacked in rows up the side of the mountain like something out of Legoland. Only ten minutes from Mamaw's and cut from the same rugged landscape, it felt like home.

We lived near the top so we had to be careful not to get going too fast down the hill or we'd find ourselves tumbling down the hard gravel drive like a Slinky toy on a staircase.

Mama's threats to leave Daddy if he didn't bring home some money and quit spending what little he made on beer spurred him into working odd jobs with Gene in direct proportion to her warnings. In hindsight, I don't think their relationship stood much of a chance, especially with Daddy's upbringing.

Mamaw and Papaw Rudder raised six kids in what can only be described as third-world poverty conditions. Papaw built their first shack out of old doors that he nailed together for walls, a place without electricity or running water. Daddy and Glenda always joked that they never knew which door to go in or out.

A creek provided both their bath and drinking water, which the kids carried in buckets nearly a mile round trip. None of them attended school past the eighth grade, and they wore hand-me-down clothes and brogans that were usually two or three sizes too big. The trailer where Mamaw and Papaw lived when I was a child must have felt like Cinderella's castle compared to most of the places they'd stayed.

My mama's upbringing was quite sophisticated in comparison. Raised by a staunch Republican mother who worked for the election commission and was an avid member of the Daughters of the American Revolution, Mama had grown up in a typical late-fifties American home with all its propriety and manners and five o'clock suppers. That is, until her mother fell off the deep end into raging alcoholism—leaving Mama, her siblings, and her father to fend for themselves, managing the best they could for years on their own. Eventually her mother remarried and settled down again.

Mama ended up pregnant at age sixteen, living with her boyfriend's family and raising my brother Todd while she was still in high school and still a child herself. Mama and Todd's father did get married, but by the time Todd was six, their relationship was imploding and she moved back in with her mom. That's when she met my daddy, which was like going from the frying pan to the fire.

After Mama fixed my bangs, I headed outside to find Sister or some of the kids down the hill in the trailer park. We were deep into throwing rocks at a stack of old tires just outside the door when Daddy came flying up the road and braked hard in front of the house. I followed Daddy, grabbing Sister's hand against her will so she wouldn't end up outside by herself. I knew by the looks of Daddy that he'd been drinking and that something bad was bound to happen. I thought if Sister and I were around, he might be nicer.

"I don't guess you made any supper worth eatin', did you, ole girl?" Daddy said to Mama in a tone that usually put her in the mood to fight back. He walked into the kitchen, sniffing around the pan on the stove and making faces.

"Listen, you can eat what I made or not, I don't really care. I didn't cook for you anyhow; I made it for these kids," she said, in the same voice that would protect me for years, avoiding eye contact with him and shooing us toward the bedroom.

The pork chops apparently didn't suit him, so he grabbed a can of Campbell's tomato soup out of the cabinet and brandished it like he was going to hit her with it.

Mama saw it coming, and before he could land the swing, she clocked him in the right eye, knocking him flat to the ground. Part proud of her and part sad for him, I didn't quite know what to do with myself. I made a movement to go toward him, but she quickly herded us outside to the car.

We could hear Daddy moaning and cussing as we drove off, but Mama didn't let that slow her down. I couldn't help but feel sorry for him in a way. He only acted mean like that when he was really drunk, and he only did stupid things like that to Mama— not to us. She told me when I was much older that it was as if he took all the collective rage from his whole life out on her, never threatening to hurt anyone else. At least she had graduated from beauty school and finally had a ticket out.

Mama took us to Tarbett Hill, where we spent the night with Aunt Glenda, the usual routine when Mama and Daddy fought.

Within days, Mama moved us from our trailer to another in the same trailer park—one that was closer to the bottom of the hill and didn't include Daddy.

It would be months before their divorce was final, but Daddy never lived with us again after the soup can wrangle.

Two babies and a lot of heartache later, Daddy's charm had run out for Mama. She found herself in an almost impossible situation, trying to make a marriage work with Daddy and his whiskey ways while working two jobs and long hours to try to feed three kids. Daddy was like an unpredictable wildfire, and Mama knew it. She finally had the courage to cut and run.

Todd, Sister, and I took to the new trailer like flies to watermelon, glad to be on flat ground and happier still to be right in the middle of a swarm of kids. Daddy moved back to Mamaw's, although one could argue that he had never fully moved out in the first place, the way he and his siblings clung too close to Mamaw and each other at that trailer.

We passed the days building rock forts and playing kick the can or capture the flag. We were outside from daylight till dark, and Todd was usually in charge of making sure we didn't get into any trouble.

One afternoon, a few of us decided to build a playhouse. We looked around, and someone pointed out a stack of old cinder blocks, the kind used to level up the foundations on the trailers.

"Those will work," someone said, and we raced over to get our needed supplies. I reached to pick one up and nearly toppled over from the weight of it. An older boy dragged one off, leaving ruts in the dirt marking his path. The other neighbor kids worked to do their part while Sister mostly watched.

With all my might, I hoisted a cinder block up onto my knees to get a good grip on it, but it was too much. I dropped the block with a thud right onto my foot. Blood squirted everywhere. I couldn't move because of the weight crushing my foot, and the pain set me to screaming at the top of my lungs.

Somehow Mama appeared before the other kids got to me. She lifted the cinder block off me and gasped at the gash splayed open on my bare foot. I was hysterical.

"Honey, Mama's right here—it's going to be okay. The doctors can fix it all back together."

Mama picked me up and carried me to the car, yelling for Todd to grab a dishtowel and a cup of water. He and Sister came running out, and the look on their faces told me I was right to be worried. Todd raced back in and got the water and a towel while Mama consoled me in the backseat.

"I just need to clean it," Mama said, scooting me to the end of the seat so that my foot dangled out of the car. As Mama poured the water, I screamed in pain and Sister started crying.

Mama wrapped my foot in the towel and told Todd to keep it covered and hold it while she drove us to the hospital.

Everything got fuzzy on the drive to the hospital. Before I knew it, we were inside with strangers leaning over my foot and saying words meant to comfort me.

I must have screamed for three solid hours while doctors and nurses hovered over me, digging tiny pieces of rock out of my foot.

Mama held my hand and rubbed my face and hair, trying to keep me from seeing all the torn flesh and drying blood. Every time I caught a glimpse of it, my screams rose to a fever pitch. The digging around finally ended, and then came the flushing with saline and the stitching up.

With the stitches finally in, I calmed down, and the room fell quiet. Mama sat in a chair right beside me. Todd and Sister were gone now, having gone home with Aunt Glenda. At first, I didn't know what to make of the silence in the room. Outside the door, I heard muffled voices and the movement of wheeled carts. In my room, there was a TV up by the ceiling. The bed had buttons that moved it up and down. And the blankets and sheets were folded and tucked in perfectly.

The room was so clean and bright, with everything organized and in its place.

I looked down at the crisscrossed stitches across the top of my foot.

A nurse came into my room to apply some medicine to the wound and bandage it. I was so struck by how nice everyone was and how kindly they all spoke to me. A few minutes later, another nurse came in with a huge tray in her hands.

"I bet you are hungry after all of that," she said.

"Yes, ma'am." I sat up and watched as she moved a table over my bed and set down the tray. As she lifted the lid covering the food, I watched wide-eyed like it was some kind of secret surprise. There was soup and crackers, a dinner roll, some red Jell-O, and a Popsicle, and even chocolate milk.

"This is all for me?" I asked, looking at Mama, who smiled.

"It sure is, sweetheart," said the nurse with the tray.

"What are these?" I asked picking up little paper packets.

"That's your salt and pepper."

I was in awe and ate everything up, like it was my last meal.

At some point, I got to wishing Daddy were there to say something funny and make us laugh.

"Mama, does Daddy know I'm hurt? Where is he?" I asked, thinking he would've loved that dinner roll. I could've put the tiny butter on it for him, like I did the mayonnaise for the bologna sandwiches I made for him at Mamaw's.

"Probably somewhere drunk, if I had to venture a guess. Don't worry about him. You're always getting worked up over him, when he's the one that should be worried about you. Just concentrate on getting this foot better, which is not going to be easy, as much as you run around and play all the time."

More doctors came in to check on me, leaning over my foot and talking all nice to me, like I was somebody important.

"Mama, I wish we could stay all night here. What do you think they have for breakfast?"

"Honey, I don't know that they're going to let you stay all night. I don't know why you'd want to anyway."

Before I left the bright lights and the white walls, the nurses let me pick a treat from their treasure box. As I limped over to choose my toy, I felt so happy to see this place, even if it meant getting my foot hurt to come here. Before we left, I hugged my nurse, and then Mama picked me up and carried me through those big double doors toward the car.

Mama lowered me into the car and kissed me on the cheek as I bit into the oversized Tootsie Roll the nurses had given me. I wondered what Daddy would say about my foot or if he'd be in his right mind enough when I saw him to even notice. It wouldn't be long before I'd be on the wrong side of another cinder block, and this time on the wrong side of Daddy, too.

5

MAMA TRIED

THE FIRST WEEKEND AFTER I got stitched up, Mama dropped us off at Mamaw's. I ran toward the trailer with a gimp in my step, excited to tell Daddy all about what had happened, figuring that maybe since I was hurt, some concessions might be made for the weekend. Like maybe we'd just have a quiet night and Daddy wouldn't drink or leave or take us to the beer joint.

"Don't drag your foot through that dirty gravel, honey. You'll get it infected," Mama hollered before me and Sister disappeared into the trailer.

"And keep those bandages on, too, okay? I love you girls, and I'll see you in a day or two."

"Okay, bye," I said, already spying Daddy sitting on the couch tying his shoes. My heart sank. He looked like he was getting ready to go somewhere.

"Daddy, look at my foot. Did Mama tell you I had to get a bunch of stitches? They dug in there for three hours, trying to get all the rocks out," I said proudly, taking my shoe off and beginning to unwrap the bandages.

"Wrap that back up, Nise. Me and you's gotta go look at some parts off an old truck so I can fix that alternator of mine this weekend," Daddy said, barely glancing at my foot and looking antsy. His eyes searched around for his keys like he was already late for something.

He hadn't been drinking yet, but I could tell by how faraway he was that he had one thing on his mind. And it wasn't me or Sister or my stitches or anything else but finding beer. I was old enough to know the signs and old enough to feel the sting, but I wasn't yet old enough to know that it wasn't my fault and that there would never be anything I could do to make it right.

I was too hurt to tag along—not so much over my foot, but everything else. Daddy disappeared out the door without hesitating.

A month later, on another Friday night, I was working the twist top off of Sister's RC Cola while the two of us dangled our legs from the front seat of Daddy's red Ford truck, parked in the front row at Mary Knox Tavern.

We must have looked like twins, the two of us—me five years old and Sister barely three-and-a-half. Gina Hope, Daddy called her. Mama gave her the family name Hope, and she would grow to stand tall into every glorious inch of it. We were close like survivors of trauma are close, welded together like metal, each one responsible for holding the other one upright, parts of our souls and past so inextricably intertwined that sometimes I wondered if I felt part of her pain along with my own.

Mama didn't know that on Friday nights after she dropped Sister and me off at Mamaw's, Daddy would usually load up one or both of us and take us to the bar with him. He normally had enough sense to leave us in the car with RC Colas and potato chips, which I found to be a nearly irresistible offer.

"Take care of yer sister, and I'll be back in two shakes of a hound's tail," Daddy said this night as he disappeared inside, the country music blaring out of the bar so loud I couldn't hear Sister talk when she asked me to open up her potato chips.

When I finally got our drinks and chips opened, we settled back into our seats with our loot, occasionally scooting up to the edge to peek over the dashboard to see if Daddy was ready to go. I was wearing my favorite hand-me-down dress, the one with the permanent Coca-Cola stains dribbled down the front, and we hummed along to the music. Eventually the RC had me squirming to go to the bathroom.

"I'm going inside to pee and check on Daddy. Don't move. I'll be right back. You can have the rest of my chips, but don't drink my Coke," I said.

Sister nodded but didn't make a peep, her mouth stuffed plumb full, chips dribbling out like the foam off Daddy's beer. I hopped out and slammed Daddy's heavy door with both hands, making sure it shut tight.

When I pulled the door open, a heavy swath of cigarette smoke and Hank Williams blaring from the jukebox greeted me. The iron bars that covered the doors and windows made it look like you were entering a jail. Before I could get to the bathroom, I heard Daddy.

I crept forward and saw him across the room, all shirtless and unstable and hollering out stuff I knew would probably get him in trouble.

I had to get him out of there, but it was hard to get his attention with all the cussing and carrying on he was doing. My heart was beating hard. I was scared for him but scared for myself, too. What if he got into a fight with me standing in the middle of the bar trying to help him?

Finally, I ran up and pulled on his arm. Daddy stared down at me as if he wasn't sure who or what I was for a moment. I felt embarrassed that I had to be doing this to begin with, but with him and Mama separated, I was all he had, and I needed to take care of him. I tried to get him to leave the only way I knew how.

"Daddy, Gina's sick in the truck. You have to come out here right now; I think she's going to puke all over your seats. We need to get her back to the trailer. Please, Daddy, please."

"Nise, it's Howdy Doody time," he said, taking me by the hand and trying to twirl me like he would do on Mamaw's front porch.

"Besides, I ain't finished in here yet. Your daddy's got some business to take care of with these here fellers. Now you run on back outside and take care of your little sister and let your daddy take care of business." He slurred his words and could hardly stand.

I pulled on him hard and made him walk toward the door. When he resisted me, I maneuvered behind him and pushed on his pants pockets, saying, "Daddy, we have to take Sister home, she's sick. Come on, let's go. I'll help you drive. Mama will be mad if she knows we didn't take care of Sister when she was sick."

Finally, I got him to the truck. He opened the driver's door and stumbled in, me pushing his legs in and shutting his door.

I raced around to the other side and climbed over Sister so I could help Daddy drive. I sat propped up on my knees in the front seat and leaned over to reach the steering wheel so I could help him get us home. I probably should have been more scared than I was, but there was something about taking care of all of us that fueled me onward, like some deep-seated need of mine was being met too. I felt proud to be getting us back safely.

Daddy never asked if Sister was really sick, but when he tried to sing to us, his breath smelled like rotten fruit.

Next to his hard, calloused hands, mine looked too small for the task, but Daddy told me I was a heck of a driver and that someday he'd give me that old red truck.

"Nise, you make your daddy proud, and I love you better'n anything. Me and you ort to pull this truck over and dance a jig."

"Not tonight, Daddy. You need to go to bed."

How we managed to get back to Mamaw's trailer and up that mountain in one piece I'll never know. I even got Daddy up the porch steps without him falling backwards, but before we opened the screen door, we heard Mama peel up the driveway.

Since it was Daddy's weekend, I knew something must be wrong.

Mama probably heard he had us at the beer joint, since she worked down the road from Mary Knox.

"Edie, don't go in that trailer. You get your sister and come get in my car right now."

"Oh, Sharon Kay, what have you got your tail feathers all in a ruffle for? Them girls is fine, and that oldest one's a heckuva driver, too."

Daddy swayed and then shored himself against the wall of the trailer. He patted me on the head and told me to run on in and fix him some grub.

"Jim, you ought to be ashamed of yourself, dragging them two little girls out to a beer joint and spending what little money you made this week on liquor when these girls don't even have good food in their bellies."

Then Mama turned her attention my way. "Edie, don't you listen to your daddy. You bring your sister down those stairs right now." Mama looked at me like she meant what she was saying.

I looked back at Daddy, a tipsy mess, leaning by the door trying not to fall, and then back at Mama coming toward us before we had a chance to walk through the trailer door.

I did what Mama said and grabbed Sister's hand. We jumped into the front seat of Mama's rusted-out blue Monte Carlo, while Daddy spun in slow circles trying to get his balance.

He stumbled down the steps, stopping to put out the cigarette he'd been too drunk to smoke. We could hear him bellowing in the background.

Daddy was not just Pabst Blue Ribbon drunk—he was

brown-liquor drunk, which meant that his funny demeanor was now exchanged for somebody mean, somebody we hardly recognized.

He was threatening Mama that if she didn't stop the car and let us stay the night he'd hurt her, going on about how we were his kids too and she didn't have any right to keep us from him when it was his weekend.

Mama squealed the tires as she turned around behind Mamaw's trailer.

Daddy picked up a cinder block and chased us down the driveway—screaming and carrying on with the kind of profanity that made me cover both my ears. He called Mama names and ranted on about how she had no right to take his girls away and that he could take us wherever he blankety-blank well pleased.

Mama told us to never mind him, that the drinking had made him crazy.

"Just look straight ahead," she said. "Everything's going to be fine."

Of course, I did turn around to look. Daddy's eyes were fiery and wild—like the eyes of a stranger, some kind of crazy man.

Daddy suddenly hurled the cinder block at the back of the car and shattered the back windshield to pieces. The block landed with a thud on the floorboard and we sat stunned, covered in shards of broken glass of every size and shape. I was shocked. Daddy had never, in all the times I had seen him drunk, done anything on purpose that could have hurt me. My mind was reeling with how to make sense of it. It was one thing for him to fight with Mama, but I was devastated that his anger would come so close to hurting Sister and me.

Mama didn't flinch. She pushed the gas pedal as hard as she could and left Daddy stammering in a whirlwind of gravel dust.

As soon as we got home, Mama called the police for a restraining order against Daddy. Moments after she called, Daddy pulled up in his truck, looking as mad as when we left him.

Mama bolted the doors, turned off the lights, and told us to wait in the closet. While Sister picked broken glass from our clothes, I cried against a stack of winter coats and eventually nodded off to sleep.

Sirens startled me awake, and I could hear Daddy outside banging on the windows, threatening to break down the door if Mama didn't let him in to see us.

The lights from the police car made a funny pattern through the slats in the closet door. We kept our breathing hushed and waited for something else to break, but that night, at least, the wounds were mostly invisible.

Daddy was hauled off to jail, and Mama put Sister and me in the bathtub together to get us cleaned up, picking pieces of broken glass out of our hair for what seemed like hours.

The next morning, Mamaw and Uncle Gene bailed Daddy out of jail, and a handful of times after that. His incarcerations were mostly for public drunkenness or DUI, and Mama didn't hesitate to call the law when the brown liquor turned him mean. Mama also had him put in jail once for not paying his child support, but when he showed up in the courtroom with forty disgruntled relatives ready to plead his case, she figured the hassle wasn't worth the twenty dollars she might get out of it. He paid it once, and then as long as he wasn't violent with her, Mama left him alone.

Though Mama had a soft spot for Mamaw and Aunt Glenda and the whole Rudder family, she was no longer one of them. She could call on Aunt Glenda in emergencies that pertained to us, but any former allegiances between her and the clan were severed with the final divorce papers, the child support case, and the phone calls Mama made to the police about Daddy.

But life was soon to change because I was about to meet Mrs. Murphy, a woman who would introduce me to a world full of books and watercolor paints.

6

KEEP ON THE SUNNY SIDE

WHAT WAS TORN APART ON the weekends got patched back together on Mondays the year I started school.

Mama took me on the first day of kindergarten and walked with me to make sure I could find the room, which was one in a row of several portable classrooms that backed up to the road. When I first stepped into Mrs. Murphy's class in the fall of 1975, I was completely mesmerized by her. Her squinty eyes flickered like fireflies and her jet-black bob framed the flawless almond skin on her face. Her smile lit up the room.

She greeted Mama and me and told her not to worry, that she would take good care of me.

"Todd will come by after school and walk home with you, honey. I know you'll have a good day," Mama said as she turned to leave, heading just down the street to the beauty shop where she worked during the day, hoping soon to give up the night job at Genie's.

That year was magical. Mrs. Murphy hovered over me like a gentle mother hen, praising my letters and speaking in a voice like an angel's. I was hypnotized by her whispery words when she read aloud to the class and the thoughtful way she held the book, making sure we could see every page.

During story time, I scooted up to the front and sat on my knees to be closer to her, admiring the way her long skirt trailed over her sandals and how her pretty polished fingernails pointed to the words. She would read from a stack of books, one after another, and I sat spellbound, listening to the stories, the cadence of her voice almost lyrical. Two of the boys got antsy and squirmed around, making noise and keeping the rest of us from hearing, and I shot them a glare to shush them.

I lived for reading time for the rest of the year, rubbing the hem of her dress between my fingers if it draped low enough, counting the books on her lap, and wishing that the circle on the floor would last forever.

Less than a month into the school year, I was standing by my cubby when Mrs. Murphy put her hands on my shoulders and leaned around so I could see her kind eyes. She had a special job just for me.

"Edie, because you're doing so well in your reading, I thought it would be such a treat if you would read the book to us today before we start snack time. You don't have to, but I know how much you love to read. Would you like to? You can go to the back of class and practice if you'd like."

I was mesmerized by the thought.

"Okay, I'll do it," I said in a voice like I was accepting a special mission.

I practiced the words in the back of the class, and when Mrs. Murphy called me forward, I walked to the front of the room with my head held high.

I read each page and tried to hold the book like Mrs. Murphy did, but my hands were too small. My little classmates watched me with rapt attention. As I read the final page, Mrs. Murphy clapped and the other kids joined her.

"Very good, Edie," Mrs. Murphy said.

I returned to the carpet, switching places with Mrs. Murphy. A sense of pride and awe hung over me all day.

Reading to the class felt like the most exciting thing I'd ever done. It gave me the first hint that I was good at something and that I had something to offer others.

After that, during our play time, I chose books to practice reading to an eager audience of stuffed animals, hoping to be as good as Mrs. Murphy someday.

One day when I walked into class, the air was charged with excitement.

My heart beat fast when I saw the electric griddle and all the food and snacks Mrs. Murphy had brought for us. She gathered the class into a huddle and told us what to expect.

"Boys and girls, today is a very special day. It's the hundredth day of school!"

I looked at my friend Leticia, both of us grinning from ear to ear, knowing this meant something special.

"I am so proud of how much you've all learned already, so this special celebration is in honor of you. We'll start the day by reading *Green Eggs and Ham* by Dr. Seuss, and then we'll make green eggs and ham and let you try them! Doesn't that sound like fun? And don't worry, if you don't like the green eggs and ham, you can eat something else for a snack."

"Green eggs and ham, yuck!" one of the boys shouted from the back. "I'm not eating green eggs and ham."

"Don't worry, Ben, you don't have to try it if you don't want to," she said gently, as she opened the book and started reading.

The book made all of us laugh and chant "I will not, will not, Sam-I-am." We cheered at the end when the character finally tried the green eggs and ham and liked them.

After the story, we followed Mrs. Murphy to the table, where she began cracking eggs and warning us not to get too close to the hot griddle. Her face lit up like Christmas lights when she added green food coloring to those eggs, like it was just as surprising to her as it was to us when the fluffy glob turned green.

Unlike a few of my classmates who turned down the chance to eat green eggs, I scarfed them down in no time and wiped the last drippings onto my shirtsleeve, a habit Mrs. Murphy was always gently reproving me for.

After the eggs and ham, we ate fruit and cookies and even drank punch. I had rarely seen so much food at one time, other than my meals at the hospital, and I had certainly never seen food become a source of fun and play.

That classroom gave me a sense of belonging that I didn't feel anywhere I had ever been. It was where I discovered the magic of watercolors and paints and crayons. In that room, I felt the enchantment of childhood for the first time, as if life had been flowing by in black and white until Mrs. Murphy infused it with every color of the rainbow.

My kindergarten days were filled with wonder and new discoveries, and no matter what kind of debauchery took place on the weekends, Mrs. Murphy's class righted all the wrongs come Monday morning. Like a game of chase on the playground where you are "safe" on base, I walked into school after a weekend with Daddy and the Rudder clan and felt relief. Kindergarten was my safe house where breakfast was served, books were read, we played with adults watching over us, and we had more food at lunch. The day was cut into organized pieces where we'd nap and draw and read and sing and play dress up. I had never lived with such order and routine. It seemed too good to be true.

Then kindergarten came to an end. On the last day of school, when all the other kids were packing up their artwork and running out the door with their parents, giddy about summer vacation, I sat beside my cubby and cried.

Mrs. Murphy tried to console me, but I could feel the weight of what I was losing. Maybe it was the books I would miss so terribly. Or Mrs. Murphy and her kindness, unlike any I'd known. Maybe I knew that the relief I felt on Mondays would be gone now, at least for the summer. Maybe forever.

Mrs. Murphy opened the door to a world of books and crayons and papier-mâché—a world that took me beyond the sirens and moonshine and disappointment at Mamaw's trailer. It was the beginning of my love affair with school, a place that was more dependable and steady than anything I had known, a place that would become a lifeline.

7

A BROKEN FLOWER

SITTING CROSS-LEGGED ON the trailer porch, I held the packet of daisy seeds in my hand, imagining scores and scores of bright yellow and white blooms, popping up right through the ground around me. What would it be like to be surrounded by so many pretty things? We had planted some beans and watched them sprout in Mrs. Murphy's class, but I had never seen flowers grow before.

"Don't open that packet up, Edie. We're going plant them flowers tomorrow," Mamaw said, somehow reading my mind and stopping my daydream right in its tracks.

"Where are we going to plant them, Mamaw, where they won't get run over or broke?" I said, looking around at the rough ground. With only a few sparse patches of grass visible in any direction, I couldn't picture flowers anywhere near the trailer. They needed something more to grow in than hard, red clay and gravel, didn't they?

"You girls is gonna plant 'em tomorrow in that box over there," she said, pointing to a small wooden rectangle on the edge of the porch. "You'll have to put 'em in there, because this ground is harder'n a rock. It won't grow nothin' but weeds and thistles."

All night I thought about the picture on the front of that seed packet and the bunches of daisies that would soon be filling up that box.

It was 1977 and we were regulars at Mamaw's—the routine, however dysfunctional, was familiar and at times oddly comforting. But I was old enough now to sense a growing divide—the chasm between my life at home with Mama and school and hot lunches and the life at Mamaw's where we were at the mercy of the demons that haunted that mountain.

I had just finished first grade, and Mama met with my teacher, Mrs. Post, on the last day of school. While I sat on Mama's lap, my teacher told her that I was a very sweet girl but that I would probably never be book smart. Mama swears to this day that it must have been those words that lit a fire in me, because from then on, it seemed like I was on a mission to prove Mrs. Post wrong.

The end of school might have been a welcome break for most first graders, but for me and Sister it meant long days at the trailer while Mama worked—a place where there were no books, no paintbrushes, no crayons, and a less-than-bountiful food supply. At least that summer we had the flower seeds.

The high-pitched creak of Mamaw's screen door when we walked in on Fridays matched the gnawing growl I had in my belly every time I walked through it.

Sister and I shared a twin bed in the back bedroom, the same room where Mamaw and Aunt Darlene slept, the two of them somehow managing to share the other twin bed. Sister and I fought a lot back then, but there was no use fighting for those blankets, even in winter. They were floral seventies bedspreads made with something resembling fishing line for thread, too scratchy to keep next to your skin long enough to get you warm. After squabbling over who was rolled over on whose side of the bed, one of us would inevitably wind up on the floor, whining about the injustices incurred by the one who was hogging the whole bed.

Less than two feet separated us from the twin bed where Aunt Darlene would lie and get a hankering to worry over her eternal destiny. She would ask us repeatedly if we thought she was going to hell. Afflicted with cerebral palsy and raised on the hellfire and brimstone of old country preachers, her mind went to demons as soon as her head hit the pillow.

"Edie, do you think I'm goin' to hell?"

Mamaw would quickly pipe up, "No, you ain't goin' to hell, Darlene. I wish't you wouldn't carry on about that. You're gonna skeer them two little girls, goin' on all night about that."

"Edie, do you think I'm goin' to hell?" she repeated.

"You've tortured her to death over that, Darlene. Now turn over and go on to sleep and let them girls alone. Why do you think *they* know whether or not you're going to hell? They ain't nothin' but little 'uns."

During summers, the air became more oppressive in that room as Mamaw chain-smoked while lying on her side in the bed, the ashes often falling onto the linoleum floor and glowing like lightning bugs until they finally dwindled to vapors. We knew one thing for sure—that was not the last cigarette of the night, and that was not the last we'd hear about hell, either.

When she'd ask again, I'd reassure Aunt Darlene that no, she wasn't going to hell. And usually I meant it, except for the time she chased me around the yard with the butcher knife, trying to steal my baby doll. That day I contemplated saying yes, but I had a soft spot for her from as early as I could remember. I felt sure the cerebral palsy was such an injustice as to render Aunt Darlene forever absolved for all moments of meanness.

Her mental sharpness and sensibilities made us forget her physical frailties, but I figured that surely God loved the infirm because everybody was always talking about how pitiful she was and making concessions when she got hateful. So I comforted her as much as a seven-year-old could. Besides, she gave us Juicy Fruit gum if we were nice so I tried to stay on good terms.

I lay there thinking about Daddy and wondering where he was. He never told me much about his comings and goings unless he wanted to take me with him. Between Mamaw's chain-smoking, Aunt Darlene's obsession with her eternal destiny, and me and Sister fighting and wriggling around trying to stay off the floor, both of us missing Mama and Daddy, sleep was hard to come by.

And it was always too hot or too cold. The air in that room sat on your chest like an elephant.

The first week of June, the weekend after school let out, Mamaw let Sister and me plant those daisy seeds in the flower box.

It was a perfect day—the sun bright and high in the sky, not too hot or humid. The seeds we planted had come in a benevolence Easter basket brought to the family by a local preacher and his wife.

The pastor served at a country church just across the railroad tracks, where we occasionally attended gospel singings and family reunions. Usually only Mamaw and Darlene went for the singings, but our whole family went if it was a reunion.

Sister, Jamie, and I loved when the church people came and brought food of any kind, especially if there were homemade sweets.

The Easter baskets they brought were filled with a cluster of chocolate bunnies and Easter Peeps as well as flower seeds. The seeds didn't interest me at the time, but for some reason Mamaw was determined that each of us kids would plant daisy seeds and watch them grow.

Every weekend, Sister and I waited for those fragile shoots to come through the dirt and debated whose flower would be taller and prettier than whose. The promise of those delicate petals was the entertainment of that summer and the only hope of color in a place more often decorated with broken beer bottles and cigarette butts.

When the shoots first peeked through the dirt, I ran in to tell Mamaw the thrilling news, but it didn't seem like a good time.

Another one of Daddy's sisters, Johnny, was sitting at the kitchen table smoking a freshly rolled Bugler cigarette, drinking coffee, and lamenting the past night's events. Johnny's oldest son, Sonny, and Daddy had been out drinking together.

Aunt Johnny took a long draw from her cigarette and said, "My life ain't nothin' but pure hell."

"What are you talkin' about, Johnny?" Mamaw grumbled, taking a swig of coffee.

"I just wish't I was dead."

"What for?"

"Both of them come in dog drunk last night and busted out one of the winders in the back of my house, and I ain't got the money to fix it. I told 'em both that they was no account and that they ought to be ashamed for treatin' me that way, tearin' up what little I've got."

"Well, did you call the law?" Mamaw asked, her idea of a good solution unless it happened to be my mama calling the police about Daddy.

"No, because I can't afford to get either one of 'em out of jail, and they wouldn't let me alone until I did. Last time Sonny got put in jail, he tortured me to death by callin' me every day until I got him out."

Mamaw fidgeted with the buttons on her shirt and then said, "Well, my nerves is shot, too, because your brother can't stay sober enough to take care of them girls or else he runs around all weekend wantin' to take them with him to every beer joint in Knoxville. Beats all I've ever seen."

While Sister watched the last of the morning's cartoons, I walked back outside and dangled my legs off the side of the porch, admiring the tender green shoots while Mamaw and Aunt Johnny talked about how pitiful it was that Sister and me didn't really have a daddy. Through the screen door, I could see the deep lines in Mamaw's face when she talked, like the pain of her life had decided to write its words in the crevices around her mouth.

Mamaw was one of those old Appalachian souls who seldom smiled and always sounded mad, even if she was just talking about the weather or what she was cooking for supper. Her skin was leathery and her hair was the texture of straw, mostly gray and white but yellowed in places, just like her teeth.

Every Friday when Mama dropped us off, we'd run to check on our flowers first thing. Soon those shoots stood tall and full of life in the middle of an otherwise dingy landscape. My daisy was knee high by early July, the shining star of the three of them, its yellow petals the color of sunshine itself.

"Look, my daisy is way bigger than yours, Sister. Mamaw, ain't mine the best?"

When we got home, I told Mama and Todd about my flower growing taller and looking better than the others. Sister said that hers was better, but there was no denying the truth.

A few Saturdays later, while we were at the kitchen table waiting with grumbling stomachs for Mamaw to scramble up a few eggs, my little rebel sister, who was as fearless as a summer storm blowing through a trailer park, marched right outside and broke my yellow daisy off at dirt level.

I saw the whole thing through the screen door.

I sat paralyzed, too scared to say anything for fear that she'd get in trouble but hoping that surely someone would notice the injustice. I pretended I didn't see anything, only feeling an ache at the loss and a foreboding about what might happen when Mamaw finally saw it.

After breakfast, we all went outside.

While Sister and I played in the yard, Mamaw squatted down beside the porch, smoking her Pall Malls and nursing the last of her coffee. Before she could blow out all the smoke from her first puff, she was up and cussing a blue streak, eyeing around for whoever was wearing a guilty conscience.

"Who in tarnation broke off Edie's flower? Gina Hope Rudder, did you do that meanness? Because you're about to get a whoopin' if you did."

My face got hot and red because Sister was guilty and I knew she was about to be in a mess of trouble.

Sister didn't flinch or so much as turn around to acknowledge Mamaw's accusation. She kept playing in the dirt, guilt scrawled proudly on her face.

"You look at me right now when I'm talkin' to you, little girl. Did you or did you not tear up her flower that's been growin' on this porch all summer long?"

Gina turned around and looked her straight in the eyes and nodded her head, then went back to digging.

Mamaw came unglued. She was as mad as I'd ever seen her—maybe as mad as that time she had to use the last of her Social Security check to bail my cousin Ricky out of jail for driving drunk. The sins my sister was about to pay for, I was sure weren't just her own.

Mamaw was not a mean woman, only strong and calloused over from years of living with alcoholics who had a tendency to get violent. But when she saw that broken flower, something inside her snapped—as if all the hope for every tomorrow was somehow growing up that velvety stem right toward heaven itself, and was now and forever cut off at its root.

I raced after Mamaw as she marched to the edge of the hillside, where the towels were snapping in the wind. She broke off a switch by Smoky's doghouse and stripped off the leaves.

"Please, please don't whoop her, Mamaw. I didn't really like that flower too much anyway, and I know she didn't mean to. She's just little. Please don't hurt her."

"You just hush up. She needs her butt busted, and her mama or daddy ain't neither one here to do it."

To Mamaw, nothing would do but for the daisy breaker to feel the weight of her transgressions. Sister was tough as nails too—stone-faced with eyes glued straight ahead ready to take her punishment without so much as a wince.

I tried to get in front of Mamaw and got the edge of my arm switched in the mayhem before I decided that standing up for the accused was too dangerous. I turned my head and covered my eyes, wailing and hollering for Mamaw to stop.

My little sister was too stubborn to shed the first tear. I wished I were made of whatever stuff she was because I was completely crushed just by watching it and she never made a solitary peep. At least not until she was made to apologize to me, which Sister willingly did though I insisted it was completely unnecessary. That apology finally brought her bottled-up tears to the surface.

Sister didn't seem any too shaken by the affair but it broke my heart. For the rest of the day, I watched her play while holding back winces and moving carefully with the bright welts on her legs. As much as a young child could, I nursed a grudge toward Mamaw for months after that—though to be fair, I never saw her punish any of her grandchildren again.

That night, I lay in the twin bed beside Sister and felt the heat coming off the welts on her little legs. Despair came over me, and I wanted to ease this pain for Sister but was unable even to articulate the pain I felt myself. I hoped Aunt Glenda would come and get us the next day so we could play with Jamie and get out of this place. I wanted to go home, even if Mama had to leave us by ourselves all day and night. I wanted to be anywhere but here. If only it could be my legs that were hot with stripes, and not Sister's.

We just lay there, both of us staring down a hard reality—that so little in our lives could be rightly accounted for.

I wanted to hug Sister and tell her that we all do bad things and that Mamaw had whipped her too hard. Or tell her I wanted the nerve to break a daisy off at its root, which was the kind of outright rebellion I would never have the stomach for.

But I didn't do or say anything. I lay awake, alone with my regret and emptiness, mad at myself for not protecting her, inching over to the edge of the bed to give her plenty of room to sleep, careful not to rub up against her legs.

8

ALL MY ROWDY FRIENDS

A WATER MOCCASIN AS big around as my arm slid off into the water just as we were rounding the corner to our campsite near the Little Tennessee River. Like the daisies had been the year before, camping was a respite from the long and dry summer days at the trailer.

It was the middle of July—hotter than the pepper sprout Johnny Cash had been singing about on the radio—when we rolled into the campsite. And not surprisingly, there wasn't a sober adult with us.

While the adults stumbled around like the Three Stooges, trying to put up the tent, Jamie, Sister, and I had headed for the river. Within minutes, we were scrambling up the clay bank and racing back to camp to tell them about the snake. Water moccasins are the fearsome venomous water snakes of the South, with legends of people falling into nests of them or that one bite from the reptile could kill a grown man before he could find help.

"Daddy, there's a giant snake over here. I think it's the same one I saw when we pulled up," I yelled, running toward the tent.

"That ain't just a snake, that's a dadblame water moccasin, Edie Nise," Daddy said with a grin on his face.

"That ain't no water moccasin, Jim; you're gonna skeer them girls," Aunt Glenda said, without much worry in her eyes as she sat smoking at the picnic table.

"I'd bet my old truck on it. That's a water moccasin as sure as I'm the handsomest feller at this campsite," Daddy said, looking at us and winking.

While they continued to work on the tent and the tarp they were using for shade, Uncle George pulled up with his pop-up trailer, and the adults started laughing and telling stories they'd heard of snake handling preachers being bit and falling over dead.

Just about the time they got the tent nearly up, Daddy fell into it and knocked the whole thing over, making a spectacle of himself like he was wont to do. A champ at turning a misfortune into an opportunity, he got up and flat-foot danced on the blue tarp and circled around the fledgling campfire, as he shouted, "Well, it's Howdy Doody time, I reckon."

Daddy was a master at making people laugh in almost every circumstance, me most of all.

Camping in the 1970s with my family was not a scene of picturesque mountains with rushing rivers, canoe trips, and campfires with s'mores like you might see in an ad for the Great Smoky Mountains. Whatever creek or lake we swam in could best be expressed the way Aunt Glenda sometimes described her intestinal problems: "This ain't nothin' but muddy water."

There was no sunscreen and no designated swimwear. We wore cutoff denim shorts and tank tops or whatever else we could find, and our skin burned to a crisp. There were no life jackets that I recall, and if there were, no responsible adults were around to make us wear them. No bug spray, no antibacterial soap, no bottled water, no "healthy snacks," and no one who gave two hoots about whether or not the kids were having a good time.

Mamaw and Aunt Johnny never went camping because neither

of them drank alcohol and both of them had a tendency toward bad nerves, which meant that we kids went largely unsupervised the entire weekend. While Daddy, Uncle George, and Uncle Gene started back on the booze, their friends Hayes Whaley and his wife strummed on their guitars and sang old country songs loud and off key. That was enough to drive off Jamie, Sister, and me to find some adventures of our own.

We meandered around the campground for a while, but always ended up back in the river, the threat of water moccasins not stopping us. The weather was so hot and humid we had to get in the water to dry off.

'Long about dusk and what should have been dinnertime, we found our way back to where our campsite should have been, only to discover no campsite whatsoever—only beer bottles strewn around, intoxicated adults, and Daddy facedown, tangled up in the tarp.

Nobody had cooked any supper, and the other adults were preoccupied with music and booze, so we stepped over Daddy's legs and rummaged around in the back of the car and found enough Beanee Weenees and chips to feed the three of us.

Sundown brought its usual trouble—a fight brewed between Aunt Glenda and Uncle George about who knows what. We snuck back down to the river's edge until it was too dark to see each other's faces. Snakes weren't too terrifying when matched against boredom and a campsite full of drunks.

Finally, we headed back and climbed into Uncle George's pop-up camper, the three of us sharing one of the beds. Daddy was still on the ground in the tarp when we turned in and the unhappy couple must have made up, because we fell asleep to the sound of someone's guitar.

In the morning, I woke Sister up and we raced to the communal bathrooms, seeing who could get there first. When we got back, Jamie and everybody else were still asleep, except for Daddy, who offered us corn straight out of a can and Vienna sausages for breakfast, with RC Colas to wash it down. Daddy was as jolly as ever, making coffee and trying to fix the blue tarp tent he'd knocked over the night before.

"Nise, me and you and Gina are gonna set off some farcrackers tonight. I bought them just for you two."

"Great, Daddy," I said. Sister pretended to be excited too.

But I knew that Daddy wouldn't be sober enough for fireworks that night. And I was right. All of the men were passed out by the time it got good and dark.

I suppose it was the preferable ending because there was always a fifty-fifty chance that the liquor would incite a domestic altercation or two, in which case we might wake up in the morning to a camping version of the apocalypse, with the worst perpetrator sleeping off his whiskey in the car by himself and broken beer bottles littering the campsite like confetti.

Intoxicated adults or not, camping was a welcome respite from the dry and dusty summer days at the trailer. The water was its own sort of baptism, though far removed from the decency of the church house I would soon learn to love.

One weekend that summer I chose to stay behind at Mamaw's while Daddy and the others took off for the river. That weekend would swallow up my innocence like a snake swallows his supper; a weekend that would live in my nightmares. It would be many years before the truth surfaced about what had happened or I told anyone about it. But when my family returned, full of stories of their adventures, I wished for all the world that I had gone camping with the rest of them.

9

SUMMER IN DIXIE

THE SUMMER WORE ON, and one night I woke up while it was still dark, listening close for any signs that Daddy might be making biscuits and gravy, but the only sound I heard was Mamaw snoring. Without rustling the covers, I got out of bed, moving in tiny increments to keep the bed from creaking.

Finally, I was standing upright looking around the dark room. Tiptoeing past the twin bed where Mamaw and Aunt Darlene were still sleeping, I looked back to make sure Sister hadn't woken up. Her hands were tucked up under her chin, making it look like she was praying.

I snuck into the kitchen hoping Daddy was just being extra quiet. He wasn't there, which meant he probably hadn't come back last night. Uncle Gene's bedroom door was closed so I sat at the kitchen table and hugged my knees to my chest, wondering where Daddy had stayed and, more importantly, wondering what there would be to eat and who would cook it.

It would be an exaggeration to say I was always hungry, but I always felt a gnawing sense of never enough—this lingering, hollow ache that felt more like my stomach was always growling.

Maybe it was because Mamaw had the barest refrigerator I have ever seen. Or maybe it was because hunger is easier to give voice to than pain. Either way, I was aware that somewhere deep down, I was empty.

Depending on who was living with Mamaw at the time and who had an actual job or had been approved for a government check, food was rationed accordingly. The one thing that Mamaw always kept on hand was leaf lard, which she used for frying potatoes and making biscuits. Usually there were dried pinto beans and a bag of potatoes. Sometimes there was milk and eggs, and on very rare occasions, Wampler's sausage.

Though Mamaw's trailer was Daddy's landing pad, he increasingly found other places to be besides there, and I didn't blame him for that. My single largest complaint about staying with Mamaw was the lack of food. It became my obsession.

Mamaw's check came the first of every month, and she cashed it the day it arrived, always requesting the money in crisp twenty-dollar bills, which she kept in a worn envelope tucked away in her pocketbook.

The pantry, or the open shelves where the pantry had once been enclosed, had been busted out when Uncle Gene came home drunk one night and fell into it before he could find his way to the couch. That meant that the green Plexiglas that came standard on the pantries in single-wide trailers was gone, leaving the potatoes and the macaroni in full view—that is, if it was near enough to the first of the month to still have them around. If there was government cheese and peanut butter—well, I can't even tell you the joy in my heart.

I broke off a piece of leftover cornbread that Mamaw had made the day before and curled myself into a ball on the green vinyl couch, hoping it wouldn't be too long before Daddy drove up. The crumbs dribbled onto the linoleum.

Just before lunchtime, Sister and I were watching Saturday morning cartoons when I heard a car drive up. I ran to the window, hoping it was Daddy's red truck, but it was his sister Aunt Johnny and her husband, Uncle Reford. My cousin Tim drove them, and his brother Mark, the only cousin my exact age, rode in the backseat. Tim chauffeured everyone around because neither Aunt Johnny nor Mamaw had a driver's license and Uncle Reford would rather have walked than driven.

"There's Tim, Mama," Aunt Darlene said to Mamaw. "I want him to go get me somethin' to eat."

"Edie, bring me my pocketbook," Mamaw said. Money could be coaxed out of her spontaneously by almost no one but Aunt Darlene. Anybody else got a good cussing to go along with what little money she reluctantly forked over. I'm sure that's the only reason there was anything at all in her upper cupboards, which usually housed a large can of JFG coffee, dried pinto beans, and rarely anything else.

"Darlene, you've tortured me to death," she said, sorting through her purse. "What do you want? I can't understand what you're sayin'."

"Fish, from Long John Silver's," Aunt Darlene managed to get out.

"Fish! Why, I couldn't eat a bite of some old fish."

Mamaw turned to Tim—her go-to driver for errands—who was now watching TV.

"Tim, can you go get Darlene her fish?"

"I don't know if I've got the gas to get over there, Mamaw," Tim said, irritated at having to leave so soon when he had just gotten comfortable.

"Well, here—take whatever's left over and buy you a little gas."

My mouth was already watering at the mention of the fish dinner, but to no avail. There was never enough money to feed us all, so I knew that Tim would bring back a sack of food for Darlene while the rest of us would eat cornbread and whatever else Mamaw managed to rustle up.

An hour later, Tim came back with the dinner for Aunt Darlene. My stomach was growling from the smell alone. I would have given anything for that fish, but Sister and I sat there in that tiny trailer while she ate it in front of us.

We pretended that we didn't care while staring wide-eyed as she finished every last bite. I looked around at the scattering of people—Aunt Johnny, Uncle Reford, cousins Tim and Mark, cousin Sis and her daughter, and Uncle Gene, who got up from the couch and walked out to the porch.

Before he let the door slam, he piped up, "I don't know why y'uns bring food in here like that when there ain't enough for them kids."

Something welled up inside of me.

For the first time, Uncle Gene spoke up for us.

I wanted to cry but I didn't. I got up and motioned for Sister to follow me. At least the smell wouldn't be so strong outside. Uncle Gene was leaning against the edge of the porch. He didn't say anything, and I didn't either. Sister and I walked across the driveway to where Smoky was tied up by his doghouse and petted his head, then meandered behind the trailer and pulled sheets of clay off the bank, the crumbles of dirt tumbling to the ground and filling our shoes.

I was surprised by the passion that rose in my belly.

I was angry . . . with Daddy.

I blamed him—for not being there, for not buying us Long John Silver's fish, for hardly ever buying any food for us at all. Whatever it was that fathers were supposed to do, I was sure that feeding their kids was probably at the top of the list.

To make matters worse, he didn't show up at the trailer at all that entire weekend.

I wanted him. Or Mama. Or maybe just fried fish.

Early the next day, Sister and I were pulling pancake-sized slabs of clay from the bank behind the trailer when Mamaw hollered for me. "Edie, get in here and clean up so you can go on the Easter Seals bus with Aunt Darlene again. That way somebody's there to help her in the bathroom at the bowling alley. You don't keer to go, do you?"

"No, I don't mind helping her, Mamaw," I said, secretly dreading it but never wanting to do anything to cause Mamaw or anybody else any trouble.

Easter Seals was a nonprofit group dedicated to bettering the lives of people with disabilities. One way was to take them on field trips. Usually I had to go with Aunt Darlene because Sister was too young, Jamie refused, and none of the boy cousins could help her in the bathroom.

Most of the time I really didn't mind that much, but today I had fish and missing Mama and Daddy on my mind.

I heard the Easter Seals bus pull up while wiping the clay off my hands and Darlene was already chomping at the bit by the door. I don't know why she always insisted on wearing heeled sandals because just getting her down the steps of the trailer safely was a job. The bus driver took it from there and got her loaded onto the bus.

By the time the bus arrived at the bowling alley, I was almost over my hurt feelings, trying my best to have a good attitude. I could never nurse a grudge for very long, especially when it came to Aunt Darlene. It seemed like her life was hard enough, without me acting like I didn't want to be there with her.

I got the handicapped contraption that Easter Seals provided for bowling set up for her and her friends and helped them get their balls lined up and ready to roll. Before long, I was enjoying myself as I watched them play.

After we finished up the games and spent the next half hour getting all the wheelchairs loaded back onto the bus, I started to get excited because I knew that lunch was next. We always went to Shoney's buffet, which is probably why I so readily agreed to go. It was quite an ordeal, getting the wheelchairs all out and set up at the tables, but it was worth it.

I filled up Darlene's plate for her and then piled enough food onto my plate for two people, eyeing the dessert bar as I walked back to my seat. I feasted like a queen, stopping intermittently to help Aunt Darlene with her drink and her napkin. After a bowl of red Jell-O, two cookies, and some vanilla soft-serve ice cream, I was beginning to feel sick. Sick, but happy. And not a bit hungry.

The food situation at home with Mama was a little better. She did the best she could—a single mom often working two jobs without any kind of child support from Daddy. Most of our childhood years, Todd, Sister, and I ate suppers alone consisting of whatever we could forage from the cupboards or refrigerator. Campbell's tomato soup, grilled cheese, Cocoa Puffs, and bologna were standard fare. Pop-Tarts were found in the cupboard only after Mama's payday.

By now, we had moved from the trailer park to a tiny cracker-box house across the street from the Boys Club where Todd played sports after school. Sister and I soon discovered the keen survival skill of eating before he came home all sweaty and shirtless and starving. Todd could empty a box of cereal in one sitting, with his Jethro Bodine–sized portions.

During the week, I lived for school lunches. Unlike my class-mates, who made unkind remarks about what was served in the cafeteria, I saw a veritable feast in the lunch line. A school lunch consisting of Salisbury steak with mashed potatoes and a home-made roll was my love language. The girls I ate with usually picked at the food on their trays, and I was often the recipient of their leftovers. Even in high school, when it was cool for girls to skip lunch, I would have rather taken a beating from one of Mamaw's switches than give up the bounty.

I don't remember when I stopped feeling hungry for food, but I do remember a vague sense that something important was just out of reach.

10

STILL DOIN' TIME

THERE WERE TOO MANY cop cars to count, and before I could catch my breath, a sound crashed in around us like a loud box fan that had a piece of paper stuck in it. It hovered closer and closer until the helicopter came into view, looking like a giant spider from underneath, its legs threatening to rapture us. Everything turned in slow motion. I felt dizzy, like I might throw up, so I sat down on the ground and buried my face in my lap.

"Get in the house, Edie!" Mamaw and Aunt Johnny screamed. Sister huddled by the edge of the porch holding on to Aunt Johnny's pant leg, covering her ears to muffle the loud sirens. I wanted to go to her, but I couldn't. I was too scared to move.

Legions of men in uniforms with angry faces and drawn guns swarmed the yard.

I heard them say Sonny, my cousin's name.

It was Aunt Johnny's son they wanted, her oldest child, then only nineteen years old. The police told her they'd find Sonny if they had to search the entire mountain to do it. When the helicopter landed and shut off its engines, I could finally move. I ran up to the porch and grabbed Mamaw's arm.

"What has he done that you'd send an army like this to find him?" Aunt Johnny cried.

"We have a warrant for his arrest, and it'll be way worse than it has to be if your family doesn't cooperate with us."

"Oh dear God, please don't take him, he ain't nothin' but a boy," Aunt Johnny pleaded. "He wouldn't hurt nobody."

The policemen swarmed the mountain, and less than an hour later brought Sonny down the steep ridge behind the trailer. We all watched in horror as they handcuffed and arrested him.

Sonny was like most of the other Rudder men, with some brushes with the law and a wild streak when he drank. He smoked pot (sometimes in their house) and did recreational drugs, but I couldn't imagine what he had done to warrant that kind of arrest.

He was hauled off to jail and months later was convicted of armed robbery. He was sentenced to sixteen years in federal prison.

I feared Aunt Johnny and Mamaw might not survive the heartache of Sonny being shipped off to Brushy Mountain Prison, one of the harshest places on earth for a young man to spend the bulk of his early life. But despite the fact that both of them had an occasional tender side that made them seem fragile, their Appalachian toughness shone through and their strength surprised me. Mamaw had seen a lot of pain in her life, and a prison sentence for her grandson didn't seem to be the worst of it. She weathered it like a farmer weathers a drought.

Prison visits became our regular weekend outing. On Saturday mornings we loaded up the car and headed to Brushy Mountain.

We were packed like sardines in Uncle Gene's car. I really didn't mind the two-hour drive to the prison, except I would get carsick when we snaked up the winding mountain roads as we got close to our destination. But I kept telling myself I could endure it all for the reward at the end: ice-cold bottles of Coca-Cola and bags of Cheetos from the vending machine in the visitors' area.

Jamie made the trek only one time. After the prison guard made her cover up her Daisy Dukes cutoff shorts with prison-issue work pants, she never went back. Jamie was smarter than the rest of us—or at least old enough to speak her mind.

I was too intrigued to make up an excuse to stay home. Usually it was Aunt Johnny; Uncle Reford; Uncle Gene; and an assortment of brothers, sisters, and cousins who caravanned to the prison gates. Daddy rarely went because even when he was sober, a long day pent up with a carload of people was not a good place for a man with a tendency toward the shakes.

One particular weekend it was me, Mamaw, Aunt Johnny, Uncle Gene, and Sonny's younger brothers, Tim and Mark.

As I walked with my family toward the building, which looked like it had been plopped right down between two ridges with its imposing fences and barbed wire and guard towers looming above, it dawned on me. *Sonny lives here now in this big, scary place.* I tried reconciling myself to this truth—made all the more difficult after walking through a series of security checks, with alarms to doors that locked loudly behind us. We entered a room of inmates, most of them with creepy tattoos and eyes full of hate.

The smell took my breath away. It was as if old men and coffee and anger had mingled with cigarette smoke and been bottled and sprayed into the visiting area to suffocate the weak. The room was littered with scuffed metal tables lined up in rows like a grown-up lunchroom where visitors could bring food and eat with their loved ones on the inside.

When Sonny walked in, tears formed in the corners of my eyes.

His blue jumpsuit hung off him; he looked too young and scrawny to be in prison. He hugged us and got all choked up when he hugged his mama.

I was probably only seven or eight, but I could felt the weight of that moment. All the things they couldn't say. All the tears unnoticed. His fears. Her heartache. The whole of it was almost too much to see.

We'd brought a sackful of sandwiches, so we sat down at the metal table by the window, eating our food and grabbing chips from the vending machine until the quarters ran out. I loved having lunch there—so many of us linked by blood and heartache and shared food.

As Aunt Johnny caught Sonny up on all the family news, my eyes darted around the room, studying the plethora of tattoos on the prisoners.

I'd never seen so many—lots of skulls and curvy women and a host of ill-formed women's names that looked like a child had penned them. It was the animals and the crosses I liked most. The animals made me think of the Daffy Duck that was tattooed on Daddy's forearm, which he had gotten during his short stint in the service. I'm guessing he may have been intoxicated at the time because nobody—not even Daddy—could ever explain the significance of the duck.

After losing interest in the ink, I turned my attention to the colorful people at the other tables, trying to figure out their relationships to one other. I listened to every conversation I could overhear and watched for body language and eye contact, trying to guess what the men had done to get themselves here in the first place. I was even more fascinated with the people who came to visit the inmates. At one table I heard some angry words and wondered if there'd be a scuffle, while down the row there was a lot of kissing going on.

"Let's go outside," Mamaw said, eyeing the make-out session happening nearby.

We walked into the sunshine and onto the green lawn of the courtyard. I took a deep breath, thankful to be free from all the smoke and body odor in the room. As long as I ignored the tower guards with their assault rifles that loomed overhead, the courtyard was beautiful, with its flowering trees, green grass, and the mountains rising up around us on all sides.

When visitation was over, Sonny hugged Mamaw and Aunt Johnny good-bye. I saw the way they steeled themselves against the pain, their hearts broken in two. My cousin rubbed the top of my head. Uncle Gene patted him on the back.

"You be smart in there now," Uncle Gene said.

We all tried to be brave as Sonny clenched his jaw and lined up at the door to go back to his cell, looking like a child compared to those hardened criminals.

On the drive home, I had a lonely, empty feeling—wondering what awful things must be happening to Sonny in there and wishing for all the world he could come back with us.

Mamaw and Aunt Johnny didn't speak a word the whole way home. They must have been thinking the same thing—the look of grief was hanging heavy on their faces.

Peeking out the back window, I stared at the prison for as long as I could see it, the cream-colored structure like a castle in some fairy tale. Only this castle was not part of a fairy tale, it was like nothing I'd ever seen and a place I prayed I'd never get locked up in. The next sixteen years would worry Mamaw and Aunt Johnny nearly to death.

As we snaked along the mountain roads in silence, my mind reeled with thoughts of what it would be like to live in a place so cruel. Perhaps worse was imagining what it would be like knowing your son was locked up there. I thought of how Mama would feel if Todd were there and how devastating it would be to walk off and leave your teenager in some awful lion's den such as that place surely was.

I closed my eyes to try to think of something else—anything else.

Drifting off to sleep, I couldn't help but think about Daddy, wondering if he would ever do anything that would land him in Brushy Mountain. The thought of it was like a knife scraping my insides. Lately he kept talking about God, so I doubted anything like that would ever happen to him, but then he really only opened up his Bible when he was drunk. I wasn't sure if the one cancelled out the other. I guess that's why I was so glad when Daddy took us to meet Shirley.

I'LL FLY AWAY, O GLORY

One Saturday I was studying tattoos at the federal prison, and the next I was watching my stepmom, Shirley, open up a half gallon of ice cream and slice it into twelve equal pieces, like you'd slice a loaf of bread.

Shirley lived in Hankins Hollow, on a meandering country road cut between two ridges in the heart of a tiny backwater town an hour northeast of Knoxville. I don't think Daddy even told us they were married until he was driving us to her house, but it wouldn't have meant much to us anyway. At six and eight years old, Sister and I were used to riding along with Daddy without asking too many questions.

We would soon become endeared to Shirley if for no other reason than she had a way of keeping Daddy sober. A recent widow with seven kids of her own and pregnant with my soon-to-be-born half brother, she was unlike anyone I had ever met—a strict, God-fearing woman who grew all her own food, raised all her own animals for slaughter, and still had a working outhouse.

The holler was home to her entire family—her parents lived just beyond the garden and all her siblings' homes peppered the hills and ridges along the creek where I would soon learn to gig a frog and catch a crawdad.

Daddy married Shirley without any fanfare or forewarning, shedding his drifter ways for a quiet life in the country. I got a strange feeling that the arrangement might be temporary, like most good things with Daddy tended to be. But sober he was, and for as long a stretch as I had ever witnessed.

When Jim Bob was born six weeks premature with Down syndrome, I wondered if that might keep Daddy on his best behavior for a good long while. Daddy seemed to be a changed man—sober, shirt on and buttoned, in love with his baby boy, and brand new at being a churchgoing man.

The first night we stayed in the holler, Shirley made a big pot of soup beans and some cornbread, and for a special treat she had Daddy run to the store to get ice cream. The slices of ice cream made me appreciate her dedication to fairness where food was concerned. After all, with all her kids and us there, too, it was a lot of people to feed. Sister and I looked at each other and then made quick work of those perfect slices.

The next morning, after a hearty breakfast of biscuits and country ham, we loaded up into Daddy's old Buick and headed to church.

The church was only a few miles up the highway from the house, but you had to come down the ridge and wind through those curvy country roads in the valley to get there. Thickets of trees and rows of tobacco dotted the landscape next to cleared-out fields bordered by silos. Even with the windows down, beads of grimy sweat rolled down the back of my shirt, and I rubbed my back against the seat to try to wick them dry.

When we got there, Daddy threw the old Buick in park on the gravel lot and helped Shirley get the baby out.

"Come on, Daddy's little man," he said as he sang Jim Bob

a little ditty and lifted him in the air, his small, spindly legs dangling.

It was one of those churches with a marquee out front always sporting a pithy saying like "Turn or Burn" or "Don't Wait for the Hearse to Bring You to Church."

Before we reached the door, I could hear somebody banging away on the upright piano. The smell of tobacco and men's shaving cream greeted us as Daddy swung open the door and single-filed us in. It was the middle of summer in the South but no air-conditioning cooled the stifling air inside the building—so burning we were, no matter which way we turned.

We made our way up the center aisle to an open pew and sat down. Several men in overalls were scattered throughout the sanctuary, holding places for their family like tokens on a board game. As the pianist began playing an upbeat gospel song, the women visited and hugged and went on about the heat and crops and whatever it was that country women talked about in 1978. The preacher started the service by asking if there was somebody who had a song on their heart from the Lord.

Of course there was.

A lady about Mama's age made her way to the microphone and belted out a charged rendition of "I'll Fly Away," a song I had heard Aunt Darlene play on her eight-track tape player.

At the start of the next song, women began to dance in the aisles and the men shouted, "Amen!" and scooted their feet like they were two-stepping. I thought to myself that Daddy *would* be right at home here, except he usually only danced when he was drinking.

A few younger women got "struck by the Spirit," as Shirley later referred to it, and landed right in the middle of the floor in a coma-like state.

When all the music and talking in tongues settled down, the preacher took his place behind the wobbly pulpit. I had never heard anyone speak in tongues before, but I would learn that some religious folks did this as a sign that they were filled with God's Spirit. It sounded mostly like gibberish to me, but I was intrigued by the flurry of high emotions that filled the room when people did it.

The preacher's presence settled like a blanket on the room, rendering folks of every age quiet and still. He loomed tall over us and opened his Bible—a book so massive that it dangled over both sides of the wooden podium. The cadence of the preacher's voice rose and throbbed like a passionate auctioneer desperate to off-load his wares to the weary farmers and their families. He preached on the Lord's sure and severe punishment for those who continued to follow the devil into the vile grips of sin and damnation, shouting phrases that ended with *huh*. "AND NOW IF YOU-huh . . . WANT TO ESCAPE-huh . . . THE FIRES OF HELL-huh . . ."

His message built into an angry swell, his face looking like he'd been holding his breath underwater for too long, while sweat dripped from his hairline in rivulets big enough to drown the housefly he was swatting. Sister squirmed in her seat the whole time, but I couldn't take my eyes off him. I don't know if it was fear or the need to belong or my deep desire to please, but I knew beyond a doubt that whatever it was he was so passionate about us doing, I needed to be the first one in line.

The preacher went on about being baptized in the Spirit and how those who had forsaken their sins would be snatched up in the twinkling of an eye in a sure and sudden rapture. Those who were left would face a fiery tribulation, and according to John the Revelator, they'd be forced to take a mark of the Beast, which sounded like a terrifying fate.

When the preacher had exhausted himself, he gave an altar call—that haunting hour of the church service that for years after would reduce me to nerves and guilt, no matter how sincerely I repented. By the seventh verse of "Just as I Am," I found myself twisted up inside. Red-faced, with eyes full of tears, and eager to turn from my wicked ways and give my heart to Jesus, I glanced over at Sister. I was disappointed to see that she was leaned over on Daddy's lap, twirling her hair and not even paying attention, but I wasn't about to take any chances on being left behind for the fire and the Beast.

I blubbered my way to the front, while the choir sang and cried and said amen for a good half hour.

Although unsure of what giving your heart to Jesus might entail, I was eager to be part of God's family, so I repeated the prayer and didn't ask any questions. The preacher introduced me to the congregation as a brand-new child of God and welcomed me to the family by giving me my very own Bible. Daddy winked at me from the pew, and I knew I had made the right decision.

A week later, I got baptized in a nearby creek. As Daddy stood at the edge of the water holding a towel for me, he told me he'd been baptized when he was young, too, and that we all needed Jesus, but especially if your last name was Rudder. We both chuckled. When I returned home that autumn, I started carrying my Bible to school. I took to church like a duck to water and found in its walls a place and a people to which I could belong.

This new world of Daddy's had me in its clutches. Maybe I was just enamored that he was sober; maybe it was the tiniest sliver of the gospel message that first planted itself in my heart; or maybe it was Jim Bob, the most darling little angel I had ever laid eyes on. I can't say for sure, but something about their rugged, simple way of life seemed to wake something in me.

The gritty, self-sustaining ways of Shirley and her mom and siblings were a different kind of poor than I had known. This was poor, but not hopeless; penniless, but not indigent. Hard work was Shirley's life and now Daddy's life, too, as evidenced by the multitude of chickens and pigs she kept; the monstrous garden that we weeded, laid out in endless rows behind the house; and the working smokehouse where they cured their meat.

Sister and I stayed most of that summer with Daddy and

Shirley, picking tomatoes, cucumbers, and zucchini, and hauling them by the bucketful into the kitchen to be washed and processed for canning day. We sat on the front porch and shucked corn and broke beans during the day and then spent those pitch-black Appalachian nights running outside with Randy and Penny, Shirley's two youngest. Often we were trying to see if we could spot the ghost that Randy swore he'd seen in the road a few nights before. We lay perfectly still on the gravel drive, waiting for its reappearance, until we heard Shirley holler.

"Randy, Penny, girls! Y'uns get in yeer right now and get in bed. There's ghosts around yeer aplenty, but you cain't set out there all night. I'm aimin' to take you kids blackberry pickin' tomorrow by sunrise, and I don't want to hear nothin' 'bout how tarred y'uns are," she said, sweeping off the front porch and spitting tobacco juice into the grass.

We came in and got a drink of water from the dipper she left hanging over the sink and then climbed into the upper loft above where Shirley and Daddy slept, a room so stifling it was hard to breathe.

There was something about those nights at their house that made me lonely—the heat, the stillness, the pitch-dark, the newness of it all. And maybe my lack of direct access to Daddy too. It might be odd to say I missed him because I knew he was asleep in the bed downstairs, but I missed *the him* I had always known. He wasn't mine at Shirley's. But he was always within reach and always sober—and there was something about it that made me happy.

I had heard people call Daddy a no-good-for-nothing drunk more times than I could count, but here he was a new man, or a new creation, as the preacher put it. Old things had passed away, at least for a time. I was shocked that Daddy had remained sober for nearly a year, not to mention well-behaved enough to badger a churchgoing woman to marry him and keep him around.

During those early months of their marriage, Daddy was the

kind of sober I had always dreamed about—the kind of sober that makes you wonder if someone has kidnapped your father and replaced him with the likes of Andy Griffith; the kind of sober that makes you happy because you realize that maybe this was how life was supposed to be all along. It also made me a little sad that the way of life I'd known with him might be gone.

I saw Daddy in a new light as I sat beside him on the porch swing and watched him cradle Jim Bob between his knees and sing and talk and whistle—the birds serenading in full voice in the background. Nobody could make that baby smile and laugh like Daddy. Nobody could make me smile and laugh like him either.

In hindsight, I'm sure the church people had heard about Daddy's wild living ways. They probably had him on a short leash, watching for signs of backsliding. If that wasn't enough pressure on him, Mama's call to him after we returned home in August probably didn't help.

Much to Mama's chagrin, I had learned a lot at the country church, now gracing the family with my new skill of speaking in tongues.

Jamie was staying the night after missing us at Mamaw's most of the summer. Sister and I were telling her all about our adventures, including our time at church.

Egged on by Sister, I was trying to teach Jamie and Todd how to speak in tongues. I conjured up what I could remember from my favorite church ladies, dizzying myself into a stupor right there on the living room floor.

"Mom, you've got to come in here right now! Something's bad wrong with Edie," Todd yelled into the kitchen.

Mama was cooking pork chops when my brother bolted into the kitchen out of breath. Mama raced into the living room.

"Edie, wake up! You answer me, what in the world is wrong with you, child?" Mama slapped my cheeks and broke my trance. I opened my eyes to see Jamie and Todd staring at me and Sister snickering away in the corner.

Mama immediately got Daddy on the phone.

"Listen, Jim, I'm glad you sobered up and married what looks to be a decent woman," Mama said. "But whatever crazy church you've taken these children to, you're gonna have to stop. Edie was carryin' on today like she was having some kind of seizure, and it scared us half to death. When she gets older, if she wants to join the Holy Rollers, that's her business, but she's just a child and don't even know what she's doing."

Whatever Daddy said to Mama must have pacified her, but he didn't keep us away from church. I just stopped speaking in tongues at home for fear that we wouldn't get to visit Daddy anymore.

His year of being sober was the strangest thing. It felt like knowing Daddy for the first time, but in some visceral way, it felt like losing him too. I wondered if we'd ever sing Johnny Cash on Mamaw's porch again or if he'd get us all laughing by pulling over on the side of the road to dance one off. I wondered if what I loved so much about him was something he could only access when he was drinking.

Would things ever be the same again? And more confusing than that, why would I wish them to be?

When school started, the two-hour drive was too far a trek to see Daddy every weekend. I was bound and determined to keep up my end of the giving-my-heart-to-Jesus bargain, and I needed help with the questions about Daddy I was wrestling with. I made Mama promise to take me to the church around the corner from us. She kept the promise but made me take Sister. Of course, since Sister was only six and quite bullheaded for her age, I was skeptical of her commitment to the cause and was not at all sure she had the wherewithal to throw off her worldly ways. I had not forgotten how spiteful she had been when she broke off my daisy, and she was always talking back to Mama. But I took her with me and hoped she'd want to get baptized too.

The new church took us in and put us through whatever their

normal system was for making converts—which put me in line for my second baptism. Eager as always for some friendly competition, I promptly joined the Bible drill team and became a regular at Sunday school. They gave me a Bible to study, and I won first place in the county-wide drill, which was the first small victory in my lifelong quest to figure out how religion worked and how to get good at it. I was sure this would make the Lord proud and prove how wholehearted my devotion was to Him.

This church was worlds apart from the country church— heavy with ornate architecture, with a choir that wore robes and a preacher who wore a suit and didn't sweat. A few months after our first visit, Mama dropped us off for a Sunday night service, and Sister and I both got baptized—my second time, her first.

At first, the church became my home away from home, a safe house much like school.

But after hearing so many fire-and-brimstone sermons, I eventually emerged from those early years with this vague sense that God was angry with me, that I was always failing to measure up to some standard of behavior and decorum. Worse yet was the burden that surely many in my family would never make the cut. For good or bad, the things you learn while young tend to stick, so there I was with a gloomy sense that God must surely be a lot like the scary, sweaty preacher from Shirley's church who would be happier if I could manage to quit sinning.

So I kept on getting saved and baptized and walking the aisles to rededicate my life to the Lord. By my eighth profession of faith, I wondered if I was the only one who couldn't manage to live the life I wanted.

When Daddy fell off the wagon the next summer, I knew I wasn't alone.

12

WHISKEY BENT AND HELL BOUND

WE SPENT MOST OF the following summer at Shirley's, too, holding Jim Bob's hands as we tried teaching him how to walk across the length of the front porch and wagering with Randy and Penny on who could jump over the creek without landing in the water. It would be a while yet before Jim Bob would walk on his own, but Randy won the creek-jumping contest every time, being two years older and two heads taller than the rest of us. To prove I was becoming a real country girl, I didn't hesitate when he dared me to jump off the top of the chicken coop, and I must have cried for half an hour when I sliced my hand wide open on a piece of old rusted tin that was hiding in the tall grass.

Shirley washed it out and wrapped it up with a torn piece of white T-shirt, and we went on with our business. It finally healed with a plump scar, but when Sister broke her arm a few weeks later, our country summer ended abruptly.

Mama raced out to get us, and we rode an hour to the hospital in Knoxville, Sister's arm sinking down in the middle into a

U shape. Trying not to get sick from looking at it, I kept patting her hair and telling her it was going to be okay, and when we finally got to the ER she was casted in no time.

Less than a month later, Daddy fell off the wagon and landed back at Mamaw's. He went back and forth to Shirley's that year, welcomed only as long as he could stay sober. Eventually, Shirley tired of his shenanigans.

The next summer, Mama decided we were old enough to stay home with Todd during the day, at least part of the time. So I devoted myself wholeheartedly to softball and put creek jumping and frog gigging, with the question of Daddy's sobriety far from my mind.

The half-mile walk to the ballpark from our house was a trek I made hundreds of times, usually with my glove slipped over my left hand, tossing up a softball with the right, my Blue Jays cap adjusted snugly over my fresh new perm.

My fourth grade school picture confirmed that the perm was a bad decision (although much begged for). But neither my perm nor the fourteen warts on my right middle finger slowed me down in the least.

Unlike most of the other girls on my softball team, I was hungry to win, as if somehow my own self-worth was tied up in winning. Maybe it was the fact that I could finally control the outcome of something, but I had a competitive streak that most of my teammates didn't have—coming early to run laps around the field, staying late for more batting practice, and throwing the ball as hard as I could over and over to first base.

A time or two, I even smudged black grease under my eyes like the pros did, sure it would help when the sun was glaring on the infield. Thanks to Rocky Balboa and Apollo Creed, we called my kind of drive "the eye of the tiger." I played shortstop like my life depended on it.

Our team made it to the finals in the Little League tournament.

I wanted to win it all. I had never wanted anything with such raw passion.

The tournament was held over the weekend, with the big game Saturday night, and that game felt like everything to me.

Daddy was a nomad that summer, living with whoever would have him while he tried to convince Shirley to let him come back. She forbade alcohol at her house, and Daddy had apparently stayed sober for as long as he could.

I called Mamaw's the day before the game, and Daddy was there.

"Hey, Daddy! I'm playing in a tournament tomorrow at four at Eagleton Ball Park. Can you come?" I asked, almost afraid that he'd say yes.

I was hoping it might boost his spirits from his mess-up with his family, but I knew it was a risky proposition, especially on account of it being a Saturday night and him not being on a sober streak.

"Woo doggies, yeah, I can come. If I can get that old truck to start, I'll be there, and if I can't, I'll have somebody bring me. I wouldn't miss it, Nise," he said, with just the slightest slur in his voice.

Sister and I walked to the ballpark so I could warm up by running laps around the perimeter of the field.

Because it was a tournament game, we were playing on the boys' Little League field, which meant that an announcer would call the game, introducing us as we took our positions. This added to my already rattled nerves. Once our team hit the dugout, I kept sneaking looks toward the stands to see if there was any sign of Daddy.

Fans who had watched the Little League boys' game stayed in their seats and now peppered the bleachers, which filled quickly. I saw at least five school friends who were staying for the game and glanced around for Sister, but didn't see her. I was technically in charge of keeping an eye on her, but she didn't need much help. As soon as her duties as my warm-up partner were over, she ran around with her friends, stopping by the field only when she needed another Blow Pop from the concession stand.

As the umpire shouted, "Play ball!" I made a final glance to the stands and felt both relieved and disappointed that Daddy hadn't shown up.

What matters is this game, I told myself. *It'll only be trouble if he shows up.*

After our team huddled by the dugout and chanted some sassy cheer that girls' softball teams did back then, I raced out to my position at shortstop, ready to play with more grit and hustle than raw talent.

With every hit that came my direction during the first inning, I snagged the ball and nailed my throws to first base.

The air felt electric, and playing under those lights was a dream come true, since I'd watched hundreds of boys' games there. We made three outs without a run from the other team, and I tucked my mitt under my arm as we ran off the field.

I was third in the lineup and cheered with my team as both girls before me made it to base. Now it was my first at bat. The pitcher was hurling them low and fast. I knew that if I made contact, I could bring the runners home.

"You got this," my coach said as we slapped hands. The girls cheered me on from the dugout. I nodded and clenched my jaw as I walked to the plate and gave the pitcher my best steely gaze.

I nailed a line drive down the third-base line that got past the left fielder. I raced to first and barely hesitated before making the turn to second. The left fielder was just getting the ball in her hand as I headed for third base and beat her throw without even hitting the ground. I'd landed a triple, putting us on the scoreboard, 2–0.

In the next inning, we held them to one run. As I raced back toward the dugout and paused, I saw Daddy and his friend Fred Owens taking their seats on the top row of the stands, both shirtless and tatted up, looking like a couple of ex-cons.

Well, actually, they *were* ex-cons, both of them having been jailed and then released in the last few months for public drunkenness and driving while intoxicated.

Trying not to be distracted, I took a deep breath and pretended I didn't see them, although plenty of people took a second glance when Daddy and Fred made their entrance.

"There she is, Fred—that's my girl right there! Come on, Nise, show your daddy how Rudders play ball," he said, standing up briefly to make sure I saw him.

When I got to the dugout, I acted like I was looking at the batting lineup, then dropped onto the bench.

"Is that your dad up in the bleachers, Edie?" asked one of my teammates, who must have seen the horrified look on my face.

"Ummm, yeah," I said without looking at her.

"Who's that with him?"

"I don't know, some guy he works with, I think," I said with my eyes on the mitt on my lap. What I didn't say was that Fred Owens was one of the creepiest guys my dad hung out with when he was drinking too much and that neither one of them had steady jobs.

As I heard my daddy's voice, I bit my bottom lip and fought back tears. I jumped up to join my team in the next cheer, focusing on the game.

By the ripe old age of ten, I knew how to handle a drunk with confidence and even compassion. But I didn't know how to deal with one while playing a championship ball game.

When my next at bat came, I shuddered at the hootin' and hollerin' that started before I reached the batter's box.

"Let's go, Nise! That right there is Jim Rudder's girl, and I bet she's gonna knock one out of the park. Woo doggies, hit it hard, Edie Nise."

For a moment, my stomach tightened and my hands felt locked around the bat. I didn't look in Daddy's direction and tried to ignore him, but hiding emotions was never my strong suit. Tears came faster than I could stop them, and for only the second time all year, I struck out.

I caught the disappointment in my coach's face as I walked back to the dugout with my cheeks burning with embarrassment. Daddy yelled out his encouragement from the top of the bleachers. "Awww, don't worry about it, girl! That umpire couldn't tell a strike if it hit him right between the eyes."

At the bottom of the sixth inning, our last chance to redeem ourselves, I was batting again. We were still just down a run, with a runner on base. Coach noticed I cringed every time Daddy and Fred yelled my name, so before I walked out, he called a time-out to the umpire.

Coach leaned close to me and said, "I know how hard it probably is to keep your head in this game."

I nodded but couldn't speak.

"Do you want me to have someone escort your daddy and his friend out of here? I can do that."

"No, please, don't do that. He'll be okay, I promise."

I knew Daddy would not leave without making an even bigger spectacle in front of all of us.

"Listen, Edie, this is our most important game of the year, and we need you. I'm sorry your daddy showed up like this, but don't let him ruin what you and your teammates have worked so hard for. You gotta dig down deep and find a reason to get your head back in this game. These girls follow you, and when you're not in it, they're not either. When it's over, I don't care what you say to him."

I nodded and walked to the batter's box. I shut everything out around me, and when the ball released from the pitcher's hand, I was ready. I smacked a line drive over the third baseman's head. It won the game for us.

The team went wild—jumping up and down and high-fiving each other, hollering and cheering almost loud enough to drown Daddy out. Coach wasn't happy with our overzealous celebration and told us to line up like good sportsmen to shake the other team's hands. After about fifteen "good games," I walked off the field toward the bleachers where Daddy and Fred were standing.

What I said to Daddy when the game was over was the same thing I said whenever he embarrassed me or didn't show up or showed up drunk or forgot my birthday or forgot Christmas— nothing. I would say nothing that implicated him or made him feel bad or worsened what pain he must have felt after losing Shirley and the life he could have had with her and Jim Bob.

"Thanks for coming, Daddy," I said as I hugged his bare, sweaty chest.

"Nise, 'at right 'air is how you do it. You hit that ball harder'n I've ever seen for a girl. That coach don't know how lucky he is to have a ballplayer like you," he said, patting me on the top of my ball cap.

Daddy and Fred took me and Sister to Pizza Hut to celebrate. We climbed into the bed of Daddy's truck and rode across town, the two of them in the front seat with the windows rolled down and George Jones blaring from the radio. The summer night air was hot and wet.

When we arrived, I asked Daddy to put his shirt on.

"Anythang for you, Nise," Daddy said. He left his shirt unbuttoned all the way down, which was always his custom when he was forced to wear one.

We found a table, and Daddy promptly told the waitress about the game.

"You don't know this, but Jim Rudder ain't raisin' no losers. This girl o' mine hit a home run before I even got to the game, and then you ort to have seen the way she slung that ball from shortstop to first base."

I didn't correct him on the home run. It was a triple, but keeping facts straight was not his forte, and he seemed so happy, I didn't want to spoil it.

"Give me and old Fred Owens two pitchers of Budweiser, and

then brang these girls whatever they want and as much as they want of it."

Despite the evening's events, I was delighted to be at this feast with Daddy. We ordered a pitcher of Mountain Dew and three large pizzas because none of us had the good sense to know how much pizza two adults and two kids could eat. Daddy didn't care and told the waitress to take the rest home for her family.

Whatever hurt or disappointment I felt toward Daddy was forgotten when he put his arm around me and said, "When did you get to be such a ballplayer, Nise?" He looked over to Fred. "She's got some arm for a girl, ain't she, Fred?"

On the way home, the night air was so humid it felt like a wet blanket that might suffocate us, even with Sister and me sticking our faces right into the wind from the back of Daddy's truck. Johnny Cash came on the radio, and Daddy had to make the most of "Folsom Prison Blues." He yelled the lyrics out the window so we could hear from the truck bed.

"Sang it, Nise!" and together we belted out the words like we were on stage at the Opry.

Then, in perfect Jim Rudder style, he pulled over to the side of the road. I thought at first maybe he needed to throw up, but when he got out of car, he came back toward us.

"You never know when you just need to dance one off," he said and began flat-foot dancing up and down the shoulder of the road. I knew he wouldn't be satisfied until I got out of the truck, so I climbed over the tailgate and onto the ground. Fred watched from the cab and Sister leaned against the side of the truck bed as Daddy and I jigged in the gravel and dirt.

We finally got Daddy back into the truck, and Sister and I bounced up and down in the back to the loud music coming from the cab until Daddy dropped us off at home.

"Nise, I'm gonna tell you one thang right now. You tell your daddy next time you're playin', and I'll be down here. You made

Jim Rudder proud tonight, ole girl," he said, flicking the ash of his cigarette.

"Okay, Daddy, I'll let you know. Love you."

He turned and peeled out of the driveway.

The daddy I knew best was back in full swing, and I wondered if it was too late to go back to those quiet, black-as-charcoal summer nights in Union County, where the only thing you could hear were whip-poor-wills and Daddy—stone-cold sober—whistling with baby Jim Bob on his lap.

But it was too late.

And the next time we would dance on the side of the road, I would be twelve and trying to figure out how to get us home.

13

ON THE ROAD AGAIN

It was late June of 1982, the day before Daddy's birthday. The Queen Anne's Lace stood as tall as me in the field by the railroad tracks, and it seemed like it was in a race with the chicory to see who could take over the field first.

Daddy took the curves on Rudder Road like he was one of the Duke boys being chased by Boss Hogg. Sister bounced along in the middle of the bench seat, and I hung my arm out the rolled-down window, trying to snatch up a bouquet of those white sprigs.

As we flew over the tracks, we passed the block house where Daddy grew up. He'd never talked much about it, but Aunt Glenda told me that at one time ten people lived in that tiny house with Mamaw, Papaw, and Aunt Darlene sharing the same bed, Daddy and Uncle Gene sleeping on couches and chairs, and Aunt Johnny and her family sharing the only other bed in the house.

The house had burned down in the middle of the night just ten years before—Mamaw, Papaw, and Aunt Darlene barely escaping out of the backroom window. Daddy and Uncle Gene were known for starting fires, but this one seemed to be pure chance and bad luck. The insurance money from that fire was how they rallied enough cash to buy the trailer that sat on the crook of Brown's Mountain, the land that all Papaw's brothers lived on. How someone ever hauled that trailer up that narrow driveway is still a mystery to me.

We threw up a cloud of dust as we jumped the ruts on Mamaw's driveway. Sister and I headed inside, and before the screen door had slammed, Daddy was gone again, out of sight before we could register what happened.

"I meant to tell Daddy happy birthday but I forgot to tell him before he left," I said to Mamaw. She was standing at the stove making coffee, shoulders slumped, seeming to echo the misery she felt.

"Birthdays ain't nothin' but a reminder of the pure hell I live in ever' day," she said.

It was evident from the tone of her voice that Mamaw had had enough of Daddy just leaving us there.

On Saturday morning, Daddy pulled up the driveway, honking his horn in sync with whatever was blasting from his radio. It set Mamaw off, and she pushed up from the table with two hands like a woman about to right some long-overdue wrong. Perhaps it was the years of Daddy leaving us or dragging us along to the bars, or maybe it was her visits to Brushy Mountain Prison, but Mamaw had fury in her eyes like I hadn't seen since she'd striped Sister's legs over the flower.

"Well, there's that good-for-nothin' sot, pullin' in here after he's laid up drunk somewhere all night," she said, walking toward the screen door.

Daddy had stopped the car and hollered out the window, "Nise, Gina! Come on, girls, we're goin' for hamburgers!"

Mamaw met him before he ever made it to the porch. Sister and I followed behind her.

"Jim Rudder, I'm gonna tell you one thang right now. You ain't takin' these girls nowhere if you aim to lay drunk all weekend.

You can forget it, ole boy. You ain't no earthly account, leavin' these children here without a dime to help buy anything to eat. Then you waltz in wantin' to take them to get a hamburger. I've had to use what little bit of money I've got to get some bread and milk and eggs so they'd have a bite. If I was you, I'd be ashamed of myself, and I wouldn't blame these two girls if they didn't never have nothin' to do with you again."

"Well, that's what I'm doin', Mama. I'm takin' these girls and gettin' them a hamburger."

"You'll take them over my dead body. You smell like a whiskey bottle, and ever'body you run with is either a drunk or on dope, and them kids don't need to be around it. Ever' time you leave here, you take them girls somewhere that they don't need to be," she finished, kicking a stray cigarette butt into the yard.

Daddy looked at us, standing on either side of Mamaw.

"Come on, girls, get in the car with your daddy. I'm takin' you for a Krystal hamburger and a Co-Cola."

Sister didn't budge. We both knew by now that the price for getting that burger was pretty steep, and the chances of us making it back to the trailer before nightfall were slim to none.

I didn't want to make Mamaw mad, but I couldn't stand the thought of Daddy leaving without me. I tried to act like I was deciding, but it was never much of a choice for me. Besides, it was his birthday, and I figured he'd be less likely to end up in trouble if I went with him.

I ran to his truck and hopped into the front seat, leaving Sister and Mamaw on the porch. A drinking daddy was better than no daddy, and I was convinced that somehow I could protect him if he really got into trouble.

Mamaw cussed and hollered until we got far enough out of sight that we couldn't hear her anymore. Daddy chuckled under his breath.

"She may whoop me when she sees me again, Nise." Daddy shifted the gear, peeling out at the bottom of the driveway.

"Yeah, I think she was pretty mad, Daddy. Are you okay to drive?" I asked, noticing that familiar glazed look in his eyes and how he reeked of alcohol, just like Mamaw said.

"Nise, your daddy's always fit to drive. Why, I could drive this old truck blindfolded with both of my arms tied behind my back," he said, lifting his hands off the wheel to prove his point.

"I'm sure you could, Daddy," I said, grabbing the steering wheel to keep us between the lines.

After we left the burger joint, Daddy drove to a seedy part of town where the government housing projects corralled some of the scariest people I'd ever seen.

"Where are we going, Daddy? Someplace for your birthday?"

"Naw, just gonna stop by ole Doyle's place," Daddy said.

Doyle was a mean drunk, and I hated going to his ramshackle mess of an apartment, certifiably the creepiest place I had ever laid eyes on—worse by far than the prison cafeteria.

A scantily clad and scantily toothed woman answered the door, covered in perverted tattoos as far as the eye could see. As soon as we walked in, I regretted my decision on the hamburger and wished I was at Mamaw's, helping her hang laundry out on the line.

"Doyle's in the kitchen, tryin' to get the lid off that moonshine, Jim. Boy, that girl looks just like you. How old is she now?" Her voice was scary sweet.

"I don't rightly know. Nise, how old are you? You look to be just about a grown woman."

"I'm twelve, Daddy."

The woman kissed Daddy on the cheek and patted the side of my arm, then scampered into the back bedroom while Daddy wandered into the kitchen to find Doyle.

I stood close to Daddy. Doyle was working on getting the top off a quart jar and looked like he hadn't showered in days. His jet-black, greasy hair was swiped back in a middle part and his handlebar mustache was greased to a point on both ends.

When Doyle saw me, he had a sort of intensity in his eyes that made me feel dirty, like I had done something wrong. I hoped I never saw him anywhere without Daddy around.

Doyle and Daddy downed a few shots at the kitchen table. *Fat Albert* entertained me on TV while I sat on the very edge of Doyle's grimy couch, careful not to let my bare legs touch it. The smell of beer and cat pee made it hard to think about anything else.

Finally we left Doyle's and slowly rambled through town, stopping to restock Daddy's quarts of beer and talk to Daddy's friends who lived nearby. Nobody ever mentioned his birthday, but he didn't seem to notice or care.

Then he took a turn for the worse. Daddy had a habit of falling into a strange seizure-like state when he drank too much too fast, and though it scared me, I had learned how to handle him. But his nodding off at the wheel finally got the best of me.

"Daddy, pull over by Genie's and let me drive. You're falling asleep."

"You want to drive this truck, Nise? I'll let you drive it. Matter of fact, you can have it. This will make you a good car," he slurred as he eased the truck to the shoulder of the road.

"Yeah, I'm sure it will, Daddy." I hopped out of the truck and came around to the driver's side as he somehow scooted over. I made him put out the cigarette that was teetering on his lips, then his head fell against the passenger window with a thud.

Daddy probably had no idea it would be four years before I could legally drive. But my inexperience behind the wheel had to be better than the swerving and bobbing he was currently doing. I'd watched Daddy shift the gears in that red Ford truck a hundred times, and I was sure I could do it.

As I pushed in the clutch, Daddy lifted his head to stare at the road, then over at me.

I put the truck in first gear and released the clutch. With only a few jerks of the engine, we were rolling.

"Nise, now listen here. Let off the gas and mash the clutch in, then throw her in second gear and give her gas like Richard

Petty," he said, showing me with his feet what he was wanting me to do.

The fact that I was taking driving lessons from a drunk man was not lost on me, but Daddy had a way of making everything seem like fun, so I listened and tried to follow his instructions.

The truck died a dozen times at stop signs and red lights until we reached the last tough grade below Mamaw's.

"You did it, Nise. I never doubted you, girl. You've got your daddy in you—there ain't nothin' you can't do," he said, as proud as he could be of me.

He leaned his head back and passed out in the passenger's seat at the bottom of Mamaw's driveway, one hand stuck in the air like it was pointing up toward heaven.

No way was I going to try driving that truck up the hill. I shut off the engine and pulled out the keys, then rustled Daddy enough to get him out of the truck. He could barely walk, so I helped him up the hill and into the trailer. He took his second good cussing of the day from both Mamaw and Uncle Gene, but he was asleep on the couch before I could get his shoes off.

"Happy birthday, Daddy," I whispered as I pulled a blanket up over him and patted his forehead.

Uncle Gene, Sister, and I watched *Hee Haw* as the sun faded over the mountain and I replayed the day's events in my head. I told Daddy the next morning that I didn't ever want to go to Doyle's apartment again.

"Well, Nise, ole Doyle couldn't stay outta jail for more than a week if he tried, so you ain't got nothin' to worry about. He ain't a bad feller when he's sober, though."

The truth was, I had never seen Doyle sober, which led me to count how many times I had ever seen Daddy sober. It was probably a number that could be tallied without much trouble, and mostly surrounding his stint with Shirley in the holler.

Still, I couldn't help but think in some way that I was a pretty lucky girl, not just for driving Daddy's truck way before I should have, but for being the person always by his side, for better or worse.

But there was a price to be paid for being someone's "person," and I began to wonder if the cost was more than any of us could keep paying. Somewhere down deep, I doubted Daddy would ever really change, and I wondered what that would mean for Sister and me and everybody else who loved him. Maybe the worst part about growing up was being forced to see things like they really were. And sometimes I wondered if a part of me would always refuse to do that.

Something was so right about Daddy and me, but something was so wrong, too. It's a lonely kind of ache to miss someone who is standing right in front of you. I couldn't quite give a name to what was wrong with us, but soon enough I'd find somebody who could.

14

ROSE COLORED GLASSES

I PUSHED MY WAY THROUGH the front door for the first time and couldn't believe how spacious it all seemed—dark wooden floors, a fireplace in the living room, two screened porches, and enough bedrooms that Todd wouldn't have to sleep with me and Sister anymore.

It was early autumn when we moved into a Craftsman-style bungalow on a main thoroughfare in Maryville, Tennessee, and the year Todd was a senior in high school. Nestled beneath two big sugar maples with a large yard of lush green grass, this house seemed like everything to me and at the same time nothing we could ever afford, if not for Gary, our new stepdad. Mama's marriage to Gary was as much of a surprise to us as Shirley and Daddy's had been, and as fast, too.

Our new house was next door to a church, which may have lent to the sacred space it occupied in my mind. If Shirley inspired me toward the art of homemaking, this house woke up something in me that would begin to crave beauty. Boxwood shrubs guarded the windows like armored soldiers, and it had the prettiest front door of any house I'd ever seen, looming tall and stately with its thick, dark wood and heavy cut-glass knob.

Besides the beautiful house, we got a new dad and two new sisters. Gary worked on the railroad and looked like Burt Reynolds, with long, shaggy black hair and a few snazzy polyester shirts that he unbuttoned at the top for effect. He was handsome and wore a watch and a gold chain that always had wiry chest hairs poking through it.

My new sister Kristie was my age, and Misty was only four. Sister and I shared a room with them when they came on weekends. With them around, our nights at Mamaw's became few and far between, mostly because it must have been easier to have all of us around to entertain each other. And visits to Mamaw's were beginning to feel like drudgery.

I don't rightly know if it was the champagne-colored Cadillac that Gary drove, the new cowhide that draped the living room floor, or the lava lamp he hung in the living room, but all of a sudden, we felt rich. The lava lamp was the sole object of my curiosity for a solid week, not to be outdone by the giant ornate bar that was delivered to our dining room, complete with a crystal whiskey decanter and a fancy set of brandy snifters.

Gary had a lavish set of white furniture with gold-leaf edges delivered to our bedroom. Sister and I spent half an afternoon folding our clothes into respectable piles and stashing them in tidy stacks in the dresser drawers. We had lived in hand-me-down spaces with hand-me-down furniture and couldn't get over the feeling that this new life was somehow too dreamy to last. Like maybe it was on temporary loan.

Now that we weren't going to Mamaw's as often, Sister and I bartended for hours on end—pouring chocolate milk, apple juice, and sweet tea into brandy snifters, and swirling our cocktail creations with fancy swizzle sticks, while Todd endlessly played his KISS records too loud from his bedroom.

Besides all the pretty things that came with my new family that year, Mama and Gary toted us all on a streak of family outings, including a trip to Cades Cove in the Great Smoky Mountains and a horseback-riding escapade. They even took us on a real camping vacation to Fall Creek Falls State Park that was everything a camping vacation should be, minus drunks and beer bottles strewn around the campsite.

The best part of our new family lifestyle was our regular walks on the local greenbelt. Gary was an honest-to-goodness jogger, with track shorts and special running shoes and a nice steady pace. As a girl missing her daddy and already nurturing a taste for the pounding of earth beneath her feet, I was determined to keep up with Gary, tracking him by the thick mop of curly black hair when his pace was too fast for the earnest attempts of my short legs. We ran countless laps around the greenbelt together, and when he created a wide gap between us, he'd wait for me.

When I couldn't run another step and would fall over my knees gasping for breath, he'd remind me, "Don't think about how far you have to go; just keep putting one foot in front of the other."

That advice made running easier. And many other things too.

I liked the way the house felt with a man around, as if his presence somehow shored up the foundation and squared up the walls. He was kind to me, but having him there had its downsides.

Todd and Sister and I sometimes grumbled among ourselves about *how* different it was having him around—the constant parade of adults that came and went onto the screen porch drinking and talking too late into the night, Gary's obsession with order and chores, and his singular purpose to keep Mama's door closed and to protect her from us when he wanted her to himself. Before he came along, us kids mostly fended for ourselves, had free rein with Mama when she wasn't working, and had become accustomed to our wide-open freedom to do as we pleased. The security he brought came with restrictions and rules that we didn't easily accommodate.

And Mama wasn't quite the same either—more preoccupied or something. Although, as I got older, I wondered if we were being selfish, wishing we still had her to ourselves.

Then there was the following summer, when Gary lost his job at the railroad and became our full-time, stay-at-home dad. With his military background, he treated us like recruits in a boot camp, waylaying us with lists of household chores we soundly resented, if on no other account than because he wasn't a blood relative.

We were always mumbling "What right does he have?" and "Who does he think he is?" under our breath to one other.

Mama must have been under Gary's spell, because our defense "But he's not our daddy" never held enough sway for her to rescue us from Gary's stronghold; he wrung out our summer freedom like a dishcloth. Which is how Todd, Sister, Kristie, and I ended up spending the summer climbing ladders and scraping shards of old white paint off of second-floor windows, prepping them for a refresh. The painting was less painful, and Mama was so pleased with the results that it almost seemed worth the cooped-up feeling we shared all summer.

Then as fast as he came, he left.

Without explanation or fanfare, Gary packed up one day while we were at school. When we got home from ball practice, almost every trace of him was gone—the cowhide rug, the sisters, the family trips, my new "dad"—even the indoor bar. Mama was rearranging the furniture and looked relieved.

I felt certain it was our complaining that drove him out, but Mama swore it wasn't. She said she had been on her own too long to know how to live with a man, and she didn't want anybody telling her or her kids what to do. She told us it would all be just fine. And I believed her because I knew that she would somehow find a way to make everything all right again.

The house would become too much for us to afford, but we stayed long enough for the preacher man to find us.

Mama was working two jobs again, leafing through college brochures on her nights off so she could get her degree to teach cosmetology in high school and make enough money to actually raise three kids. On a scorching Saturday morning in August, while Todd was playing electronic football and talking to one of his three girlfriends on the phone, the preacher man knocked on the thick front door, wearing a suit and tie and the widest smile I'd ever seen.

"I'll get it!" I ran through the house to answer the door, noticing Sister on the couch with her softball uniform on already, her cap slightly off center and pulled too low over her eyes. I chuckled at the thought of her standing in right field, twirling around chasing lightning bugs. We were on the same team, but she only played because Mama made her.

The living room was stripped almost bare since Gary left. When I swung the door open, I found two men standing there. I hoped it wasn't someone coming to take more things away from the house.

"Hi, there, I'm Brother Cross from Victory Baptist Church, and this is Pastor Wiggins. Is your mom or dad home this lovely morning?"

I smiled at them both and said hello, hoping they wouldn't ask about the sparseness of the room behind me. Brother Cross seemed too polite for that, and I was relieved.

Mama had heard his sunny voice and came up behind me, twirling my hair and straightening my shirt.

"Hi, I'm Sharon. This is Edie, my daughter."

"Well, hello, Sharon, it sure is nice to meet both of you on this beautiful day." Brother Cross shook Mama's hand, cupping it together between his own, his eyes full of kindness.

"We wanted to let your family know that we have a church bus that drives right by your house every Sunday. We would just be honored if you or your family would like to join us this week. Do you good folks have a church home?"

"No, we sure don't," Mama said.

"How many children do you have?" the pastor asked.

"I have a son, Todd, and his younger sisters, Edie and Gina."

"Wow, what a blessing it is to have a house full of children. Such a gift from God," Brother Cross said with a sincerity that was compelling.

"Yes, yes, they are."

I had never heard anyone say that it was a blessing to have children. It seemed like a curious thing to say.

"We'd love to have your family at church on Sunday. We pick up children on the bus if Edie or any of the other children would like to come. We have a youth group for your son, a vibrant children's program for the girls, and a Bible study for mothers like yourself. I wonder if Edie here would ever like to join us," he said, nodding my way.

He looked at me and then back at Mama.

I was nodding my head yes and hoping Mama would agree to it. With Gary gone, she seemed so much more herself lately, so I felt sure she would be okay with me going.

"Edie, would you like to come tomorrow? Of course, only if it's okay with your mom. I'll actually be driving the bus myself, so you'd already know someone. Pastor Wiggins's son and daughter sometimes ride the bus with us, too, so there would be other kids near your age. How does that sound?"

I looked up at Mama, and she nodded yes. It was the beginning of something I can only describe as a miracle.

Over the next months, I hopped on that church bus with Brother Cross every Sunday, taking in everything that he taught in Sunday school, and thinking that eventually I could talk Sister and Todd into going with me too.

I sat with Sister Cross and her kids during church and hung on every word, every inflection of the pastor's voice. My chest was heavy every Sunday during the altar call, so I did the only thing I knew to do. I got saved two more times in the next six months and baptized again too. I had an uneasiness about my faith, an agonizing obsession with the growing disparity between my "new" life in faith and my real life at home and when I was back at Mamaw's. I wasn't sure those worlds could ever be reconciled, but I was drawn to church like metal to a magnet.

More than anything, I wanted whatever it was that made Brother Cross so full of joy. To him, everything was a blessing and the Lord was good and faithful. My life experience up to that point had not convinced me that everything was a blessing, but there was something about his passion and kindness that made me think maybe it was true.

I was a girl who had her father's eyes but not his days, and that loss was already taking root, twisting itself around everything. With Gary gone and Daddy absent, hope was hard to keep in view.

Brother Cross was an antidote to all that, a source of lightness and laughter, grinning from ear to ear every time I saw him, greeting me on the rickety old church bus as we bounced up and down, singing all the Sunday school songs week after week.

On most Wednesday nights Brother Cross picked me up for youth group, where he taught an in-depth class about what it meant to be a Christian. When he arrived at the house, he'd greet my family at the door and always extend an invitation to Sister and Todd, and Mama, too, if she was home, to come with us, before leading me to the car and opening the door for me.

"So, how was school today, Edie? Did you have a great day?"

Brother Cross always listened like he really cared, like I was his own daughter. I asked for his advice like a girl would ask her dad.

"Coach Moser talked me into trying out for the basketball team, so it looks like I'll be playing basketball this year. I'm excited, but kinda nervous."

"You haven't played basketball before, right?" he asked with great interest.

I shook my head. "No, but he said I was athletic and I would learn fast and that he needed me on the team."

"Well, I'm sure that's true. Coaches don't usually do things like that. But any coach would be proud to have you on their team," Brother Cross said with sincerity. "I've watched you play sports in the church gym, and you're a talented athlete as well as a gifted student, not to mention your kind and helpful attitude."

His confidence shored up my confidence. My first time playing on the school basketball team was just what I needed, and I had a feeling Brother Cross knew that.

In youth group, he talked a lot about sin and about forsaking the ungodly things in your life, but he talked in a way that was different from the fire-and-brimstone preacher man at the church in Union County. Brother Cross still didn't know anything about me and my family—the things I'd seen, the things that filled my dreams at night, the times I lied just to make someone like me.

His words wrapped me up in hope, a hope that I desperately wanted to be true.

"Edie, you are a very special girl, and I want you to know that. I want you to know that God has a plan for your life that only you can fulfill. He loved you so much He sent His Son, Jesus, to die on the cross for you, and He would have done that if you had been the only girl in the whole world. He loves you that much. From what you've shared with me, I know you've had some hard things happen in your life, but God will use them for His good. He made you for a special purpose. The way you see the world is a gift and inspires those who know you."

I wanted to ask him how he knew this, and what he meant about the way I saw the world.

But I didn't want to ask too much, for fear that in the answers something in my past would negate the promise. I wanted to believe in Brother Cross's belief in me. I wanted to believe that new stepmoms and country houses and new stepdads and cowhide rugs weren't what made us, that even with all that gone, what was important was still there.

Brother Cross taught me that the only thing wrong with me

was the same thing that was wrong with everybody else, including Daddy. Sin. And it was something I couldn't fix on my own, no matter how much I tried or how many good report cards I brought home or how many home runs I hit at the ballpark. What I needed was to forgive and be forgiven. It was just that simple and just that impossible.

Thus began my fumbling around in the dark for Truth, for something that holds when nothing else will, for someone who never leaves and never gives up, for a way to hold the loss with the hope.

Coach Moser was next in the long line of people who spread across my life like a bridge over a raging river—both soothing and deepening the ache I had for a real father.

15

REAL GOOD MAN

I COULD HEAR THE screeches from the players' shoes on the gym floor all the way in the locker room as I straddled the bench and buried my face in my hands for a good cry. The boys were warming up, and I was supposed to help Coach Moser run the concession stand during their game. He ambled over and sat down beside me, put his hand on my shoulder, and made me look him right in the eyes. Coach had come to find me after my teammate told him I was upset.

"Listen, Edie, you did your best tonight," Coach said, patting my back. "I couldn't be more proud if you were my own daughter, and I mean that. You played your heart out, girl. You hustled out there like everything depended on that game, and that's all I can ask for. And as much as I like to win, you need to remember that this isn't everything. I'll deny saying this, but you've got to remember that this is just a game," he finished, doing his best to make me feel better.

"I guess it is to some people," I replied haltingly between breaths, as I tried wiping away the tears.

"Well, I'll tell you one thing—any seventh grader who scores eighteen points in one game, gets five steals, and plays defense enough for three people doesn't have anything to be ashamed of. Now walk out there with your head up, and let's help these boys win. You gonna need a ride home later?"

"Yes, Mom's working late, and Todd had a game tonight, too, with his park and rec team," I said as I swallowed back the last of the tears and rose from the bench to follow Coach.

The boys' team lost in overtime. Coach and I finished cleaning up the concession stand while the janitor swept the entire gym floor, back and forth like he was on a riding lawn mower. After the janitor packed up, Coach turned off all the lights and we headed to his car in the hush of November's chill.

Coach Moser drove me home almost every night after games. I loved talking to him about everything and kept him entertained with stories about school and boys and basketball.

But on this night, for some reason, he asked me about Daddy.

"Does your dad live around here, Edie? I don't believe I've ever seen him," he said as he turned onto Old Knoxville Highway.

Coach was young and married but didn't have any kids of his own. He must have thought it was strange that Daddy never came around.

"He lives in Knoxville with my mamaw."

Immediately, I pictured Daddy—shirtless, thin but muscular, with ropy biceps and well-defined shoulders, jeans hovering just below the tops of his Fruit of the Looms, grinning from ear to ear. The thought of him made me homesick, the kind of homesick that twists your insides right in two, the kind of homesickness that even going home can't ease.

"Does he work late? Is that why he's not at the games?"

"Uh, I don't know. He doesn't really work that late. I mean, when he works, he usually gets done pretty early. Sometimes he paints or does wallpaper with my uncle Gene, but they don't really work that much." I fiddled with my jacket zipper, wondering if I should say anything else. "He's good at working on cars, too. He can paint them or work on the engine. And funny. He's really funny."

I looked at Coach and smiled. He looked like he was waiting for me to say something else.

"He's one of those people who'd give you the shirt off his back, if he was ever wearing one."

We both chuckled as the lights to the grocery store by my house flicked off.

"Well, I hope to meet him someday. I bet he's proud of you."

"Yeah, I guess he would be if he . . . well, yeah, I guess he is."

I thought how Daddy probably didn't know enough about me to be proud of me. He had never been to a basketball game and probably never would be. He didn't drive at night now, even when he was sober. Said he couldn't see two feet in front of his face.

As we pulled into my driveway, I thanked Coach Moser for the ride and then slung my bag over my shoulder and headed inside the little house where we now lived. Mom was at night school and often didn't remember to ask if I'd won or lost a game. I hoped she'd forget to ask tonight.

Losing a game wasn't something I could get over easily, although it seemed easy enough for most of my teammates, who'd be talking about their boyfriends or gossiping while fixing their hair and makeup as soon as the game was over. On the basketball court, or even in school for that matter, the harder I worked, the better I did. Those were the places I had control over. If I failed or succeeded, it was mine to own. And I hated accepting failure. It cut too deep, threatening me with the accusation that I'd never amount to anything. So I white-knuckled my way toward every win, every prize, every notch higher—hoping somebody would notice. Perhaps always wishing that somebody were Daddy.

I controlled what I could with my striving. The rest of my life was pretty much a crapshoot.

It was early August 1983 and the chicory was growing wild along the rural Tennessee roadsides. I'd spent most of the summer playing fast-pitch softball and wondering what it would be like to go to high school.

I sat in the backseat of my friend Nicole's car, thinking how funny it was that the cool leather seats in her family's blue Buick didn't have a single rip. The drive to her house always made me carsick, so I rolled down my window as we slithered up country roads like a garter snake climbing a willow oak.

I was thirteen years old and the new shortstop for the girls' Senior League All-Star fast-pitch team. Nicole's dad, Coach Tommy, had been my softball coach all year and was now coaching this team as well. He was tall with broad shoulders and handsome in the dad sort of way, and I had a soft spot for a man who was a good daddy.

I was spending the weekend with them so I'd have a ride to all the practices scheduled to prepare for the All-Star game. As the car hugged the yellow line that would lead to their farmhouse, I pressed my head back on the seat, hoping that if I pushed hard enough, the hollow stabbing that always made me feel hungry would die down.

By the time we reached the house, which seemed like forever, the sky was charcoal, the stars dancing like far-off Christmas lights. I could feel my chest flutter as we pulled into the driveway. The sight of their house always did that to me.

I couldn't imagine what it would feel like to live in a place so enormous. When Mama and Gary split up, we had moved into a tiny house that would have easily fit into Nicole's living room, with two bedrooms for the four of us and one small bathroom that we constantly fought over. Todd had a new job and slept on the couch until he moved out. I wasn't exactly embarrassed by what we had, but seeing Nicole's home made me wonder what she and her family must have thought when they took me home.

Do they feel sorry for me? I wondered. It didn't feel like it. Nicole's parents treated me like their own child.

I hadn't told Nicole or her family about Daddy, at least not much. I wondered what they'd think if they knew about all his drinking, or about Sonny in prison, or the clan at Mamaw's and all the other things from my past—things that were still part of my present. Their world was altogether different than where I lived.

But something strange came alive in me when I was at their house. Something I couldn't rightly name. Going there was like going to a castle—it was almost magical—the curtains and the décor and the nice furniture all giving it the feeling of something out of a fairy tale. I thought about the rooms in Nicole's house even when I wasn't there, its welcoming vibe inching its way into my dreams at night.

I shouldered my faded Adidas sports bag and paused at the sidewalk to adjust my eyes to the house lights. It was lit up like the Fourth of July, as if the place itself were cheering us on.

The two-story farmhouse had wooden horizontal clapboard siding, ordered in perfect rows of stark white, except where the rain and mud had splatter-painted along the bottom edges. The house's original windowpanes had an otherworldly feeling, like ocean waves, that made the whole house feel like it was taking you on vacation. When I entered the huge wooden double doors, I always looked at the kitchen table first. I'm sure I was the only one who had its wood grain memorized.

I loved that table, every single thing about it.

I stopped and brushed the top of it with my hand. Then I headed upstairs to Nicole's room to get some sleep.

The next morning, Nicole's mom, Judy, called us down for breakfast. Nicole was still sleeping, but I had been awake for at least an hour, lying next to her in the canopy bed, scanning the room and admiring all the white-painted pieces of matching furniture. It reminded me of the furniture Gary had bought for us that had eventually been taken away.

I got up and dressed quickly, anxious to head downstairs. I was puzzled that Nicole seemed as ambivalent about breakfast as she did about nearly everything in her life.

"Nicole, come on. Your mom said breakfast is ready," I said, rustling the covers around her face.

She turned over and pulled the covers over her head. "I'm not even hungry. I just want to sleep. You go on down."

Not even hungry? How can she not be hungry with the smell of bacon wafting from the kitchen, and the thought of those chocolate-chip pancakes that her mom promised us last night?

Next thing I knew, Nicole's dad was knocking on the door.

"Girls, come on, y'all gotta get moving. We've got early practice today and trust me, you're going to need that bacon and those pancakes. I'm coming on in!" He burst into the room and headed straight for Nicole. He nudged and bugged her till she pushed out of bed, then he chased us downstairs like a bear coming to attack.

"We're not four years old, Dad," Nicole said, pretending to be annoyed with him. All I could think of was how lucky she was.

Once in the kitchen, I saw the feast in process, with sizzling bacon on the stove and a bowl of pancake mix with a bag of chocolate chips beside it, flour splotched on the counter and on the apron around Judy's waist. She threw a kitchen towel over her shoulder and began pouring batter onto the griddle. Time stood still, as if I had telescoped out of the kitchen and was looking down on the whole glorious mess of it.

Something inside me paused, like this was a picture to hold on to. A moment of clarity came, and I knew that I wanted to be a mother. I wanted to wear an apron and make chocolate-chip pancakes. I wanted a husband who would chase my daughter down the stairs. I wanted a real wooden table.

"Judy, make sure you load those girls up because I'm gonna work them pretty hard today."

"Don't you worry, honey. I made enough chocolate-chip pancakes for an army." She flipped the pancakes onto plates and served them up.

I was becoming such a regular at their house that I had my own unspoken assigned seat. I sat on Coach Tommy's left, Judy was on his right, and Nicole was beside me. As always, the table was set with napkins and silverware and cups full of milk. Underneath my napkin was a circle of rings, formed in the grain of wood. I traced the grain's pattern next to my plate every time I sat down for a meal, losing myself in its swirly perfection.

The sun was lazy, slow to flood the room but warm on our backs. Nicole's dad came up behind us and put his hands on our shoulders, reassuring us we were his favorite players. He sat down and grabbed our hands, circling us up for prayer.

Coach Tommy said a short prayer, thanking God for the food, for his wife, for Nicole, and for me. He said he was thankful I could be with them for the weekend. I was thankful too.

Then he started talking game strategy as we dug into our breakfast. The bacon had a perfect crunch, and its saltiness drove us to drink half the pitcher of milk sitting on the table. I drizzled chocolate syrup over my fluffy short stack and delighted in every heavenly bite.

"Mrs. Judy, this is the best breakfast I have ever had," I said, chocolate leaking out of the corner of my mouth.

"Why, thank you," she said with a wink.

"Hey, Edie, who is that boy that's always hanging around the dugout trying to talk to you? I can tell he's sweet on you." Coach Tommy narrowed his eyes as if he did not approve of this.

"Oh, that's Kent. He lives over near Mt. Lebanon Church and helps his dad on the farm a lot . . ."

Nicole covered my mouth with her hand and wouldn't let me finish.

"Daddy, we don't want to talk about boys. And please don't say anything to him like you do to every boy I like."

Her dad started laughing. "What? I don't say anything. I was just thinking of telling this boy that he's going to have to go through me to get to Edie. I don't think he's good enough for her. He doesn't even play baseball."

"So that disqualifies him? Oh, great, Dad. Note to all the boys who might want to date me: You have to be good at baseball," Nicole sassed.

The joking continued, and I worked slowly through that breakfast, savoring it in ways Nicole and her family never could. They didn't know the gift those meals were to me.

This time was also bittersweet—offering something wonderful in the moment that set in motion a longing for the family life I wanted for myself someday. But the bitter came in knowing that I had never sat down to a real honest-to-goodness meal with my dad.

I certainly couldn't imagine Daddy noticing something like a boy who had a crush on me, because that would require him to be actually present. It struck me then that perhaps chocolate-chip pancakes weren't the only things absent from my life.

My eyes were starting to open to the truth about Daddy, and it was weighing heavier than it ever had. Was it a betrayal or a sin to wish for more?

I imagined a world with a daddy more like Nicole's. But then I couldn't conceive of my life without Daddy. I had his eyes and his smile and his personality and his forehead, but maybe more important, he had my heart—and there would never be anyone else like him.

My stomach churned with guilt at the momentary wish that I'd been born to another father. I tried to keep myself from finding substitutes for him, but it seemed like God was sending them left and right, almost on purpose. There was Gary, Brother Cross,

Coach Moser, Coach Tommy, and even my brother, Todd, whose presence was always a comfort to me.

Later, this desire for surrogates would become my greatest weakness—looking for love and nurture wherever it could be found, and often in all the wrong places.

16

HOPE AGAINST HOPE

Darkness wrapped around me like a snake.

I wanted to scream for help but nothing came out. *It's only a dream*, I told myself.

Or was it?

I was shaking as I stared at the night ceiling, covered in sweat from the remnant of the nightmare that had me around my neck, choking off the air. Bits and pieces of this same dream had stalked me for years, here and there invading my sleep. Lately it had me in its grip, and I'd begun to dread bedtime. Sleeping, I was at the mercy of something, someone—there on the mountain with no one to help me. I kept seeing his face and I wanted to get away, wanted to be camping with Daddy.

I sat up with a start to prove to myself I was awake.

Nothing could hurt me now.

Sister slept soundly in the bed next to me. Night hung heavy, and I needed to sleep but didn't even want to try. I pushed myself out of bed and went to the bathroom down the hall to wash my face.

I caught a glimpse of my reflection, and something cut through me like a gust of cold November air. A realization. Puzzle pieces clicked together. The truth nearly knocked me over.

The woods. I'd stayed at Mamaw's instead of going camping. Hide and seek. His hands guiding me. His smile and the odd look in his eyes. Tugs on my clothing. My innocence gone.

Always the same groping hands.

Always the same despair, sinking into nothingness, blackness.

I grabbed the sink to keep from falling. This wasn't a nightmare. This was a memory. I was sure of it, and the knowing unraveled me.

I paced the hallway, going over each detail. Every feeling. Every gesture. The violation. Then I pressed my hands against my head, trying to rattle it clear of the images. I hurried back to the bathroom, the churn in my stomach so fierce I felt sick.

I paced again. I sat in the dark living room. I tried to go back to bed.

Finally, the light broke through. It was dawn and I was safe again.

Mama woke up first, then Sister. I worried that they would see it on my face, hear it in my voice. Mama started fixing breakfast as I talked about the away football game we were cheering at that night and the arrangements I had made for Sister and me after school, trying to make it appear like nothing had changed overnight.

It took me until the following Sunday, a week and a few days of wrestling with the memory on my own, before I had the courage to talk about it. I waited until Sister was gone so I could tell Mama in private.

"Mama, I have something awful I need to share with you."

There was already a quiver in my voice and in my chest.

"Oh, Sister, what is it? You look upset," she said, using the nickname she called both of us girls.

Mama put her arm around my shoulder as we walked to the kitchen and sat down at the chrome-edged Formica table.

The weight of the memory I'd been trying to bury was more than I could bear, so I slid onto the floor and cried facedown until I couldn't cry anymore. Mama got on the floor with me, trying her best to make it all go away. She held my head in her lap, gently stroking my hair and wiping away the tears as fast as they came.

"Honey, what is it? You can tell me; I'm right here. Oh, how it hurts me to see you like this. What happened? You know you can tell me anything."

Mama knew about the dreams because I often woke her up so I wouldn't have to be alone in the dark. I would say that I was having trouble sleeping, but I never told her the details of the blurry patches of images that seeped into my bones and tormented me. She'd always been the kind of mother I could tell anything to, the kind who loved me unconditionally.

But this felt different.

I almost changed my mind until her tender nudging finally made me believe it was safe to confess.

"You know those dreams I've been having for years? The ones where it's getting dark and I'm in the woods? I was sexually abused. I remembered all of it last Friday night."

I told her who it was, and the color drained from her face. She looked like she might be sick, and then Mama started to cry too.

We made our way to the sofa and sat for what seemed like hours, each trying to comfort the other one, both of us trying to figure out what to do now. What do you do when your memories come to you in the form of patchwork nightmares? What do you do when the person involved is not only your relative, but married now with kids of his own? What if it were just a dream?

Those hard questions haunted us for months, until the whole mess erupted when both Sister and Jamie confessed that the same person had done the same thing to them.

I was relieved when we gathered together one night and shared our stories. *I wasn't making it up.* No wonder I had all those sleepless nights. No wonder my chest would tighten when he was around. The relief was slowly replaced with dread as we contemplated what all this would mean.

Eventually, we all agreed to bring our stories to light, which would later lead us to a small-town courtroom to testify against him. The grief it brought the family was almost unbearable, and there were many more tears and sleepless nights for all of us. But truth and courtrooms have a way of setting things right. Something of that Appalachian survival instinct kicked in, and we marched on, scars notwithstanding.

I wondered if this was the source of so much of my angst when I was at church. Was this the reason for the shame I felt, for my inability to make it through an altar call, for my constant doubt about being clean and forgiven? Could the God I had learned about somehow fix this, too?

I found healing in the truth—not by hiding my story but by finally finding the courage to share it. Grace and beauty were waiting for me, but the truth that I had to walk through to get there felt like a tightrope, and I was always losing my balance.

17

BLUE EYES CRYING IN THE RAIN

IT WAS CHRISTMAS DAY, and Mama was driving us up to the trailer to give Daddy, Uncle Gene, Mamaw, and Aunt Darlene their gifts.

"I hope Daddy's there," I said, glancing at Sister in the backseat. "We probably should have called."

"You mean you hope he's sober," she said matter-of-factly.

Of course that's what I meant. I immediately began to turn over in my mind what holidays must have been like for Daddy. He never had money to buy us gifts and wouldn't have known what to get anyway. Mama had always managed to make Christmas special for us, and because I couldn't stand the thought of not getting Daddy some little gift, we'd head to Mamaw's on Christmas Day. We usually left Mamaw's with that awkward, shameful feeling you have when you've injured someone's pride. Every year, I would say to myself that the next Christmas, we'd forgo gifts and not make Daddy feel bad about not getting us anything. But when the time came, Sister and I wanted him to know we loved him and thought of him, so we'd be on our way there again.

Holidays at the trailer were mostly depressing, save the benevolence baskets the church people brought without fail and the lonely white tinsel tree that sat on the end table by the couch. The tree had one strand of garland, a few worn ornaments, and a string of colored lights, all trying to wage war against the desperation that usually filled the room.

Daddy was sitting on the couch in jeans and a white undershirt when we walked in with Mama. The two of them had both managed to put the past behind them and were always cordial when in each other's company. Mamaw said hello, too, and asked Mama about her new job teaching cosmetology at the high school.

We gave Daddy his socks and undershirts and passed out the rest of their gifts—a necklace for Darlene, some house shoes for Mamaw, and a can of flavored popcorn for Uncle Gene.

"Well, you girls know that I ain't got no money for no Christmas, but I wish't I could have got you girls a little somethin'," Mamaw said, folding up the wrapping paper used for her gift into a perfect square.

Daddy said that as soon as he finished the wallpaper job he had started a week before, he would give us each twenty dollars to get whatever we wanted.

"Oh, we don't need anything, Daddy," Sister and I said, almost in unison.

The ride home was quiet, the letdown of Christmas pressing in along with the emptiness I always felt when I left Daddy.

I thought about how long it had been since we'd stayed the night at the trailer with him, probably almost two years. Something about time and distance gave me perspective, and I realized that I mostly felt sorry for him. He was a man without anything, really—having lost Shirley and the daily time with Jim Bob that I knew was special to him. Shirley hadn't remarried and was pretty strict about Jim Bob being with her. Seemed like now Daddy was losing us, too, or at least losing touch with us. I felt guilty that Sister and I weren't doing anything to stop it, but we were teenagers now, and busy with school and sports and our friends. Then there was youth group and church for me, all of which didn't leave much time for seeing Daddy anymore.

Perhaps his drinking made that decision easier, but it didn't make it easier to shoulder the guilt, though it was never consciously the reason I stayed away. Maybe that was partly why I had so much angst. Getting saved and baptized over and over again, I began to wonder whose sins I was trying to atone for and if I would ever find the peace and contentment I so desperately wanted. Still, however confused I felt, I clung to faith because it was the only thing in my life that made sense, the thing I could count on in a world that was always changing.

When we got home from the visit, I realized I hadn't said a word the whole way back, since if I did, Mama would chastise me for always feeling sorry for Daddy.

"Thanks for taking us up there to see Daddy, Mama," I said, hugging her and heading up to my room to sink into my thoughts.

A few weeks after Christmas, I agreed to give my testimony at a high school youth group retreat at Ridgecrest Retreat Center in North Carolina. It was an annual youth gathering, and I was terrified when Coach Murphy asked me to speak. I had heard other people do it at the camp I went to in the summer with Brother Cross, but I wasn't quite sure about doing it myself. I was pretty certain that my experience growing up was far from what any of the other kids had had. I wanted for all the world to back out.

"Whatcha fretting over, with all those papers?" a guy named John asked, patting me on the back as we came down the steps of the bus, after a twisting and torturous ride through part of the Smoky Mountains. John, a retreat counselor, was a Carson-Newman University football player who was a few years older than me and had sat beside me on the long ride here.

"Coach Murphy asked me to give my testimony, and I'm so nervous," I said, holding my hand over my eyes to block the sun.

"By the looks of those notes you're studying, you're going to be just fine," he said, eyeing the thick stack of papers on my lap. His sentiments were kind, but he wasn't the one about to give his testimony to hundreds of people.

"I sure hope so," I said. I took a few deep breaths; even with the sun beaming, there was a chill in the air and my breath was visible in front of my face. The camp was a beautiful place with a host of buildings rambling up the side of the ridge. As I headed toward the girls' cabins, I thought, *I wouldn't be lying to Coach Murphy if I told him that my stomach is hurting too badly to get up in front of everyone and talk.*

Lately, my mind was always wrestling with my past, and I couldn't seem to reconcile the life I had seen and lived with the one that I knew existed for other people. And starting high school only made it harder, with the constant peer pressure. So I'd dived deeper into church and into the Bible, especially since the night I remembered what had happened to me when I was little. The dreams were less frequent now, but the abuse was something I couldn't stop grappling with and visualizing. I'd gone to even more Bible studies and never missed church, hoping that somehow that would undo what had been done.

It wasn't just the abuse that had me tied in knots; it was seeing so much of my childhood from a different perspective that confused me. I just wanted to be like everybody else, but that seemed like the one wish that would never be granted. Sister must have felt some of the same things, too, but we never really talked about it together. I guess we both just wanted to be normal, and avoiding bringing up the things that made us abnormal seemed like a good start.

I sat in my room, looking over my notes and wondering what lay on the other side of telling five hundred people my story.

Every time I thought about standing on stage all by myself, my heart started to pound. Was that a sign I shouldn't be doing it or a sure sign that I was supposed to? I felt conflicted and sweaty and slightly nauseated as I walked to the dining hall by myself.

I found a few people from our youth group at a table and sat down with them, but I didn't say much and just picked at my food. As soon as dinner was over, I went straight into the auditorium to get familiar with the place. I sat on the second pew and went through every page of my notes, making sure I wanted to say what I had written down.

Could I even get the words out—things about my daddy and my family that I'd never spoken aloud in my entire life and had only recently begun to say to myself?

Maybe the memories of being violated had knocked something loose, but my need to tell the truth felt like fire in my bones despite my nervousness. It felt like I was being moved toward this by something or someone I couldn't control. In the end, the fear of being gossiped about or rejected couldn't hold a candle to the need to be free, to say the things I was most scared of saying.

The auditorium filled up fast.

John found his way to the second pew, slipped in beside me, and told me not to be nervous.

I had first met Coach Murphy when I heard him as a guest speaker at our church, and I was immediately drawn to his kind and charismatic personality. When I learned he was the husband of my beloved kindergarten teacher, he became almost saintly in my mind. I guess that's why I couldn't say no when he asked me to speak. When he saw me come into the auditorium, he gave me a wave from where he was talking to several other youth leaders. He was a football coach at a rival high school, the youth pastor at a neighboring church, and the leader of a Bible study I had just started attending.

It wasn't long before Coach Murphy headed to the stage and the last stragglers took their seats. He opened the retreat with a welcome and some introductions, and I knew it wouldn't be long before it was my turn.

I tried to believe Brother Cross and all those church messages and words about Jesus loving me, but the doubts were strong too. My struggles had brought me to this moment where I stood on the verge of crying or throwing up or running out of the auditorium and never coming back. I shuffled the stack of papers in my hands, making sure they were all in order, and then the entire crinkled pile wafted to the floor.

"Here, I'll get those for you," John said, bending down to pick up the pages before I could respond.

"Thank you," I muttered as I took the stack and put them back in order.

"It's okay. You'll do great," he gently whispered. "God gets the glory; we're just the vessels."

God gets the glory; we're just the vessels. How do words like that just roll off his tongue? I wondered.

The only things that readily rolled off my tongue were the lyrics to George Jones's or Johnny Cash's songs. I guessed this was probably not the place for displaying my giftedness at singing classic country songs.

Maybe that's how I ended up becoming such a driven student. I didn't trust what was in me, so I focused on school and learned everything I possibly could.

"I hope so," I whispered back, wondering if there'd be any glory for God in what was scribbled down on my sheets of paper. What I had learned at church had changed my life and I wanted to share it—partly because I thought it might help someone else and partly because I hoped it would help me.

More than anything, I wanted to believe that my past didn't matter. Yet, could it really all be washed away by a dunk in the river or a few words at the altar of the church? Maybe saying it all out loud would convince me as much as those who listened.

It was all Coach Murphy's fault, for asking me to speak at

this retreat, where I knew there'd be teenagers from every church in town. He'd heard me share parts of my story at a small group Bible study that one of the Fellowship of Christian Athletes (FCA) leaders held. I had recently been to an event where Coach was the main speaker, and he gave one of the most challenging messages I had ever heard about loving your neighbor. The thought of even just Coach Murphy listening to what I was going to say terrified me, not to mention the other 499 people in the room.

Two other teens gave their testimonies before me. The girl explained that after going on a missions trip, God opened her eyes to the poor and helped her have compassion toward them. The guy shared how he rededicated his life to God after getting into partying his freshman year. As my sour stomach threatened to let go of my supper, I began to have a terrible case of second thoughts.

I realized this might not be the kind of place to say my daddy was an alcoholic and I missed having him around. Or that my cousin was in prison and I spent a lot of time visiting him on weekends.

What would these people think of me after this? I didn't know very many of them, so maybe they wouldn't care. Then my thoughts turned to Daddy. Was this a betrayal? I certainly wouldn't share my experiences if there was a chance he would ever hear about it. The thought of him sitting on Mamaw's couch a few weeks before at Christmas made the guilt even worse—the humiliation he must have felt from not being able to give his kids anything.

Maybe that was part of why I was here—because I didn't know how to help him or help myself. It felt like the truth might be a good place to start.

The warring inside me came to a fever pitch when I heard, "Next we have Edie Rudder."

I felt light-headed when I stood up.

Coach Murphy's introductory words seemed to come from far

away, telling how I had been a student in his wife's class the first year she ever taught kindergarten.

As I inched past John to get out of the pew, he patted my shoulder and said he'd be praying for me. I thought that I needed more than that, but I was thankful for his kindness.

I looked like most of my peers. I was a freshman in high school with a fresh asymmetrical bob, wearing a pencil skirt and an oversized blouse with shoulder pads. Only I knew that it was the look of someone trying too hard to rise above her upbringing.

I was about to tell my story and Daddy's for the first time to a room mostly comprised of perfect strangers, and I didn't know how to tell it without the whole thing making me seem worse off than I was.

My hands were numb and sticky with sweat as I tucked my notes under my arm, walked up onto the stage, and gave Coach Murphy a hug.

"Listen, you can do this," he whispered.

I took hold of the podium and looked out across the auditorium. I was stunned by the faces looking back at me. There were supposed to be five hundred people, but it looked more like ten thousand, a tsunami threatening to drown me. I cleared my throat and started with my opening line.

"I'm fourteen years old, and I've been to prison more times than I've been to the park. I grew up in a broken home, the daughter of a wonderful man who could never manage to stay sober."

My voice was shaky, and my lips quivered at the end of every sentence.

"When I was seven, my cousin was hunted down like an animal and taken to prison while my sister and I stood there and watched. We visit him on the weekends. It's a place I hope none of you ever have to go."

You could have heard a pin drop in that auditorium. I looked around for reassurance and saw Coach Murphy sitting in the front row, eyes full of hope, nodding me on.

"Since I was a little girl I knew my daddy loved me, but his demons kept him away from us. I miss him every day and wish he wanted to be a part of our lives. The only time he ever came to one of my sporting events, he showed up drunk with one of his ex-con friends."

I kept making eye contact with Coach Murphy and finding enough strength to say the next thing on my paper.

"As hard as it's been at times to live without a father at home, Daddy did something for me that I will always be thankful to him for. He took me to church when I was eight years old where I was introduced to Someone who changed my life forever, and that Someone is Jesus. I'm learning that no matter what has happened to me, Jesus loves me."

Then I found my stride. My lip stopped quivering, and I straightened my shoulders, took a deep breath, and told about how Brother Cross and Coach Moser were both like angels to me, teaching me things and showing me how to be a leader. And then I finished with the promise from Psalm 68 that God is "a father of the fatherless."

I crumpled my papers together and hurried back to my seat, my heart flooded with relief and also a twinge of guilt for airing the truth about Daddy.

John leaned over and said, "That was amazing."

I wanted to go back to my room and hide. I was sure I'd burst into tears if anyone else said anything nice to me.

After the session was over, Coach Murphy made a beeline for me and hugged me. His words made it easy for the tears to flow.

"You are one special girl, Miz Edie, and you don't know how many teenagers you helped today. Your words are powerful and courageous. Don't ever stop sharing your story," he said as he put his arm around my shoulder and ushered me toward the back of the room. "By the way, there's somebody here who wants to see you."

Mrs. Murphy was standing there, looking at me, tears streaming down her cheeks.

I hadn't seen her in almost ten years. She kept putting her hands to my face, trying to find her words.

"You're so grown up," she said, hugging me again and again.

"I can't believe you're the same little girl who used to sit in my class and hang on every word. You're so strong, Edie, but I knew you were special, even back then. You've always had this light in your eyes."

We hugged and cried and talked for the longest time and finally said good-bye, promising to keep in touch.

Other friends and youth leaders were waiting to encourage me and to thank me for sharing my story. I thanked them but still wondered if I'd shared too much. Part of me wished I hadn't told my story while a bigger part of me wished I had had a different story to tell.

The rest of the retreat was unbelievable. People I knew and mostly people I didn't know came to me, often with tears in their eyes, thanking me for my courage and often sharing their own painful stories. It was then that I first began to realize that the painful parts of our lives are often the very things that God will use as gifts to bless and change us and the people we meet.

On Sunday evening, after a two-hour bus ride home and a ride from a friend to our new-to-us town house, I walked up the steps to the empty-looking house.

I remembered that Mama had said something about going away for a couple of days, but I wasn't sure where. Sister was probably staying at a friend's house, and Todd was no doubt at his girlfriend's. He was still living with us but wasn't around much.

I thought of Daddy, probably sleeping one off on Mamaw's couch.

With my tangled memories and my bags of wadded up clothes and crinkled papers, I climbed the stairs.

I made my way to the bedroom I shared with Sister, threw my bags on the floor, and crawled into my unmade bed. My notes fell out of my backpack, alighting like a whip-poor-will onto the stained carpet. I picked up the pages and lay on my bed, clutching those papers against my chest, while the soft colors of sunset wrapped the room in the sweetest light.

I began to reread what I claimed to believe. I read the pages out loud and realized for the first time that I was in charge of what I had written on that paper. This first telling of my story was important in forming me; I had no doubt of that.

The actual events as they unfolded could not be changed just because I wished for a new story, or a new house, or a cuter name like Tiffany or Kristi, or even for someone to be home with me right now after such a draining and life-altering experience.

But as I lay on the bed that sank too low in the middle and looked at what I had written, I was surprised.

The girl who wrote those words didn't sound angry.

She sounded okay, like she was starting to believe what she had written on those scraps of paper she doodled on at every turn, like she believed what she had spoken at the retreat.

Maybe hope, however frail, was taking root in the deepest places; maybe sunlight and peace really would shine in her heart after the rain; maybe heartache can be the birthplace of the most beautiful things.

Outside the bedroom window, a storm came on without fanfare and poured through the sun streaks in the sky.

The house creaked from the weight of the rain but I fell asleep peacefully.

MAN OF CONSTANT SORROW

AFTER A SEVEN O'CLOCK Bible study at a nearby friend's house before school, Sister and I rumbled into the high school's front parking lot in our 1978 Camaro five minutes before the bell rang. We had inherited Todd's car when his new job as a courier for a laboratory came with a company car. The doors of our hand-me-down ride creaked so loudly that they sounded like you were entering a haunted house, and the car guzzled so much gas and drank so much oil that I wasn't sure if the gift was a blessing or a curse.

The October air coming off the mountains was brisk, with fog so thick in the valley that the football field looked like it was draped in spun cotton candy. Sister was a sophomore who put the "social" in "social butterfly," dressing as fashionably as possible and teasing her hair the whole way.

"I'll buy the next few quarts of oil," Sister said, as we grabbed our stuff out of the car, "but I'm not getting up at the crack of dawn to go with you to that Bible study every mornin'. I need to find a ride with somebody who gets up at a reasonable hour."

Rambo (the nickname we'd given the car in honor of Sylvester Stallone's character in *First Blood*) had a perpetual oil leak that was costing us about three dollars a day. That was three dollars more than either of us usually had. And then there was the gas gauge, which was perpetually registering empty. Despite Rambo's obvious shortcomings, he was large on looks and we were grateful to have a car at all and the occasional five-dollar bill to maneuver us around town. My part-time job at a clothing store in the mall and Sister's dough-slinging gig at Little Caesars gave us barely enough money to keep Rambo running.

I snatched my Bible and backpack from the backseat and we ran in, both of us in cheerleading uniforms for the day's pep rally and home football game.

Something about wearing that uniform to school made me feel alive, as if I had a badge that identified me as someone who mattered. But having been on the other side most of my life, I also knew that the uniform could make others feel inferior and left out, which concerned me. Some girls wore those uniforms as weapons to wield against those who didn't meet the prescribed standards for popularity. So I was overly cautious, constantly worrying that people perceived me as one of those cheerleader types. I made every effort to avoid coming across that way.

"I told Shawna we'd spend the night with her after the game. But I need to get some clothes after school first," Sister said, checking her hair in the glass door leading into the school. Shawna was our dual best friend.

"Remember, we're seeing Daddy tomorrow, so we have to leave Shawna's as soon as we wake up."

"Why tomorrow?" Sister said, with a good amount of whine. "Mike is taking me to a bonfire tomorrow night, and I don't want to be gone all day. Why can't Daddy bring his new girlfriend to see us?"

"Yeah, that's not going to happen. He has less chance of having gas money than we do," I said, glancing at the clock and picking up my pace before the bell rang.

We'd been promising Daddy we'd come see his new apartment and his new girlfriend, Pat. Between our cheerleading schedule, my basketball practices, and my constant string of commitments to this school club or that committee, it was hard to find time to go. We needed to check in not just to see his new apartment—the first place he'd ever lived somewhat on his own—but also because Daddy's brother, Uncle Gene, had been diagnosed with lung cancer the previous month, and Daddy wasn't taking it very well.

So this weekend I was making us do it, even if Sister complained that it was cramping her social life. Sister and I were on the same cheerleading squad but not on the same life plan. Her curvy figure got her involved in relationships with boys the likes of which I wouldn't have until college. What she lacked in academic focus, she made up for in social butterflying, flitting around from one boyfriend to the next like a monarch to spring flowers.

I was working for good grades and the praise of teachers and coaches. Thank goodness I had enough Daddy in me to keep from taking myself too seriously.

We cackled most of the night at Shawna's, waking up her mom several times with our shrieks, talking about cute boys and makeup and who might ask who to the prom. We never ran out of topics. As usual, I was the first one asleep, since I inherited my daddy's propensity for going to bed early and rising before the sun.

By eight the next morning, I was ready to leave. Sister was still in bed, groaning and complaining that it was too early to get up.

"Sister, we need to go. Now come on," I said, gathering her stuff. "I'll pay for the oil and the gas to get to Daddy's." On the way out the door, we passed Shawna's brother, Mark, who was working on an old red truck, a much nicer old red truck than Daddy's.

"Nice truck," I said, loading our things into the car. Sister hardly glanced his way.

We spotted Daddy's truck as we pulled into the parking lot,

just seconds before he walked out of an upstairs apartment with no shirt or shoes on, taking a large gulp of coffee and a long draw off a Winston Light. Daddy's new apartment was part of a package deal from the government after he qualified for disability for having smoked and drunk himself half to death.

He draped his elbows over the railing so that his muscular biceps and tattooed forearms were in full view. Following right behind him was a stringy-haired woman with tinted glasses, wearing an oversized men's T-shirt and with nary a tooth or nary a bra that I could see from where I sat in the car. My first impression of Daddy's new girlfriend sat like a twenty-five-pound dumbbell on my chest.

"Well, I guess that's Pat," I said, trying to mask the despair in my voice.

"Yeah, looks like a doozy to me," Sister said. "Somehow, this doesn't surprise me. Jamie told me that Aunt Glenda's exact words were, 'Jim has took up with a woman that ain't no earthly account and cusses like a man.' I can see now how that might be true." Sister craned her neck to get a better look at the woman who might be our future stepmom.

Jamie was now married to a navy serviceman and living in New Hampshire, trying her best to be an adult without a tainted past. We sure could have used her comic relief at this moment. Pat had the general look of a woman who'd rather fight you than make you supper.

"Well . . . at least he's not alone," I said, scrambling to think of the bright side.

Slowly and without speaking a word, we climbed the stairs to greet the happy couple.

"Well, look who the dogs drug in. There's ole Nise. And Sister, too," Daddy said with one of his wide grins. "Pat, this yeer is my two girls, Gina and Edie Nise. They're perty as two dolls, ain't they? Pat here come from Ohio and ain't lived here but six months. Me and her's done made four runs of chowchow, and we're about to start another one. Come in here and taste it. It's the best stuff you ever eat."

"Hey, girls, your daddy's told me a lot about you," Pat said, dabbing out her cigarette. "And I can tell which one of you's Edie, 'cause you look just like your daddy," she said, nodding toward me.

Sister and I both smiled and tried to be polite, but I couldn't think of anything nice to say to her in return. I was glad she couldn't read my mind because I was thinking she looked like she hadn't showered in days.

The smell of cigarettes and mildew and hot vinegar was stifling as we walked through the door. The heat from the canning operation added to the discomfort. Scanning the room for anything incriminating, I was surprised to see nary a beer can—just two ashtrays sitting out on the cardboard box they were using for a coffee table. Maybe Daddy was trying to stay sober for a spell and Pat wasn't so bad for him after all.

In the kitchen, mason jars of chowchow littered every surface, evidence of his swirl of productivity.

But my stomach turned over when Daddy handed me a big spoonful of his pickled cabbage. I loved chowchow as much as the next Southerner, but something about the look and smell of the place had my stomach a little green.

"That's good, Daddy. Where did you get all the vegetables from? Uncle George and Aunt Glenda's garden?"

"Yeah, they've had enough cabbage this fall to feed south Knoxville, so me and Pat's been up there taking all their extries."

Daddy was chopping up vegetables for the next batch of chowchow, a cigarette hanging out of his mouth. Pat went into the living room and sat down on the couch to watch TV.

Once Daddy got a batch in the pressure cooker and showed me how to tighten the top, he walked over to his stack of jars, admiring his work.

"Before you girls leave, take a jar or two of that home with you, but don't grab the one with the H on it—it'll set your mouth on far."

Reaching in front of Sister, I took a jar from the counter. She wasn't about to try the chowchow for reasons she didn't have to explain to me. I could sense her eagerness to head out, and so I asked Daddy if he needed anything before we had to leave.

"What are you two in such a hurry for anyhow? All y'uns do is run the roads, ain't it? You got a boyfriend waiting for you back at home or somethin'?" he said, while he slipped on a white T-shirt and some tennis shoes.

"Gina has a boyfriend, but I don't. I'm babysitting some kids from church tonight so I've got to get back home soon," I said as I walked over to the refrigerator. "Daddy, you got anything to drink?"

"Nothin' but a pot of black coffee. You want some, Nise?"

"No, I'm good," I said as I grabbed a drink of water from the sink, further relieved that I didn't see any beer stashed in the refrigerator.

"Gina Hope, who are you a-courtin' and when are you getting married?"

"His name's Mike, Daddy. You don't know him. He plays on the football team. And I'm probably not getting married anytime soon. I'm just fifteen, you know," she said. Her eyes kept glancing toward the television.

"Well, you look like a grown woman. And you tell ole Mike he better be good to you or your daddy'll come down there and whoop him. I ain't afraid of no football player, and I'm stouter'n I look," he said, flexing his right arm.

Although he'd always been trim, I wondered if he'd lost weight. His muscles were still lean but he was even thinner than the last time I'd seen him.

"All right, Daddy, I'll tell him," she answered with a halfhearted chuckle.

"What about you, Nise, you ain't flunkin' out of school, are you? And how much money you gonna make tonight off babysittin'?"

"No, Daddy, I'm making straight As so I can get into college. And I don't charge for babysitting. I just like doing it," I said, eyeing the sink full of dishes and rummaging around the kitchen for a place to put my cup.

"Goodness, you're a downright Mother Teresa, ain't you? You're smarter than any Rudder I ever knowed. I couldn't pass the eighth grade, so you've already showed me up."

We all laughed, and then I asked Daddy again if he needed anything before we had to head out.

"Yeah, run me down to the store; my old truck wouldn't start this morning. I need to put a new alternator in it."

We grabbed our jars of chowchow, said good-bye to Pat, and then headed to the car while Daddy told us a story of him and George whooping a fella who got too big for his britches one night at Genie's Bar. Before he got too far into one of his long storytelling rants, I asked about Uncle Gene.

"So, what do the doctors say about his cancer?"

"Well, he's got the worst kind of it a feller can have, I reckon. It started in his lungs, but he's plumb eat up with it now. They say he won't live to see another year. He's having radiation, and then they're gonna try to cut that sucker out," Daddy said, as he lit up another cigarette.

"That's awful. I bet Mamaw didn't take that news too well. Or Aunt Darlene."

"No, they was all tore up over it. You girls ort to go up to your Mamaw's and see him when you get a chance, although your aunt Glenda has threatened to move him up to her house wore she can take better care of him. Your Mamaw ain't able," he said, flicking his ashes out of the window.

"We will, but we can't go today, Daddy; maybe next weekend. Maybe you can go with us." Rambo rumbled down Martin Mill Pike to the Pilot gas station, where Daddy was a regular.

"I can't imagine losing him, but it sure looks like we're goin' to," Daddy said.

When we got there, I set a twenty-dollar bill on Daddy's leg, and he slipped it in his back pocket as he got out. He bought a pack of cigarettes and a quart of beer. Sister rolled her eyes when she saw him coming out of the store carrying the brown paper bag. I told her that I was sure he was trying to stay sober, because there was no beer in the refrigerator. Sometimes a quart of beer was just enough to keep down the shakes, as any alcoholic worth his salt will tell you. At any rate, it'd be Pat's problem and not ours at this point. I was inclined to think that if Daddy was making chowchow, all was well.

"Thank you, Nise, I'll pay you back as soon as I get a paintin' job," he said, putting the change in his billfold.

"You're welcome, Daddy," I said. "How's Jim Bob doing?" I asked, noticing the picture of him that Daddy kept in the front of his billfold.

"Aw, that boy is good. I talk to him on the phone all the time. He's always askin' about you girls and always wantin' to come stay with me, but Shirley usually won't let him," he said, lighting up another Winston.

"I miss him, and I'd sure like to see him," I said, remembering his smile and the adorable way he talked.

We rounded the corner to the apartment, dropped Daddy off, and headed back home to Maryville—him waving from the second level of the building, with one arm slung around Pat, the other hand holding his beer. I thought about him the whole way home.

It seemed no matter how many accolades I told Daddy about, whether it was being elected class president or making the winning hit in a softball game, he mostly made a joke out of it. I wanted him to see how well I was doing, hoping that somehow that might make up for our family dysfunction. Maybe I thought I could inspire some miraculous change in him or maybe I just needed him to know that I was doing something right. It seemed the more I told him, the less he listened. Most of the time, I might as well have been speaking Greek. I don't know why, but I was always hoping to impress him.

It took me a while to learn that Daddy was not impressed by me and was never going to be. The things I was good at were things he didn't value, and it was futile to explain to him what any of it meant. He couldn't have cared less about student council or my invitation to a summer camp for exceptional students or my batting average on the softball team.

But he did love me, in the only ways he knew how. And in the end, I hoped I'd find that what he could give would be enough.

Still, on most days fatherlessness felt like a flame in my bones, burning endlessly on, consuming me and eventually spiraling me out of control.

The following year would mark an end to things as we had always known them.

19

ALWAYS ON MY MIND

IT WAS LATE FALL of my senior year, and the sugar maples were the color of fire. Heritage High School sat right in the foothills of the Smoky Mountains, so we weren't strangers to the perfect beauty of fall.

Daddy was on the rocks with Pat, Uncle Gene was dying from cancer, and I was on the ballot for homecoming queen—all things that would make the year unforgettable, in the best and worst ways.

It was also the year of the bangs, and mine were standing in a claw formation at a 90-degree angle to my face, blue eye shadow so thick and frosty that my overall appearance would put you in mind of the flamboyant TV personality Tammy Faye Bakker. My classmates who had nominated me were apparently undiscriminating. Or maybe they just loved Tammy Faye as much as I did.

Tammy and I shared a similar philosophy about makeup and hair, as well as the uncanny ability to spill out tears at the least provocation. I could never get my eyelashes to burst into full bloom like hers, despite a careful study of her on the Trinity

Broadcasting Network. Even with my eyelash inadequacies, I was in the running for homecoming queen and Daddy was on his 152nd try at staying sober.

It was 1987, the year that Jamie got a David Bowie haircut and acid-washed jeans ruled the world. It was also the year I scribbled in my senior memory book that I wanted to be a missionary in Africa and have six kids. Maybe that would be possible since I was dating Shawna's cousin, Darryl, a Christian musician, more than eight years older than me.

Of course I wanted to do the Lord's work. You could have blamed it on my overzealous personality, but every young evangelical Christian my age knew that if you were really serious about your faith, African missionary work was God's sure and certain will—as if it counted more in God's economy than other less spiritual jobs. I told Daddy about my aspirations, and he said something like, "Nise, your head ain't never been shaped right."

Daddy didn't have patience for long-range goal setting, but he did promise to come to the homecoming football game sober and with his teeth in. We always had to specify the teeth now that he'd had all his pulled and was sporting a brand-new set of pearly whites. He hated wearing them because they were so ill-fitting, and none of us could really blame him.

He'd never been to any event of mine since I'd started high school. He didn't know any of my friends, and they didn't know him. Only a few close friends and those who had heard me speak at Coach Murphy's retreat knew anything about my childhood, and I knew that if he showed up drunk, the damage would be hard to undo. High schoolers were pretty unforgiving, even back then. They would make assumptions about Daddy and about me that weren't entirely true. They wouldn't get to see how funny and generous he could be, and I would just be a girl with a drunk daddy. At least that was my worry.

Whether he came or not, I anticipated a night branded for tears and disappointment. In so many ways, that described every

Friday night of my childhood. Daddy probably wouldn't show and I probably wouldn't win. I braced for the worst but decided to put my best makeup face on.

Homecoming night arrived, and I toted my borrowed dress down the long hall of our high school and up a flight of stairs to the band room—tripping on the Scarlett O'Hara crinoline with every step. Sister helped me get the back of my hair teased up and my makeup finished, and after I polished off a second can of White Rain hairspray, she helped me into my dress too. It was a little strapless number made of pink taffeta and cream-colored lace, with a poofy but stiff slip.

"Now you better work on Shawna's face. I can't be the only one who looks like Tammy Faye," I said to Sister. The three of us did everything together, and I was thankful that Shawna was one of the homecoming candidates with me, making what could have been a nerve-racking night way more fun.

We laughed like hyenas while we were getting ready.

"Please don't put as much eyeliner on me as you did on Edie," Shawna instructed Sister. "Not that you look like a lady of the night or anything, but I'm just not used to wearing as much," she said, amusing herself with her own teasing.

Sister finished up Shawna's makeup while I kept checking to make sure my eyelids had enough blue on them. Could a girl ever really have enough?

When Mama came into the band room, she looked at me with an expression that matched her words. "Sister, you look absolutely beautiful." Tears pooled at the edges of her eyes. She looked over at Gina, who was applying more blush to Shawna's cheeks. "Doesn't she look just beautiful?" Mama said, nodding her head my way.

"Yes, she does, and you can thank me," said Sister. "But I've got to head back because the cheerleaders are helping with the ceremony." Sister hugged Shawna and me and left. Mama caught me looking out the band room window, and she knew exactly what I was thinking.

"Now listen, your daddy's not here yet, and he's probably not coming. Don't let that spoil your night. You've got so much mascara on that if you start squawlin', you'll look just like a raccoon."

She was right, so I tried to laugh it off. I knew no one else from the Rudder clan would come, but I had my heart set on Daddy being there, no matter how much I tried to convince myself otherwise.

Even with Mama's words, I was still worried either way—worried that if he came, he'd be drunk and shirtless in the stands with a few "friends," dancing one off while the band played. It could easily become a repeat of the softball tournament. And if he didn't show—well, let's just say I've never seen the point of trying to hold off a good cry.

Despite all that, I felt just like Cinderella in my dress and makeup and big eighties hair.

An hour later, my escort and I were standing together on the edge of the football field, floodlights blinding and band instruments blaring. The lights, the crowd, the beautiful weather, being all dressed up and treated like a princess—I'd never had a fairy-tale moment like this one.

While the band marched into their formation, the homecoming queen candidates and their escorts walked onto the field, each to her assigned yard line.

My escort and I stood on the forty, waiting for the announcement. I was hoping Daddy was somewhere in the crowd, but braced myself for the likelihood that he wasn't.

The lights bounced off the brass instruments like lightning bolts, and it felt like the whole world was watching. When they announced the runners-up and my name hadn't been called yet, I knew there was a decent chance I might be crowned queen.

I was so nervous I thought I might vomit right there on the field.

"This year's homecoming queen is . . . Edie Rudder!"

Everything went blurry—the dazzle of the lights combined with my tears made everything swirl around me like a fuzzy watercolor painting.

My escort pulled on my arm to drag me to the center of the field, where the football captain and last year's queen waited with the glittery sash and the faux rhinestone crown.

As we made our way to the fifty-yard line, that's when I saw him.

Daddy was standing on the sideline, less than twenty yards in front of me, stone-cold sober in a khaki three-piece number and smiling from ear to ear with those pearly whites just a-shinin'.

They placed the tiara on my head and the football captain did the honors of the homecoming kiss, which could have been awkward since he was the ex-boyfriend of both Sister and me. Welcome to every small high school in the South.

Then I walked with my escort off the field, and Daddy was the first person to greet me.

He smelled like aftershave and smoke and looked like he had tried to comb his hair. He kissed me on one cheek, and Mama came up from behind to kiss me on the other. She must have shown Daddy right where to wait for me.

I had never hugged that man so tightly in my life. His arms around me made me feel like the luckiest girl in the world.

"Daddy! Look at you! Where'd you get that spiffy suit, you handsome thing?" I took a step back and admired the outfit, with not even one button undone on his white button-down shirt.

"Aw, they was runnin' a special—buy a set a teeth and get a monkey suit free."

I laughed and looked at him with tears in my eyes. He didn't say anything earth-shattering to me that night. He didn't have to, because his presence was all the gift I needed.

Daddy mentioned he'd probably leave pretty quick on account of his teeth being loose and his monkey suit driving him crazy. But he showed up for me on that Friday night, sober and handsome and perfect—not because I was proving myself to be smart or dedicated or anything else I was striving for.

It was one of those moments that stop time, when everything is right in the world; one of those moments when you know you are loved and nothing else really matters. It was rare and beautiful and perfect.

And then, like all moments, it was gone. Senior year was coming to a close, Daddy was sleeping wherever he could find a place, and Uncle Gene was about to leave us.

FREE BIRD

UNCLE GENE DIED three days before my senior banquet, landing his funeral on the same night. The first thing I thought of when Aunt Glenda called to tell me was how hard it was going to be for her, Daddy, and Aunt Darlene to lose their brother. And especially how hard it was going to be for Mamaw to lose another son. Despite the fact that her oldest son, Ed, had died before I was born, she still talked about him like it had happened just yesterday.

Uncle Gene was a permanent fixture in my childhood and had always been quiet, but in his later years, after giving up drinking, he had become sullen and downright irritable. If memory serves me right, when he was drinking he'd pester us by saying, "You hate me, don't ya?" We teased each other for years with that phrase.

I often thought to myself that I'd almost rather have Daddy drinking than grouchy like Uncle Gene, but regardless, we were all sad to watch Uncle Gene die the cruel way he did—cancer rendering him lifeless and pitiful.

Jamie flew home from New Hampshire. We hadn't seen her in almost a year, so we made plans to ride to the funeral home together. Then she and Sister would take me to Gatlinburg for my banquet. There, we'd spend the night in a hotel with the rest of my graduating class.

Before heading to the funeral home, we made an obligatory stop at Aunt Glenda's.

She gave us a morbid minute-by-minute account of Uncle Gene's last few hours. The image of him being "blowed up like a balloon from all the fluid they was pumpin' in him" was more detail than any of us asked for. We made a quick escape, coughing through a cloud of cigarette smoke, Jamie mumbling about the lung cancer we were all destined to have, thanks to the years of secondhand smoke we had inhaled.

Sister was the designated driver because, in Jamie's words, "She's the only one with enough sense to get us where we're going." I climbed into the backseat of Rambo, and Jamie rode shotgun. We had instructions to meet the family at Berry's Funeral Home in less than an hour.

Sister and Jamie had always been bosom buddies despite their six-year age difference, and I was the odd man out—way more interested in their eternal destiny than I was in party-ing with them at The Library, a popular bar on the University of Tennessee's campus. How the two of them put up with my self-righteousness is hard to say, but they were no picnic either. I knew what they were doing and tried to ignore it, hoping that the way I clung to my faith throughout my high school years would someday rub off on the two of them. We enjoyed banter-ing about our differences, but there was part of me that always worried about them.

"I could've gone my whole life without hearing the story of Uncle Gene's last gasping hours," Jamie said, finishing her makeup while we drove. "Who wants to wager on somebody being drunk at the funeral home?"

We all chuckled, none of us willing to take that bet.

"Okay, after the funeral we'll drive Edie to her banquet and then we'll meet Jill somewhere in Gatlinburg," Jamie said, smiling at Sister. The two of them were scheming things that I wasn't sure I wanted to know about, though I was sure the plan involved illegally getting Sister into some adult establishment that sold booze. Jill was Jamie's best friend from high school, and the two of them together usually meant even more trouble than Jamie and Sister alone.

Sister mumbled something, and then Jamie piped up, "You look more like a grown woman than I do, so I don't reckon we'll have any trouble." She rolled down her window so that her spiked red hair stood on its ends.

They yammered on about their strategy to get Sister into the bar in case the Gatlinburg bouncers actually paid attention.

Sister was only sixteen, so being the collective moral compass, I leaned forward and interrupted. "Hello, I'm sitting right here. And y'all better be careful with all your carousing. You'll end up like everybody else in this family—drunk and poor, or even worse, in jail."

They rolled their eyes, but I wasn't finished.

"I'm not as naive as y'all think. I know exactly what you did last year the night I came home from church visitation. And Mama didn't have to be the one to tell me, either. You think I didn't see the twenty boys sneak out the back door and the coolers of beer on the porch?"

"Oh hush, preacher girl," Jamie said. "Listen, there are two things that I will not be when it's all said and done—drunk is one of them and poor is the other. You'll notice that I got out of this hellhole as soon as I could, and if you've got any sense, you'll do the same thing when you turn eighteen. Me and Sister just like to have fun, unlike somebody we know."

Jamie's tone said that as much as we disagreed, she loved me no matter how much preaching I did.

I thought she'd said her piece as she flipped down the visor mirror to reapply her lip gloss and powder the freckles on her nose to invisibility, but she kept on.

"And you want to know the funniest thing about that night last year? Your mom found us first, and the only thing she was worried about was you finding out. 'You two better get this place cleaned up before Edie gets home' is all she said." Jamie nodded her head in defiance.

The two of them laughed and I couldn't help smiling, too, because I knew that was probably true.

"We could have had a lot of fun that night if you weren't such a Bible thumper, old Edie Nise," Jamie said as she laughed. Everybody called me Nise because of Daddy, and I had gotten old enough not to mind.

Jamie cranked up Pink Floyd on the radio. She and Sister danced in the front seat while I stared out the window, thinking about what we might be in for at Berry's and how I would ever get myself together for the senior banquet after leaving a funeral.

She turned the radio down long enough to say, "And remind me on the way to Gatlinburg to tell you about my run-in with religion. I'm not as bad off as you may think."

She motioned for Sister to pull off at the Krystal for a burger.

"I know I'll be deathly sick for doing this, but I haven't had one in at least six months," Jamie said as she grabbed some cash from her purse.

We all knew that Krystal burgers tasted good going in, but you might live to regret the decision an hour later.

We ate in the car, talking about Jamie's new life in New Hampshire and how devastating it was that there were no Krystals there. I got to thinking that if she had had a run-in with Jesus, I didn't know anything about it, so I made a mental note to ask her before the day was done.

Ten minutes later, we pulled into the funeral home's parking lot. It felt like pulling into a relative's driveway. I had been to Berry's Funeral Home more times than I had been to a doctor's office by a long shot, partly because neither longevity nor preventive care seemed to be our family's strong suit, and partly because we attended funerals of anyone even remotely related to us.

The family's general tendencies toward health and wellness were nearly nonexistent, but they brought their A game to sickness and death. The constant alcohol, poor diet, drug use, and reckless behavior meant death and dying were no strangers to the clan.

Nothing could invigorate the family quite like a funeral.

I walked through those heavy double doors and immediately thought of Daddy. Something about Uncle Gene's death made it clear to me that we would be doing this someday for him—sooner rather than later, if he didn't change his ways. Losing his last brother wasn't easy for Daddy either, so I was halfway worried that he'd be drunk at the funeral.

As soon as we signed the guest book, I saw the whole clan—Mamaw and Aunt Darlene on the couch by the casket, with Aunt Johnny and her kids in chairs nearby. Mark, her youngest, was my age and wasn't looking so good. Rumor had it he was mainlining drugs, and by the looks of him, that was not just a rumor. Aunt Glenda, Uncle George, and Jamie's brother Jeff were over talking to some of Daddy's cousins, but I hadn't spotted Daddy.

Daddy's friend Doyle was standing by my cousin Tim, looking half lit and talking some nonsense about how he and Daddy were going to open up a body shop in Vestal. I couldn't recall going to a family funeral where somebody didn't show up drunk and drape themselves over the open casket in pitiful sobs, trying to resurrect their beloved with pleas to God for just one more chance. But Uncle Gene didn't have any kids and had never been married, so the funeral was turning out to be pretty civil. Or at least it was while we were there.

Aunt Glenda hugged us all as we walked in and ushered Sister and me to the front of the viewing room, right up to Uncle Gene's cold body. Jamie had always been enraged by the family's insistence on an open casket at funerals, and feeling a little nauseated from the burgers, she found a place to sit down, saying she felt faint. She always seemed to feel faint when the whole family was together.

I walked right up to the casket and put my hand on Uncle Gene's, thinking how terribly sad it was to see him like this. He lay there in what looked to be a borrowed black suit, which I was sure was on loan from the funeral home, his neck and face swollen and his thinning hair more slicked back than normal.

It looked like Uncle Gene, but a sick and pitiable version of him.

I stood there for the longest time, trying to wrap my mind around how quickly life is gone. So many Saturday nights I'd sat on the same green vinyl couch with him at Mamaw's, watching the news and *The Lawrence Welk Show*, and noticing how he never said much and always fell asleep before anybody else.

Mostly, I noticed how different he was in every way from Daddy—so stoic, never smiling, while Daddy was always grinning from ear to ear and usually going on with some tomfoolery. Uncle Gene grumbled a lot about having us kids around, always telling us to shut the door and quit runnin' in and out, and find somewhere to light.

I loved him, but I couldn't imagine being his daughter.

Still, I felt Daddy's loss.

I turned around, and there was Daddy—sober, with little ten-year-old Jim Bob at his side.

"Oh, I'm so happy to see you," I said to my little brother, hugging him and thinking how much I missed him.

"I know, S-s-sister, I miss you, too. M-m-mama Shirley brought me here, but I wish she'd let me stay with my d-d-daddy all the time," he said, stuttering some of his words.

I noticed Daddy's hands shaking as he patted Jim Bob on the back, the two of them inseparable when they were together. Jim Bob took my hand and walked me back up toward the casket to see Uncle Gene. He waved toward Shirley standing in the back so she'd know where he was. I smiled and waved, too, thinking how sad it was that her and Daddy's marriage hadn't lasted.

After seeing the two of them, I was even more thankful Daddy was sober. His face was clammy, and I wondered if a beer might do him good right now, but I knew that seemed too wrong to even think.

Shirley was anxious to take Jim Bob home, so Daddy hugged Sister and me and then walked them outside to her car. Daddy stayed out of the fray and left before any of us said good-bye, probably making a beeline for the nearest store that had a tall one.

At least he came to the funeral home sober. I was proud of him for that.

Aunt Glenda put her arm around my shoulder, and looking toward the casket, said, "He looks good. I think they did a good job with him, for how swolled up he was before he died. And I'll tell you what, this has about killed me, and Mama, too. Ain't none of us, includin' Aunt Johnny, been able to eat a bite for a week. Our nerves is all shot."

Aunt Glenda was the collective voice of our family, her idioms so fixed in my brain that her voice in my head was more reliable to me than my own. She bent over the casket and patted Uncle Gene's hands.

"You girls don't know what it's like watchin' your own brother suffer when they ain't nothin' in this world you can do about it. I know he was not always nice to you girls, but he didn't never have no kind of a good life. He lived with Mama and Daddy and worked what little bit he could. At least he sobered up the last few years of his life, which is more than I can say for some of the rest of 'em."

She was right—Uncle Gene had a hard life, but he did have his good side. I remembered his occasional tenderness toward us—the time he stood up for us at Mamaw's and the times he picked up a half gallon of Blue Band Ice Milk for us from Cas Walker's grocery store on Fridays when he got paid.

Beside us stood a red carnation flower spray in the shape of a cross with a red plastic phone nestled at the center and a sign that said, "Jesus Called." Such was the charm of a funeral in Appalachia. Jamie, of course, had noticed it right off and was snickering in the back of the room. I finally had a chance to walk back to see how she was doing.

"I'm fine, but please tell me why we always have to have the 'Jesus Called' spray. I'm holding you personally responsible if that ends up at my funeral. But never mind, because I'm not having a funeral. I'm getting cremated to prevent any of this from happening when I die. And I give you full permission to have a party for me and show up drunk," she said, as full of the family wit as any of us.

We heard Aunt Darlene making her way to the casket, crying intermittently about how much she was going to miss Uncle Gene, a brother she had lived in the same house with for forty years. Her gait was more labored than normal, so I helped her to the side of the room where she could sit with Mamaw, who was miserable in her grief.

"None of y'uns know what it's like to bury your own child. I've already buried one son. This may put me in the ground," Mamaw said.

I found Mamaw a box of Kleenex and sat with her awhile, trying to console her and Aunt Darlene while dabbing at my own tears, too, and feeling the weight of this loss for them. Eventually, Jamie and Sister told me it was time to go if I was going to make it to my banquet in Gatlinburg. We said our good-byes and talked on the way to the car about the miracle that no one had showed up drunk, not even Daddy.

I slid into the backseat, feeling a heaviness and guilt for what we were leaving behind. Before we were out of the parking lot, I was sobbing, and I really didn't even know why. Maybe it was seeing the family all together again and thinking how sad it was to live a life that seemed so unfulfilled. Or the loneliness of watching Daddy leave by himself, without Jim Bob or us or Uncle Gene to keep him company.

I cried off and on the whole way to Gatlinburg. I apologized to Sister and Jamie for being such a mess, but I knew they didn't care.

"Oh, you're always squawlin'; we're used to it by now. You're really gonna squawl when I tell you my church story," Jamie said, as she shifted in her seat to start her tale. "I don't think I've ever told another soul. It's pitiful and also hilarious."

Sister and I were now all ears.

"Okay, well tell us. We could use some laughter about now," Sister said.

"Well, what happened was, some nice man driving a church bus picked me up from the trailer park one Sunday morning and told me all about not going to hell and asked me on the way if I wanted to get baptized the next Sunday. I thought that sounded like a great idea, except for the fact that I was terrified of water. The only thing I can tell you is, I was terrified of hell more. So the next week, he picked me up again and I got myself baptized."

"I did not know that. Did Aunt Glenda or your dad go with you?" I asked.

"No, just me. I just went and got myself baptized and sat in the back of the church with my hair wringing wet. And to my recollection, I never went back after that."

That's when Sister and I told how we had done the same thing at a different church before I ever met Brother Cross, both of us baptized without so much as a parent, or a towel, or a change of clothes.

The thought of us three girls sitting in the back of some church, maybe just a Sunday or two apart from each other, dripping wet, sent us into a fit of laughter that we could not get under control no matter how hard we tried.

By the time we reached the banquet, I was a wreck, having cried and laughed all my makeup off. The rest of the night was a blur, except for my friends and teachers repeatedly asking me if I was okay. I remember gathering my awards and spreading them over the hotel bed, pretty proud of myself for the hard work they represented. In the wake of Uncle Gene's death, I knew it was self-ish to feel sorry for myself, but it hurt that none of those awards mattered much in our family's economy.

The next morning, I woke up before anyone else and went onto the balcony to sit with my thoughts. I held the joy close and the grief closer, not knowing that the pain behind me wouldn't hold a candle to the heartache that was to come.

21

A THOUSAND MILES FROM NOWHERE

THE DECISION STUNNED ALL OF US, including me. But I was the one who made it. At the beginning of the summer, I had applied and been accepted to the University of Tennessee, but I had just announced to my family that I was now heading to Tennessee Temple, a tiny Baptist college in Chattanooga.

I had never heard of the school until some kids from my church youth group mentioned it, snickering about its stringent code of conduct. Maybe that's what intrigued me at first. In August at a Christian camp I learned more about it from the camp director, who happened to be an alumnus and recruiter. He told me about the fledgling sports program and said he could guarantee me a basketball scholarship if I went there.

Without hesitation, I said yes.

But now, facing my family with the college handbook, I began to worry about my wobbly decision-making. I mean, who does that—changes colleges two weeks before classes start because somebody thinks you're decent at basketball?

After hearing me read some of the policies, Daddy said, "I don't know even what half of them rules mean, Nise, but if I's you I wouldn't tell 'em I was a Rudder. They'll throw your backside out of there on that account alone."

Only he didn't say "backside."

I made a mental note to keep Daddy away from the place. And deep down, I wondered if I could even cut it.

Sister's response was a puzzled and irritated, "Why did you decide to do that?"

"I don't know," I said. "It just sounds like fun to be able to keep playing sports and to get a scholarship to do it."

"Well, we don't call you preacher for nothing. I'm sure you'll be fine," Sister said, half teasing, as we walked toward our bedroom.

"The problem is going to be this right here," she said as she sat on the bed, where our shared ragtag collection of clothes was spread out.

I was glad I only had a couple of weeks to think about what it would be like to leave Sister. She had been the only real constant in my life, and my leaving wouldn't be easy for either of us. Sure, we sometimes fought over clothes, but we also were there for each other. We shared everything, literally—clothes, a car, cheerleading uniforms, friends, the occasional boyfriend, and Daddy. Neither of us could claim one single article of clothing solely as our own. Both of us were about to lose a best friend and half our wardrobe simultaneously.

In the end, I took all the skirts and dresses and left the rest, agreeing to switch out the clothes when I came home for holidays and breaks. With that taken care of, I didn't want to think about it anymore. The next couple of weeks were spent gathering transcripts and recommendations and test scores to make the last-minute transfer to one of the strictest Baptist colleges south of the Mason-Dixon.

Mama and I drove to Chattanooga on a hot, humid August morning. I could hardly contain my excitement. *I am going to college. I am going to college. I AM GOING TO COLLEGE!* I thought to myself as we rounded the corner of the campus and saw my dorm, Ruby Hall.

As much as the budding spiritual and intellectual part of me tried to be breezy and nonchalant, the "Yeehaw! It's Howdy Doody time 'cause Nise is going to college" part of me wanted Daddy here so he could make me laugh and finish the college send-off by dancing a jig on the sidewalk.

But he wasn't, and it was probably for the best.

Though I worried that Sister would now be his sole caretaker—or at least the sole provider of his beer and cigarettes on the weekends—I was a smidge relieved that I would be relatively unavailable for the next year. It felt self-indulgent, to be honest, but it had all the makings of the ever-elusive fresh start—where I could be whoever I wanted to be, with no baggage to tie me down to my past. I even thought of having everyone call me by my middle name, Denise, but Mama said it would never work. And besides, Nise was Daddy's name for me. Even entering school as plain old Edie, I couldn't have been more excited.

Mama and I sat in the car in front of the dorm without saying a word, holding the moment for as long as we could, both of us feeling its weight. She reached over to hug me and then finally said, "You just don't know how proud I am of you, Sis." Her voice cracked. "You had such a rough start into this world, and it's hard to believe that you turned out like this, so tender and smart and capable of making a good life for yourself. I don't know what to say except that I'm so incredibly thankful." She hugged me for the longest time.

Something in me knew that it was the end and that I would never really go back home, at least not as the same person. We pulled out my mismatched bags and headed into the building, my insides swirling with jitters and anticipation.

I looked around and saw large families piling out of station wagons and vans—the dads all dressed like pastors, the moms with shampoo-and-set hairdos, wearing perfectly pressed knee-length skirts. The kids were serious-looking, the boys in their neckties and the girls wearing their best Sunday shoes. These looked like the kind of families that had beef stew every night at a solid-oak table, holding hands while the dad said grace. The girls who got out of those station wagons did not look like girls who had visited Brushy Mountain Prison or girls whose dads came to their ball games drunk and shirtless. My heart began to race. The tune "One of These Things Is Not Like the Others" kept running through my mind. I was the other.

As we unloaded my stuff inside the lobby and waited for my room assignment, I looked at Mama and me. She was wearing black pants and a denim jacket with her short pixie cut, while I was wearing a summer dress. *I should have thought this through more. I should have asked Mama to wear a skirt.* And I should have worn black or navy blue, not the far too flowy and colorful dress I had on. And my makeup was too flashy—too much eyeliner, blue eye shadow, red lipstick. My hair was more teased than everyone else's. I quickly scanned the other students, making mental notes of girls I should try to emulate.

Maybe the one with the tidy updo, now headed to the fourth floor, or the one with a metal banana clip, wearing the long prairie skirt, bobby socks, and just a hint of powder and mascara. Or the one standing outside who looked like an airline stewardess in a business casual suit, her daddy heaving her oversized suitcase up the sidewalk to the dorm entrance. I found myself wishing for enough money for a whole new wardrobe—one that might broadcast to the whole campus that I was one of the conservative girls. The thought crossed my mind that maybe a new last name would help, too, but that didn't seem possible.

If there was any trait of mine that I was proud of in almost any circumstance, it was my abiding optimism, so I tried to put out of my mind all the ways I didn't fit in. I figured my peers would like me once they got to know me, and I tried my best to be myself. Mama left as soon as she helped me unload my stuff, and I sat on my new twin bed, wondering who my roommate would be and how I would ever survive in this alien world I had been dropped into. More important, I worried about Sister and Daddy and how we'd all manage to get along without each other.

Despite the initial shock and fleeting waves of fear, I actually adapted to my new life pretty well. My roommate was a wonderful girl from Michigan who loved to hear me talk. I made friends with remarkable ease and found many of my classmates to be delightful, despite the perfection I had been sure would separate us when I'd first laid eyes on them. After promptly losing my copy of the student handbook, I repeatedly questioned the girls on my floor about what we could and couldn't do. I had never seen so many written rules in my life.

No physical contact between unmarried members of the opposite sex.

Freshmen may not leave campus without written permission from the permissions office.

Women may not wear pants. Skirts and dresses must come to the knees.

And so on and so forth, for at least forty pages.

I wanted to follow the rules, but they were so foreign to how I had grown up that it was hard to remember them on common-sense grounds alone. It became my life's goal to avoid getting any demerits, which I managed to do for an entire year.

The no-pants rule made it impossible for me to be warm in the winter; the mandatory panty hose, which could be found in various and sundry places in my dorm room, poking out of drawers and bags and balled up under the bed, didn't provide much in the way of insulation. My family made plenty of jokes about my basketball shorts, which came down to my knees, although to my knowledge, they only ever made it to one game. The six-inch rule between boys and girls, the ban on movies, and the mandatory curfew were easy enough to adapt to, but forbidding all secular music was a pill that was hard to swallow, mostly because of Johnny Cash, George Jones, and Merle Haggard. How could listening to "Folsom Prison Blues" or "Mama Tried" possibly be wrong?

To make matters worse, nobody had ever been so concerned about what I was wearing or where I was going or why I was going there as they were now. In order to leave campus, you had to have an actual permission slip from a flesh-and-blood person who worked in the permissions office. It wasn't that I was ever trying to break the rules, but it just never occurred to me to ask somebody if I could drive to the drugstore to get a pair of black tights. Once, when I needed to get some shampoo, I actually remembered that I needed permission after I was sitting in the parking lot of the drugstore. Always a rule keeper, I drove back to school to get official permission and then promptly drove back to the store. It all seemed so unnecessary. Mama had never even imposed a curfew on us, and for all practical purposes, we'd come and gone as we pleased since we'd been old enough to walk home from school.

Still, it only added to the foreignness and the charm of this entire college experience. I would catch myself staring off into space at the marvel of it all—that I was an actual college student with an actual scholarship and a dorm room and a very generous meal plan. If anyone was made for college life, it was me, and I didn't take one ounce of it for granted.

I breezed through most of my classes and joined a social club, the Christian version of a sorority. Whatever I forfeited in the way of music or movies or freedom to come and go as I pleased, I gained in shared experience and friendship in a place more sheltered and cocooned than anything I'd known. In some ways it felt like coming home, and I eased into place like I had lived there all my life.

22

THAT'S THE WAY LOVE GOES

A COUPLE OF MONTHS after college started, I began dating a tall, cute basketball player named Jeff. (And by dating, I mean we sat together in chapel and at meals in the dining hall, and I all but wrote his English essays in exchange for lessons in three-point shooting.) We were the same age but came from very different backgrounds—Jeff from one of those seemingly perfect Christian families with six talented kids and a pastor/coach dad.

Mama really liked him. A lot. She met him one weekend when she drove down to watch a Friday night basketball tournament. Truth was, I was falling hard for him too.

I had broken it off with my hometown boyfriend, Darryl, convinced by everyone, especially Mama, that I needed to fully immerse myself in life at college. With Uncle Gene dying five months earlier, it had been a rough year, and as much as I wanted to go to college and chase down some dreams, I also wanted to make my life into everything it had never been. The American dream, in my mind, was a husband and kids and maybe a dog or two.

I wanted stability and a real family so bad I could taste it. Mama had been glad when I chose the school away from home, thinking if I went away I wouldn't end up married and pregnant at eighteen, like a lot of girls from my high school. And since Darryl was quite a bit older than me, I think she feared I'd choose him over college. She probably felt like I was out of the woods, so to speak—away at college and now dating another eighteen-year-old, someone who had no interest in getting married any time soon.

I was, however, glad to be at college since school was not exactly on our family's priority list. Daddy never finished eighth grade, and most of my cousins didn't finish high school. Mama had gotten pregnant at sixteen, although she did finally manage to get her GED and then take college classes. Sure that I would somehow manage to mess something up, I had recurring dreams of getting kicked out of school or discovering that I had registered for a class that I never attended or that I had missed my final exams.

But none of those bad dreams came true, and I hummed along in my new life with a kind of tempered hope—hope that maybe this place was the key that would unlock the door to that magical world I dreamed about called *Normal*.

So everybody, including me, was caught off guard when I saw Darryl while I was home on semester break and he proposed to me on Christmas Eve. The only thing more surprising than the proposal was the fact that I said yes, without an ounce of obvious hesitation.

Maybe it was the fact that he did it at his parents' house, two people I adored. Maybe it was the giant diamond and my dream of having a real family. Maybe it was my utter paralysis when it came to any kind of confrontation. Whatever my reasons, I said yes to a marriage proposal while my heart was twisted up inside from a torrent of very strong feelings for Jeff, the basketball player I had been dating back at school.

Jeff called me the following day to wish me a merry Christmas, and I didn't have the heart to tell him the truth. *What kind of monster am I? And how am I going to get out of this impossible situation?*

I wasn't the only one confused and in a panic. I had never seen Mama so heartbroken and so at a loss for words. She said almost nothing to me the whole week I was home, probably in an attempt to avoid saying something hurtful. A death in the family wouldn't have put a stronger damper on the house.

Always in tune with everyone else's emotional anguish, I could feel the heat of everything Mama couldn't say. I was saying the same things to myself. *What in the world am I doing? How have I gotten myself into such a convoluted mess?*

That Christmas break was the worst and longest stretch of days I could remember, and I couldn't seem to find my way out of it.

When I returned to school early for basketball practice before the second semester began, I had worked out a plan for how I would handle this awful predicament. I'd phone Darryl and call off the engagement. Then I'd tell Jeff that I had gotten engaged, but thought it over and realized what a huge mistake I was making and called it off. Maybe Jeff would somehow forgive me if I was unengaged by the time I talked to him.

I set the plan in motion within twenty-four hours. The phone call to Darryl was by far the worst thing I had ever done. I knew I was such a mixed-up coward. I wanted to pretend like none of it had ever happened, but I was so distraught over what I had done, I couldn't even think straight. My stomach was in so many knots, I couldn't eat. I figured while I was such a mess, I'd get all the bad news out of the way, so I called Jeff and told him the whole story, how I'd gotten engaged and then unengaged in the span of a few days. He was devastated and hung up the phone without really saying good-bye. I was crying so hard I could barely see to get back up to my dorm room. I sat there on the bed for what felt like hours, wishing I could make it all go away.

I'm not sure what I expected, but it was way worse than I thought it would be.

I needed to call Mama.

I was standing in the middle of my dorm room in my stocking feet, staring out the window, watching tiny spits of snow fall like confetti, wondering how in the world everything had spun so out of control in a matter of two weeks. I headed back down to the lobby and the phone.

The January wind was blowing harder, swirling to a whistle, causing the shrubs to scratch eerily against the lobby windows. Nobody was working the dorm desk, so I sat alone and dialed the number.

It seemed like forever before Mama picked up the phone. She must have thought somebody was holding a gun to my head from the mangled words I managed to get out between sobs. I curled up on the metal chair, hugging my knees and holding the phone receiver in the crook of my arm.

"Sister, what in the world is wrong? Are you okay?" Mama said in her I'll-take-care-of-everything voice.

"I'll be okay, but . . . ," I managed to squeak out.

"Honey, don't be so upset; whatever it is, we'll get through it together. We always do. Do I need to come down there?" She waited patiently for me to pull myself together.

"I just broke off my engagement, and I wondered if you could meet me somewhere tonight."

The words ran together as I buried my head in my lap to muffle my wailing.

As I cleared my throat and dabbed my face with my jacket sleeve, I looked up to see the lights from the Commons flickering across the street. It was otherwise pitch black and empty on campus.

"Did you already have basketball practice today?" Mama asked.

"Yes, it's time for dinner, but I'm not hungry, and I can't go in there like this."

"Just stay right there, and I'll be there in two hours," Mama said.

I didn't think I could wait two hours, and I didn't want her to have to drive the whole way. So we decided to meet halfway, in Cleveland, Tennessee.

I headed out to the parking lot in sweatpants, my basketball sweatshirt, and a red peacoat with only a few dollars for gas crumpled in my pocket. There was no one around to give me permission to leave campus, but that was the furthest thing from my mind. Fortunately, the car started on the third try in the frigid temperature.

Driving on autopilot with a million thoughts running through my head, I was so preoccupied that I realized about halfway to Cleveland that I was still shivering. I had never turned the heater on. I flipped on the radio and hummed along in an almost dreamlike state, mulling over everything that had happened, until I saw the sign for exit 25. I pulled into the Pilot gas station to wait for Mama. I parked and reclined my seat, dozing off until I heard her tap on the window. I got out of the car, and we hugged and cried.

"Sweetheart, you're doing the right thing," Mama comforted me. "You don't need to be getting married right now. What's the hurry?"

We climbed in her car and talked for what seemed like hours. She didn't scold me at all for what I had done. She was gentle, promising that this would all be okay and that in time, the hurt and guilt would heal.

"I want you to go back to that school and have the time of your life. Don't worry about all this. Play basketball, make good grades, enjoy your friends, and apologize to Jeff. This is just a hiccup, and things will work out. Don't worry so much about other people. Worry about yourself, for once."

"Thank you, Mama. I love you. Make sure you tell Sister that I'm giving the ring back, and make sure she tells Daddy."

"Yes, I'll tell her. Now, get back to school, you hear me?"

We hugged one last time, and I got into my car and drove back to campus, ready to face Jeff and the embarrassment and shame of what I had done. I was doubtful that he would forgive me, but I had to try.

When I got back to campus, I saw the lights from the gym as I pulled into the parking lot at Ruby Hall. I managed to run up to my dorm room without anyone seeing me and change into a skirt. Fortified by my talk with Mama, I knew that I needed to find Jeff as quickly as I could.

A handful of players were shooting hoops, and as I walked over, my teammate Wendy said, "Jeff's in Coach's office. I don't think he's in a talking mood."

"Pray for me," I said as I took a deep breath, half hoping I'd run into him when no one else was around and half hoping he had already left. Sure enough, I came around the corner and saw him in the office. Our eyes met, and I could see that his were full of hurt. Neither of us said a word.

He leaned against the doorjamb, jaw clenched and eyes averted. We both just stood there. *Can he hear my heart pounding?* I was trying to find words that would somehow undo what I'd done. His arms were folded tight against his chest, and he could only glance at me before looking away.

"Jeff, I'm so sorry for what I've done. I know I made a huge mistake. I'm begging you to forgive me. I'm praying that we can at least eventually be friends again. I can't imagine being here at school without you."

How could I have ruined such a wonderful thing? I touched his arm.

Jeff turned and looked right into my eyes and said, "I can't believe you did it, Edie. You even talked to me on the phone the night after it happened. Everything seemed fine. I missed you so much over break, and I thought you felt the same way. At least, that's what you've been saying for the past few months. And then you go and get engaged? Who would do something like that? It doesn't even make any sense to me. I feel like I don't know you at all."

His words cut to the quick, and they were all true. What kind of person *would* do something like that? My heart was beating out of my chest.

He walked behind the desk and sat down, his hands pressing hard against his temples. I so wanted to hug him, to make him see that my feelings for him hadn't changed. My throat felt hot, the words burning me from the inside out. Finally, I found the courage to speak up.

"Jeff, none of it makes any sense to me either. My whole life has been so messed up. But you have to believe that it has nothing to do with you. You are so amazing, and if I could take it back, I would. All I can do now is say that I'm sorry and that I made a huge mistake. I don't know what's wrong with me. I pray that you will find a way to forgive me."

We stood there with broken hearts, neither of us able to find the magic combination of words to put this totally behind us. I could see forgiveness in his eyes. I felt it in my bones, but I knew he had too much self-respect to let me off the hook so easily. I left the gym that night convinced that this was unfixable. I was too messed up for someone like him.

Within two weeks Jeff and I were dating again, but this time he was more cautious. The hurt was evident in everything he said, and things were never the same. Deep down, I figured it was only a matter of time before he moved on. It was probably for the best because I could feel myself being pulled back home.

I finished the semester in May, told Jeff good-bye, and never went back.

I was married by the end of July.

23

SING ME BACK HOME

OH, DADDY, DON'T DO THIS TO ME AGAIN, I said to myself, pacing in the back of the church, waiting for my man in black to arrive.

Waiting for Daddy to show up for my wedding felt like my high school homecoming all over again. In less than fifteen minutes I was supposed to walk down the aisle, and he was nowhere to be found. Each time the church doors opened, I held my breath, only to be disappointed. The letdown of Daddy's absence, combined with the steamy hot July air trying to melt my mascara, rekindled every childhood anxiety I'd ever felt.

Mama reassured me that Todd was ready to stand in as my escort if need be, and I tried to act like that would be just fine. Of course, the truth was it would be a knife to my heart if Daddy didn't come, so I kept pacing and sweating my way back and forth to the bathroom, wiping the black blotches from underneath my eyes.

Daddy, are you really going to stand me up on my wedding day? I couldn't imagine that happening. He had been fitted for his tux the night before and had attended the rehearsal dinner. The best any of us could tell, he had been sober all week. He wasn't even jittery and was joking with Sister about bringing a shotgun to the wedding.

"I don't think you need to, Daddy; Edie's not pregnant and these are all churchgoing people, so they might not take too kindly to firearms," I heard Sister say as she was walking him out to her car after the rehearsal dinner.

"Well, a man can never be too sure," he said, climbing into his truck.

And that was the last time anybody talked to him.

"We should have had somebody pick him up today," I said to Sister as she reteased her hair for the tenth time.

"Well, I would have, but he seemed fine last night. Jamie tried to call Aunt Glenda but nobody answered, and nobody's seen him today."

About that time, Jamie came in the front door to check on me. She had a nine-month-old baby girl named Jordan now, so cute with her headful of wiry black hair.

"No Daddy?" Jamie asked Mama.

"No Daddy. And that man will regret the day he ever met me if does not show up here in the next ten minutes," Mama said, her eyes boring a hole through the church doors.

"Well, that wouldn't be the first time you whooped him," Jamie said.

We all laughed.

"Besides, my mom's not here yet either, so don't give up hope," Jamie said. "Maybe they're together. You know how slow they are. Has anybody even checked the parking lot? They're probably both out there smoking." She disappeared out the door to see if she could find them.

"Do you think the pressure of it all drove him to binge?" I asked, searching Sister's face for an answer.

"The pressure of what?" Mama piped up. "All he has to do is

show up. He hasn't paid for anything or planned anything or even so much as asked any questions about it."

"He'll show up. I know he will," I said to myself a hundred times.

Five minutes passed, and it felt like five hours. I stood in front of the bathroom mirror and thought, *If Daddy doesn't show up, it will be okay. It will make me stronger. And Todd will be happy to step in.*

But deep down, I was crushed—a feeling I knew all too well.

As I walked out of the bathroom, I saw the front door of the church open.

I could hear his whistle before I saw him. Daddy had the door propped open with one arm while he looked for a place to put out his cigarette. He flicked it on the concrete landing and ground it out with his shoe. I ducked back in the bathroom to gain my composure before I went out to meet him. Mama said what we were all thinking.

"Well, it's about time you showed up! Edie's been worried sick, Jim. Where've you been?"

"Aw, now, Sharon Kay, you know I had to get my hair just right. Where is that Nise anyways? She decide to get outta Dodge and skip this shindig?" I could hear him clear as day, but I kept patting my face with a tissue, waiting until it looked like I hadn't been crying.

"No, she didn't. She's probably in the bathroom drying her eyes *again*," Mama said, irritated with Daddy's nonchalance.

"Hey Daddy, you made it!" I said as I came out of the bathroom. I was still fighting back tears but was as giddy as a schoolgirl to see him.

"Well, there you are, Nise, I thought you mighta run off to Africa or somewhur. Wadn't that where you said you was goin' after you got outta school?" he said.

"No, Africa isn't for me just yet, Daddy. Just getting married is all. And waiting for you to show up to do it." I hugged him, straightened his tie, and asked where he was hiding his cigarettes.

"Awww, they're in my back pocket, but you can't see 'em for this straitjacket y'all've got me in. I cain't even raise my arms up," he said holding his hands out to demonstrate how restricted he was.

He was wearing a tuxedo for the first time in his life. With his big smile and brand-new haircut, he almost looked like a movie star.

"Well, listen, there's no smoking during the ceremony. Should I confiscate your lighter?"

We both laughed as the organ began playing, the signal for the ushers to escort the grandparents down the aisle. Mamaw Rudder was wearing a pretty blue dress.

"Did Jim get here?" I heard her ask.

"Yes, he made it, Mamaw," Sister assured her. "He's over there with Edie, cracking jokes as usual, talking about how we've got him a straitjacket for the day."

"Well, good; he needs to be tied up."

I made Daddy practice holding his arm just right, but every time he'd get set up, he'd act like he was going to dance a jig.

"Okay, Daddy, no cigarettes and no singing and absolutely no dancing one off down the aisle. This is my church, and you're going to have to behave yourself if it kills you," I said, patting his right arm.

"Well, it just might kill me. But I'll be quiet as a church mouse as long as they don't take up a collection; then I guess I'd just have to fork over my Winstons and put *them* in the plate."

"There won't be a collection, Daddy. Your cigarettes are safe."

It was almost time for the mothers to go inside. Mama came over to Daddy and me. I had my forehead buried in his shoulder, trying to fight off my nerves. Mama tapped my arm and hugged me hard, like it was the last time she'd ever see me.

"Edie, I would feel like I was doing you a grave disservice if I didn't say this to you. I don't want you to start crying or get upset. Just hear me out."

My heart started pounding.

What is she going to say?

"I'm not trying to tell you what to do, but I love you more than life itself. I think you're making a mistake. You're too young. You don't know what you want, and I think you're caught up in the emotions. You don't know anything about being married, and you've got your whole life ahead of you. If you want to leave right now, I'll pick up all the pieces. I'll do all the explaining, I'll return all the gifts, I'll make all the apologies. I don't want you to do this if you felt pressured into it, or if you just wanted to escape something. Don't do something that you're going to regret for the rest of your life. I will love and support you like I always have no matter what, but I'm giving you a way out if you want it."

My knees felt like they might buckle underneath me, and my ears and neck felt hot. I was afraid she might be right. Maybe I was making a mistake, acting out of fear or impulse or just a desire for something better than I'd known.

But I knew just as well that I didn't have the courage to do what she was asking, and I hated that part of myself, the part that always avoided confrontation at all costs. I thought about all the people who had bought dresses and gifts and airline tickets and more. I thought about my future in-laws and how disappointed they would be in me for being so flighty.

And I thought about Daddy, standing right here beside me, and how he had managed to get here to walk me down the aisle.

I just didn't have the stomach to run away, so I said, "Mama, I'm okay. Really I am. We are going to move to Nashville so Darryl can make it in the music business, and I'm going to finish school, and this is all going to be fine. I know you don't think I'm ready, but I'm more grown up than you think."

But you can't lie to your mama. No matter how hard you try.

"Okay, then, I'll be your biggest supporter."

She kissed my cheek and looked at me with those eyes that know everything and said she'd never say another word about it. She found Todd and they got ready.

Soon enough, Daddy and I were the only ones left.

I held my bouquet to my nose and took in the fragrance of the white roses mixed with daisies. Daddy smelled it too. Then we heard our musical cue.

I kissed him on the cheek. "Thank you for coming, Daddy. I love you."

"Well, I love you, too, Nise, and I guess if you ain't changed your mind by now, we're gonna walk down this aisle like two Rudder stooges. Now don't get down there and cause a scene and get woozy or nothin' 'cause I ain't able to pick you up. I reckon you weigh more than I do," he said, making us both chuckle.

"I won't, Daddy. You won't have to carry me, I promise."

It all went off without a hitch. A month later, we were living in Nashville, and my feelings of regret were already creeping to the surface.

I enrolled in the nursing program at Middle Tennessee State University and began working at a nursing home at night for extra money.

Later that fall, my cousin Mark hung himself from an oak tree in his front yard after a drug binge, right before his twentieth birthday. At the funeral, Aunt Johnny's face was the saddest one I ever laid eyes on, and I began to wonder if self-destruction was just part of the inheritance that came with being born a Rudder.

24

MAMAS, DON'T LET YOUR BABIES GROW UP TO BE COWBOYS

IN EARLY FALL OF 1989, just about the time the ragweed was in full bloom to torment my allergies, I began to feel more tired than usual. And then I noticed that I was getting thick around the middle. As I thought back over the past two months, things started to add up. *Is it possible that I'm pregnant?*

I stopped at the drugstore and bought a pregnancy test. I didn't want to wait until I got home, so I pulled into McDonald's and ran into the bathroom.

Within moments, I saw the pink line on the white stick. Positive. I was 90 percent sure. But then I began to second-guess myself. *Is the line too faint? I'm probably reading the test wrong somehow.* I rubbed my stomach, trying to imagine a tiny human being tucked inside of my body. Maybe it was some weird fluke or imagining, but I instantly felt a strange sensation come over me—like someone was hovering over me or near me or in me. I dismissed it quickly, but wondered if that's what it felt like to have another life growing inside of you.

Scared to death, I wanted to vomit. I wanted to cry. I wanted to go back home to Mama. Instead, I gathered up the empty box, the instructions, and the stick, and flew out of the bathroom stall like I was being chased by a band of outlaws.

I needed to talk to Mama, but I couldn't bring myself to tell her.

Instead, I drove around Nashville, wallowing in uncertainty, thinking about how every little thing would change if the test result was accurate. *How will I finish school? Will I even know how to be a mother?* And how would this complicate the already-difficult situation we were in—living in Nashville where we knew no one, with very part-time jobs and no serious opportunities for our future?

Mama would know what to do, but I still hesitated to call her for fear that she would be disappointed that I was pregnant already.

I pulled the car over by a row of cypress trees that led into our apartment complex and parked. I grabbed the stick from the passenger's seat, rolled down my tinted window to let the sun in, and squinted.

There was definitely a line.

But it was definitely faint.

I bought another test the next day just to be sure and then another one after that. All three of them were positive. We were going to be parents. I was both thrilled and completely terrified, and all I could think about was Mama. I needed to tell her, but I knew it probably wouldn't be the news she was waiting for.

They say that once a baby gets here, no matter how dire the circumstances, everybody forgets all the worries they had about it when they see the tiny face and the impossibly small hands and feet. All true. And it didn't even take that much for Mama. When I told her the news, she was so happy about the baby and excited to be a grannie. Sister and I had decided long ago, while we were still in high school, that Grannie would be her grandma name— for what reasons I couldn't even recall. And now she was one, and from then on, everybody called her Grannie.

So despite my young age and despite her misgivings about my

marriage, Mama rallied and gave me all the advice and encouragement I needed, making the nine months fly by. Daddy seemed happy too.

At the end of May, I noticed a long row of peonies near our apartment complex bent over from holding up the heavy blooms through weeks of wind and rain. I felt spent from exhaustion too. I waddled around the nursing home where I worked at night and waddled around campus during the day. When I did try to sleep, I had nightmares about whether or not I would be able to have a natural delivery on my own. On the doctor's recommendation, I agreed to be induced.

We arrived at the hospital at 6 a.m., and I was in full labor before noon. Mama and Darryl stayed by my side the whole morning, while Sister paced around in the waiting room, coming in periodically to check on us. They called my obstetrician when the baby crowned, and he was there almost instantly, ready for the delivery. There was a baseball game on TV, and the doctor kept glancing that direction between my contractions. I wanted to tell him to pay closer attention to me than to the game, because this was the most amazing and important day of my life and I needed his full concentration. But the pressure was so excruciating that I quickly forgot about everything else. I could hardly catch my breath between the pushes and felt like there was a good chance that maybe the baby wasn't going to come out.

"Are you sure I can do this? The pressure is so intense, I don't know if I can stand it anymore. Please, can you just get him out?" I gasped, trying to find some regular rhythm for my breathing.

"Yes, he's coming out, dear; we may have to help him along with some forceps."

"I just want to see my baby," I said, wiping the sweat from underneath my eyes and laying my head over the side of the bed in defeat. My legs were quivering from muscle fatigue, and I was suddenly cold, dreading the next contraction.

"Don't give up on me yet, Miz Edie; you are one strong mama, and you have shown me how hard you can push. On this next one, I want you to give it all you've got."

Mama was beside me, wiping my head with a cool rag and clutching my right hand. She got up close to my ear and said, "I want you to hold my hand and bear down as hard as you can. You've got to fight for this baby; I know you can do it."

"Okay, deep breath in, Miz Edie. Now, push as hard as you can," the doctor said as he and a nurse squared themselves up for the moment we had all been waiting for.

From the second I laid eyes on him, I knew Taylor was "Tuesday's child, full of grace." When the doctor laid him in my arms, all warm and wet, I knew that everything I'd gone through to get to this point was worth it.

I was mother to the most perfect baby boy on the planet, and I cried tears of joy.

"Could I take him to clean him up?" The nurse smiled as she held out her hands.

"Not just yet," I said to her. "He's so content. Mama, I can't believe he's mine. He's so perfect."

I counted his toes and fingers and gently kissed his soft pink lips, snuggling with him. His daddy hovered over him, just as proud and full of gratitude as I was.

"Thank you, Lord," I kept saying over and over as I adjusted Taylor's swaddling blanket to keep him tucked in tight.

The nurse finally took him from me as they began cleaning me up.

"Is there anything you need, honey, like more ice chips or something?" Mama asked.

"Yes, I want pepperoni pizza. And some Coke," I said, as I sat up and fiddled with the IV tubing in my arms, anxious to get unhooked.

"Oh, and Sister, make sure you call Daddy and tell him."

"I already did," she said. "He asked if you cared if he called him Tater." We all laughed.

"I wish he could have been here," I said, finally untangling myself enough to get out of bed and go to the bathroom.

"Yes, me too," Sister said.

Mama spent the night at the hospital with me, sleeping on the chair beside the bed.

Less than a week after Taylor's birth, I was back in the aerobics class I had attended up until my thirty-ninth week. And within a few days, I lost all fifteen pounds I had gained. What I wasn't ready for over the next weeks was the sleep deprivation and the roller coaster of feelings I experienced—the extreme waves of emotion, the overwhelming love I had for this tiny baby, and the flood of memories from my own childhood that now seemed sad, almost cruel. I couldn't imagine leaving Taylor in some of the places I had been left as a little girl, and I surely couldn't fathom being intoxicated for most of my son's life. There was a small part of me that felt more betrayed and more hurt than I ever had. *How in the world could you not protect your own child when they come into this world so frail and tiny and vulnerable?* I would soon learn that none of parenting is easy, and blaming Daddy was only a temporary fix, and worse yet, a sorry substitute for the forgiveness I really yearned to be able to give.

Thank heavens, Mama spent the first ten days with us. She got up in the early hours to help me get comfortable so I could breast-feed Taylor, which was difficult for me from the start and resulted in multiple episodes of mastitis. Having never breast-fed herself, Mama was unfamiliar with how to help me, so we talked to a lactation consultant on the phone. Despite the volumes of advice we received, every feeding felt like torture.

I was able to get some sleep at night, with Darryl managing the midnight feedings using the pumped milk I kept in the freezer.

One Saturday morning just before dawn, Mama heard us

stirring. She met me in the living room and changed Taylor's diaper while I grabbed a cold glass of milk and two chocolate-chip cookies from the kitchen. I wolfed down the cookies while I listened to Mama talk to Taylor in the living room. She had a tenderness with him that made me stand still, straining to hear every word and inflection of her voice.

I guess Taylor was complaining about the cold baby wipes she was using, but as soon as I shuffled back to the living room and she handed him to me, he stopped fussing, right on cue with the beating of my heart near his. This was the magic of motherhood that I couldn't quite wrap my mind around—this instant knowing that I was his and he was mine, and that nothing in the world could change the sacred bond we shared.

I finally felt like I was beginning to understand God's love for me. He called me His child and said He was my Father. Now that I was sitting here holding my own flesh and blood with my heart about to explode from sheer joy, I felt nearer to knowing what it meant to be loved by God. The thought occupied my mind all summer—at every diaper change and every feeding, with every coo and smile and cry.

So this is what it's like to really love someone else, to have the sum total of everything you are and love, living and breathing outside of you?

It was my first real taste of heaven, of communion with God, and in a way, its own baptism of sorts.

As the rising sun cast shards of light through the window, I settled into the overstuffed chair, ready to begin the long, grueling process of helping Taylor feed. Mama had him perfectly swaddled when she handed him to me, kneeling down to kiss us both on the forehead.

More than once, Mama begged me to let her go to the store and get formula, but I refused. While Taylor nursed, my tears streamed onto my chest. Mama kept me company, trying her best to understand why I was so stubborn about this. But she distracted me with stories, mostly about Daddy.

"I'd say it was about a week after you were born, and we didn't have two nickels to rub together. There was no food in the house, and I was down to one can of milk for you. Your daddy had been drunk most of the week, and I was fed up. I got right up in his face and told him that he'd better well go find enough work to buy you some milk, or he might as well not bother coming home." She nodded her head at me and raised her eyebrows, leaning in just like she was saying it right to Daddy.

"What did he do?" I asked as I switched Taylor over to the other side.

"Well, he left," she said, pausing for effect. Mama could keep you on the edge of your seat with her tales, that's for sure. Then she continued.

"'Long about five o'clock I heard him come back through the door, and I could tell as soon as I saw him that he'd been drinking. He slammed a six-pack of beer down on the table with one hand and one of those dolls with the painted porcelain faces down with the other."

I had never heard this story. "A doll?"

"Yeah, I guess you can't say your daddy never bought you anything because I'll tell you right now, he probably paid a pretty penny for that crazy doll," she said. "It was about a foot tall with a big poofy dress that had to be almost two feet wide. I knew right then that there was no milk to be had, and I lost my temper with him. He was enraged that I did not appreciate the fact that he had bought his baby girl her first doll. 'Jim,' I said, 'she can't eat that blasted doll. I guess if it's up to you, this child's gonna starve to death.' Well, he didn't take too kindly to that, so he went to cussing and took that doll and ripped it right in two, and white stuffing went all over everything. It looked like that apartment was covered in snow."

By this time, she was laughing and I was laughing and neither of us could stop. I was shaking so hard that Taylor unlatched, his little head bobbing back from the crook of my arm. When Mama finally found her composure, she said, "I honestly don't know how I survived or how I didn't kill him in the four years I tried to live with him. But I'll tell you this—when he was sober, there was nobody else in the world like him. I guess that's why I kept trying to stay."

She took a deep breath, then said, "And you're just like him."

We both smiled. Everybody had always told me I was just like Daddy, and I wondered which parts they meant. He was funny, generous, charming, and gregarious, but he was also other things that I hoped I'd never be—impulsive, distracted, addicted, hopelessly irresponsible, and lacking the ability to hold down a job.

The wistful look in Mama's eyes when she said it cut to my heart, and I wasn't even sure why.

Maybe it was that things could have been so different if Daddy could have stayed sober. Maybe it was that I was in a much more stable situation than Mama ever had been, save those few years with Gary. But deep down, I was scarred and so very fragile. Maybe it was the ghost that always haunts children of divorce, that no matter how awful or wrong it was, you wish your parents could have stayed together.

What I knew for sure was that something was wrong with my marriage—or maybe just wrong with me. Mama saw it long before I did.

If I thought about it too long, it made me crazy. So I didn't. Instead, I mothered and worked and studied and found a hundred ways to fill up my emptiness and keep fear from flooding in.

Mama stayed with me as long as she could. The day she left was ten times worse than when she dropped me off at college. I was full of dread, and she knew it.

"Honey, you are a wonderful mother already, and you've been taking care of people your whole life. This comes so naturally to you. I'm so proud of you. I know you don't feel ready, but you are. Nobody knows what that little fella needs more than you do.

Trust yourself. Besides, I'll be back in two weeks." She bear-hugged Taylor and me, and then she was gone.

My legs were wobbly, ready to give out. I fought the urge to run after the car and beg her not to leave. How in the world would I manage this without her? Who would keep me company in the wee hours of the morning? What if something happened to Taylor and I didn't know what to do? I felt like I was seven years old, standing in Mamaw's driveway, watching Mama drive away, the same emptiness rising up in me like floodwaters.

I stood there, pushing back a wall of fear. I nuzzled Taylor's face, his breath making me believe that somehow this was all going to be okay.

25

FAMILY TRADITION

WE ZIGZAGGED BACK and forth on Martin Mill Pike until we reached the turnoff to Twin Creek Road, where Aunt Glenda and Uncle George's house was. Jamie and her daughter, Jordan, were visiting, and Sister, her brand-new husband, Mark, Taylor, and I were headed to a family fish fry.

Mark was driving, Sister was sitting in the back with baby Taylor (he was two now, but Jamie always called him baby Taylor, so we did too), and I was hanging out the front passenger window trying to hold on to the oversized video camera that Mark had gotten for Christmas.

"Don't fall out of the window, Edie. That camera's about as big as you are, and that's saying something," he said, laughing at my ad-lib commentary done in my best, most exaggerated Appalachian accent. I wasn't offended at the comment because I was very pregnant with my second baby.

"I won't, but what I might do is throw up if you don't quit slinging me around these curves while I'm trying to make this family documentary," I replied, laughing so hard and sliding around the front seat so much I could barely hold the camera still.

Taylor was in his car seat, chattering away to Sister about his guitar that we'd had to leave behind. The only thing Sister was better at than being a sister was being an aunt, and since she didn't have any children of her own yet, she always chose to be with Taylor when she could, backseat or not.

Just a few months earlier, our little family had moved home to Maryville so my husband could work for his family's construction business and I could get help with family babysitters while I finished school at the University of Tennessee. When I found out that I was pregnant again, I was a little nervous about having a baby so soon after classes started, but I figured I'd manage it somehow.

I steadied myself for the most treacherous part of the ride, where it felt like you might drive yourself right off a cliff.

The guardrails provided somewhat of a barrier and peace of mind from the hundred-foot drop-off to the valley below—the valley that had become a dumping ground for everything from empty milk cartons to beer cans to old worn-out couches, and even the occasional rusted-out car. The switchbacks were so narrow that if another car approached, you either had to hug the embankment to the right and pray you didn't puncture your tires from broken glass or hope one of you would be able to back up to where the road widened enough for both vehicles.

The road was clear of traffic that day, so we counted ourselves lucky. Once I knew we were home free, I made Mark lean back as far as he could so I could capture footage of the debris that lay in the valley.

When we finally pulled into the driveway, Jamie and Jordan were standing at the top of the hill, waiting impatiently for us to get there. The fish fry was being held in the garage, which had long since been converted into a smoking, crafting, and laundry room. Perhaps trying to reduce the occupational hazard of being born into a family of chain smokers, Aunt Glenda had established a no-smoking rule in her new house, which she even abided by herself. That made the small garage quite hazy with a cloud of toxins, especially in the hot summer or in the winter when no doors were propped open.

Having been away from cigarette smoke for a while now, we were all hoping to find a smoke-free zone for the kids. But with the August heat and humidity, being outside didn't feel like the best option either.

We always joked that you needed a hazmat suit to walk through that garage because of the exhaust from the dryer, the cigarette smoke, and glue guns leaking hot fluid onto every surface. Then there was the plethora of craft supplies, including a bolt of lace being used to decorate the family of ceramic ducks that had lined the dining room wall for years. Aunt Glenda could have gone into business making lacy-collared duck families, and looking back, I guess I come by my crafty side pretty honestly.

We might have declined the invitation to the August family gathering, but then we learned that Uncle George's mom, Virgie, would be there along with her two friends, Mame Lawson and Glad Gryder. Those two women liked to sing, and we knew the entertainment factor alone would be worth whatever we suffered in heat and secondhand smoke. There'd be plenty of chances for us to belt out a few of our own favorite songs, karaoke style.

"It's about time you trash showed up," Jamie said teasingly when we reached the top of the hill.

"Listen, I'm too pregnant to live right now, so don't get me any more winded than I already am," I said, the two of us posing for Mark with the video camera, proud of the matching shirts we'd bought the day before for the occasion.

"Well, I hope this shindig don't end the way the last one did. The one where your daddy had to take Darlene home early," Jamie said, giving me the side eye.

"Oh, I remember that one, but you'll need to tell Mark," I said, still trying to catch my breath.

Family gatherings had been pretty rare for us, but we'd had a reunion two years earlier where Jamie walked up to Aunt Darlene and heard her muttering, "I hate Mama."

Ironically, the reunion was at Friendly Chapel Baptist Church, but Darlene was far from friendly with regard to Mamaw. Her voice had all the vitriol we'd come to fear when we were kids. Before it escalated even more, Daddy was ordered to drive Darlene back to the trailer as punishment for her sorry attitude.

"When Uncle Jim returned and got out of the car, he looked like he'd been beat to a pulp." Jamie had Mark's attention now. "Why, his hair was standing on end, and there were scratch marks and blood all over his face. Darlene had whooped him from the backseat all the way home.

"By the way," Jamie added, "Mom told me that Uncle Jim's not coming today. I can't say that I blame him."

"Well, when I talked to him this morning, he asked me if I'd run a quart of beer over to his place so he could try to sober up," I explained. "I just said yes and didn't ask any more questions."

"All I know is Edie and I pay seventy dollars a month for life insurance on him, and at the rate he's going, we'll be needing it sooner than later," Sister said, putting Taylor down so he could join Jordan.

It was 1992, yet I still held tight to a lot of trends from the eighties. My hair was a spectacle to behold, spiked up on its ends and immovable, thanks to plenty of White Rain. Jamie, on the other hand, had tamed her David Bowie mane into a more respectable mom bob when she had Jordan, though the color was now canary yellow.

"So, where's the fish fry part of this gathering?" I asked Jamie, looking around for the fryer as the two of us helped Taylor and Jordan navigate the hill to the house.

"Mom said they borrowed the fryer from Hayes Whaley, so I guess it's set up by the garage. My dad and Jeff caught all the fish last weekend at a tournament. Apparently they go bass fishing all the time together, even at night," she said. "You could not pay me a million dollars to get in a boat in the middle of the night with those two. I've done my share of camping with my stepdad, and being stranded in a boat all night with him would not be my idea of a good time. I'd rather be shot between the eyes with a .22," she said, reaching down to straighten Jordan's poofy dress.

"Jordie, we're going to visit Poppy George and Grandma Glenda. Don't be scared when Mommy starts singing real loud," she said, picking up Jordan to carry her the last few yards.

"And I know that I'm not telling you anything you don't know, but I'll have to throw this dress away tonight because it'll be so saturated with smoke," she said to me as I scooped up Taylor, who kept stopping to pick up rocks.

We finally reached the smoky garage where everybody was gathering, toting their side dishes and whipped cream–laden desserts.

Virgie was telling her friend Mame about her moneymaking venture—setting up her own rummage sale at one of the local store parking lots.

"Listen, you can go down there and you can set up all day for four dollars. Me and Glad made thirty-seven dollars over thar last Saturday, and we didn't even have no furniture to sell," she said, scaring the little children with her loud, scruffy voice.

"Well, looky thar, that's old Jamie. Honey, what have you done to yer hair? It's right yeller lookin', ain't it, Glenda?" Virgie said, taking a big gulp of sweet tea and trying to wrangle Jordan into a hug.

"It's not my hair that matters today, Virgie, because me and Edie are here to sing. We heard Glad was going to do a number or two, so we figured we'd debut a couple of our songs too. We're trying to talk Sister into singing with us, but she didn't want any part of our matching outfits. She probably thinks she's too good to be in our sister band," Jamie said.

We ate our fill of fried fish, potato salad, and baked beans, and then hovered around the banana pudding, trying to figure out who made it and if they could be trusted with basic kitchen hygiene. Jamie turned it down, but I scooped up a heaping serving without regret or fear.

Soon after we finished dessert, Glad started in on her favorite musical numbers, Aunt Glenda harmonizing with perfect pitch.

"Okay, it's our turn," Jamie said, as we situated ourselves on the porch stoop and used plastic utensils for microphones. We belted out "Satin Sheets" at full volume and slightly off key, followed by "Coal Miner's Daughter" and then our signature number, "Stand By Your Man."

Everybody laughed, including our videographer, Mark. When we played it back later, the evidence was indisputable: Sister was mouthing the words to all of the songs in the background.

We missed seeing Mamaw and Aunt Darlene at the fish fry. After all, Aunt Darlene did like her fish. After hours of eating, storytelling, and singing, Sister, Mark, Taylor, and I said our good-byes and left to drop off a quart of beer at Daddy's. We told him about the fish fry and our band's debut, staying only a few minutes, long enough for him to get Taylor giggling. I could see that Daddy was starting to get the shakes, so that was our cue to go.

Three weeks later, on September 10, 1992, I was clinging to a chair in the hospital's waiting room, wishing the contractions would pass. Mama was sitting beside me with Taylor and timing how far apart the contractions were. By the time I was admitted to the hospital, Darryl arrived and the baby was almost crowning. It was too late for an epidural. I'm guessing my howls were so loud that they must have echoed through the whole hospital as we welcomed our baby girl into the world. She was so beautiful, and I was instantly in love with my Caiti, the pain making the joy all the sweeter.

Caiti was born on Thursday, and by Monday I was toting her to biochemistry class with me to take my first test, hoping to graduate with a chemistry degree by the spring. All semester, she was my sidekick in every class as we sat in the back and listened to the lecture while I nursed.

Later that year Mamaw went on hospice care from lung cancer. Aunt Glenda was the self-appointed nurse and caregiver in the family, so she set up a hospital bed in her spare bedroom and spent the next few weeks providing round-the-clock care for her mother. Plans were made for Aunt Darlene to enter a group home, and Mamaw willed my cousin Tim, Aunt Johnny's middle son, the trailer—a decision that caused quite a ruckus among the living siblings.

Mamaw died in peace at Aunt Glenda's, but she wasn't laid to rest in peace because Daddy showed up drunk at the funeral. As in, could-hardly-stand-up drunk. So Sister and I got on either side of him and manhandled him all night to keep him from doing anything stupid. We also kept answering his repetitious questions about where he was going to live now that his mama was gone, and more importantly to him, where he was going to get his next quart of beer. Sister and I looked at each other and sighed. He was probably looking right at the answer to both of those questions.

A few months after Mamaw died, Daddy was hospitalized for a hernia repair and then subsequently diagnosed with liver failure. His weight loss continued, and so did his drinking.

If Daddy was drowning in beer and the body fluids that were building up internally, I was drowning in my own self-imposed sea of busyness—trying to be a mama to two little ones while keeping a 4.0 GPA, volunteering at the hospital in the surgery department, and managing my new research position in the biochemistry department.

But busyness can't numb everything. I began the long, slow journey of constantly weighing the fullness and beauty of life with the loss that was always hovering over everything like a fog.

26

I SANG DIXIE

FASTER THAN THE MORNING mist burned off the valley below Brown's Mountain, Daddy began to leave us. He was visibly dwindling every time I saw him, almost as if right in front of my eyes. He was losing his appetite, losing weight, and losing the ability to drink, and especially hard was when he began losing his charisma. Stubborn as a mule, he kept refusing to go to the doctor. I guess we all wanted to delay knowing the truth. What the soul knows and what the head knows are two different things, but I think we all knew in both senses of the word.

As the pressure of having a sick father and a full schedule of classes competed with trying to raise two young kids and a growing sense that my marriage was in trouble mounted, I dove into school with all the fervor I could muster. Sometimes it was simply my way of escape, but I was also good at it. Majoring in chemistry and biochemistry with a minor in biology, I took to the sciences like I was made for them. Working in a research lab and studying all hours of the night and day, I knew I needed those good grades to get into medical school, so I tried my best to graduate at the top of my class. It also helped take the focus off everything that felt wrong in my life. I had the gnawing sense that something bad was chasing me, and I wasn't about to slow down and find out what.

Plus, I figured if I were a doctor, I'd be able to help Daddy or at least know what was wrong with him. In February of that year, I got my acceptance letter to medical school, and it felt like my ticket out—out of what, I didn't even really know, but we all celebrated like it was some kind of miracle.

Maybe in a way, it was.

A poor girl raised in a trailer park earns her way to a better life.

But what I would learn the hard way is that even when you change the outward circumstances, you can't resurrect what's dying inside. That would take many more years and a miracle that even I couldn't orchestrate.

Sister and I had been taking care of Daddy for years—paying his bills, buying his food (and beer), paying his rent, and helping him in whatever way we could—including taking out a life insurance policy on him that we paid on for a handful of years despite the fact that neither of us could really afford it. I guess Mamaw had taught us well.

Six months after we let the policy lapse, I was sitting in my living room holding Caiti when I got the call. At eighteen months old, she had climbed on my lap with her sippy cup while we watched Taylor repeatedly screech as he jumped off the couch and landed on a pile of blankets on the floor, laughing like a hyena. Caiti was an old soul even as a baby—somber and quiet and puzzled by Taylor's constant laughter and smile that seemed to fill his entire face. I felt her tiny fingers stroking the edge of one of my gold hoop earrings. Holding her with one arm and paging through my study sheets for my last final in chemistry with my other hand, I almost didn't answer the call. But after three rings, I unclasped her little hand from my ear and propped her up in front of two pillows before running to the kitchen to grab the phone.

It was Aunt Glenda.

"Edie, this is your Aunt Glenda," she said in her slow, melodic cadence.

"Hi, did you get back from the doctor with Daddy already?" I asked, knowing that with Daddy's recent blood-tinged sputum, we might be in for some bad news.

"Yeah, we did, Edie, and it ain't good. It ain't good at all. When we got up to that doctor's office, the nurse said your daddy's oxygen was dangerously low." She paused for effect.

"And your daddy was white as a ghost. What that doctor said was that besides the fact that he's got very severe C-O-P-D," she said, pronouncing each letter with the weight and gloom they deserved, "he's got a mass on his lungs the size of a baseball and his liver is eat up with tumors."

I knew it. We all knew it. But something about the pronouncement felt like it sealed our doom. I stood there motionless and watched the room go blurry, too numb to talk.

"Edie, he's gonna have to move in with me or somebody so we can try to take care of him. They've put him on oxygen, and he is not to be without it. I guess I'll take care of him like I've took care of the rest of them. Me and Jim has always been there for each other, and we always will be."

She was now in tears, neither of us talking.

My eyes stung. Here I was about to graduate from college and then move off and leave, with Daddy sicker and weaker than he'd ever been—his body full of cancer and him probably not that long for this earth. I couldn't do anything but stand there in shock, lingering quietly with the phone drooping down on my shoulder, almost out of earshot.

Just then there was a knock at the door. I told Aunt Glenda I loved her and I'd call her back. Caiti had somehow nodded off to sleep, so before I answered the door, I laid her head back on the pillow, while Taylor scampered off toward his bedroom, probably to dig out the guitar he loved that was taller than he was. When I opened the door, I saw my father-in-law, Bill, a man I had grown to love like he was my own dad. As soon as my eyes met his, he knew something was wrong.

"Honey, what is it? You look like you've seen a ghost," he said as he came through the door, patting me on the shoulder and waiting for me to speak.

But I couldn't talk. I fell down in the middle of the living room floor and blubbered like a child who just lost her daddy. I could hear Taylor in the background climbing up on his papaw asking what was wrong with Mommy, but everything felt like it was a million miles away. Bill knelt down with Taylor in his arms, trying to console both of us, since Taylor was upset to see his mommy curled up in a ball on the floor. I felt lifeless. I wanted to get up and hold my buddy boy, but I just lay there on the floor, seeking comfort in its cool wood grain. Bill was patient and knelt there with me for the longest time, almost like he knew. I finally raised my head up enough to tell him that Daddy had lung cancer and that it had spread to his liver. He wrapped Taylor and me in a bear hug and told me that he was so sorry and would do anything he could for me.

"I know how close you are to your daddy, Edie, and I know this is not going to be easy, especially with you moving and everything y'all have going on. But you are just like a daughter to me, and I want you to know that I'll do whatever I can to help you. And we will pray for you every day. You'll get through this."

I knew it was true. Bill was one of the best men I had ever known, which made it even harder when the reality of my failing marriage seeped unawares into my consciousness. Time and time again, he had given us money and helped provide a place for us to live. He had even bought my schoolbooks the previous semester, which I thought about every time I loaded them into my backpack. And that man loved his grandchildren with a fierce kind of love.

A month later, as my family was packing up and moving two hours north to Johnson City for medical school, Daddy moved into Sister's basement, about the time her little boy, Corey, was just starting to sit up. Her husband, Mark, even drilled a hole through the basement ceiling for the tubing to the oxygen concentrator to be snaked through. When Daddy came up the stairs for dinner, he was often too winded to eat, so this way he had his oxygen readily available. The only things he kept closer than that oxygen tubing were his cigarettes and ashtray. Sister and Mark managed to get him a television and a refrigerator downstairs and tried not to leave him alone with Corey too often, as Daddy had a habit of trying to feed the baby Skittles and M&M's. Other than the nutritional danger, Daddy was a gem with the little ones, making crazy noises with his mouth and always whistling little ditties he'd made up.

Not two weeks after that, our long-lost brother Jim Bob moved in with Sister, too, and he and Daddy shared a twin bed for months on end. I guess Daddy's cancer made it easier for Shirley to say yes when Jim Bob wanted to be with him. And I suppose she knew he'd be safe with Sister. Too weak with lung and liver problems to cause much of a ruckus, Daddy stayed sober almost eight months straight, until the shakes got too bad one day and he drove his beat-up blue hatchback off to who knows where to find beer and a seedy place to stay for a while. The oxygen tank was thrown in the backseat of his car; the hole in the ceiling was left open as a reminder to Sister of the longest stretch of time she'd ever lived with Daddy.

A world away from all that, I was immersed in my first year of medical school, just trying to survive the mountain of studying that needed to be done every hour, every day, every week. After the initial wave of eager anticipation, I began to be terrified about taking on such a heavy load with a two-year-old and a four-year-old in tow, but I seemed to be operating on autopilot, reaching with what felt like inexhaustible passion toward a true north that I couldn't even name.

Was it success? Money? Perhaps a way out of what felt like a false or veiled version of myself? Or maybe just a desperate attempt to stop the ache that had been with me ever since I could remember. Looking back, maybe it was just an elaborate scheme of overachievement in an effort to prove to the world that I was worthy of love.

Whatever it was I was working so hard to find was not granted to me on the day I graduated from college or even from medical school. But that didn't keep me from looking for it everywhere but where it could be found, measuring myself against every person I met, every goal I achieved.

The sicker Daddy got, the harder I worked, perhaps unconsciously thinking that if I made all As and brought homemade cupcakes to preschool, that would somehow keep him here longer. In my mind, everything always depended on me—like a grown-up version of "if you step on a crack, you'll break your mama's back." It was an exhausting and oddly self-centered way to live.

I visited as often as I could, but watching Daddy over the next couple of years suffer and dwindle down to 120 pounds was heartbreaking. During the last couple of months of his illness, he became bedridden, and Aunt Glenda decided to take care of him with the help of hospice nurses. When he was coherent enough, he would still try to tell stories and make us laugh—always the life of the party.

But the end was painfully near.

My sister called one Sunday night and said that Aunt Glenda had told her she didn't think Daddy would make it through the night and that if I wanted to say good-bye, I should hurry. I prayed and cried the whole two-hour drive that he wouldn't die before I got there. Somehow, I knew he would wait for me.

Since the beginning of my medical school career he'd always teased me in his perfect Appalachian lingo, "Nise, have you made doctor yet?"

It was pretty clear to me on that long drive to Knoxville that he was never going to see me graduate from medical school. Maybe my whole life, even while we were together, had been a long and slow grieving of everything he could never be. Now what I felt was profound sadness, the solitary emptiness of a girl soon to be truly fatherless, fighting to stay upright in what felt like an always downward-sucking current.

Daddy was dying, and I thought of a million things that'd be undone when he left this world. At the top of that list was me.

The smell of death and cigarette smoke covered the house like a fog when Darryl, the kids, and I walked in. Meandering my way through to the back room, I peeked through the door and saw his open mouth, drawn up at the corners like he had just finished the last line of some George Jones anthem. Daddy was in and out of consciousness, and his breathing was erratic. He sounded like he was trying to gargle salt water in slow motion. The only thing I had learned during my rotation as a medical student at the VA hospital was the death rattle, and Daddy had it, of that I was sure.

He was leaving us—and soon.

Sister and I stood by his side, the kids and their dads in the next room waiting quietly. I put my hand on Daddy's damp, stringy hair and smiled at how much he and Taylor reminded me of each other—those blue eyes, wide foreheads, and smiles that lit up a room. His hands were cold, so I wrapped them up in mine and told him to squeeze if he could hear me. A few seconds passed and he pried his eyes almost open like it took all the strength he had in the world, the corners of his mouth quaking toward a smile.

"Daddy, we're right here with you; me and Sister and Aunt Glenda. I know you know how much we love you," I said.

I thought of a hundred things I wanted to say. I wanted to joke with him and tell him to dance one off with St. Peter when he got to the pearly gates. I wanted to tell him not to leave me like this, with all this life yet to live, so much school left to finish, and two kids yet to raise.

I wanted to tell him to at least stay until I made doctor, for heaven sakes. But I didn't say any of that. I looked over at Sister, who was wearing more sadness on her face than I'd ever seen, and at her hands mingled in with mine and Daddy's.

The pauses in his breathing seemed to last forever, all of us holding ours, too, until he eked out another thready exhalation. We strained out a tinny verse of "Amazing Grace" when the gaps felt too uncomfortable to bear. Then I put my cheek to his and told him how much I would miss him and how life would never be the same without him. In the stillness of my breath on his face, I felt the life leave him. I looked up to catch the last light in his eyes, but they were already closed, his head tilted over in surrender. I fell to his chest and sobbed until somebody unclenched my hand from his and made me walk outside for air.

Daddy was finally at peace. No more labored breathing. No more cancer or liver failure. No more junker cars that wouldn't start or wayward couches to thrash around on, trying to get comfortable.

No more trying with all his might to stay sober.

No more yearning for a quart of beer or asking for a light for his cigarette. No more hurt, no more loss, no more tears.

Only peace.

Probably for the first time in his fifty-six years.

Waiting for me to be there with him as he crossed life's last threshold was perhaps his greatest gift to me. The sacred mystery that surrounds death is like nothing else in life, and it is a privilege to walk the last miles home with someone. It would make me a better mother and woman and a better doctor, and it is my most cherished memory with him. I knew there would never be anyone else quite like him. I also knew that my complicated relationship with him was far from over.

For as long as I could after Daddy's death, I clawed at the edges of everything, trying to find a way to stay above water, but nothing seemed to be able to stop my sure and certain unraveling. After twenty-seven years of pretending to be fine, something in me broke—like a dam too cracked and fragile to fight the constant beating rains. It felt like there was nothing I could do but stand like a spectator and watch the water rise around me, as if everything that had buoyed me to the surface of things was gone, even the faith that had once seemed unshakable. Over the next few months, my life became so unmanageable that it felt like I was trying to survive an ocean storm on a flimsy piece of driftwood.

21

I WALK THE LINE

IT HAD BEEN EIGHT MONTHS since Daddy died, and it was nearing the end of May and closing in on Taylor's eighth birthday. The breeze was infused with the fragrance from a blushing row of pink peonies, falling over on the sidewalk, filling the air with life. It was graduation day. All sixty of us graduates entered the narthex in a winding line that stretched almost to the road. It was the same stretch of road I had run hundreds of miles on during the past four years of medical school, hoping to sweat out all the stress of test after endless test, and the same road that led around to the VA hospital where I had my clinical rotations.

This day loomed in my mind like some kind of landmark that would signal something important, almost unbelievable. It seemed as unreal to me as any fairy tale. We were introduced as the 1998 graduating class of the Quillen College of Medicine. I walked through the doorway and stood up tall, straightening my emerald green stole as we made our way into the old chapel sanctuary, the iconic Edward Elgar "Pomp and Circumstance" graduation march being played by the East Tennessee State University ensemble. There were rows and rows of parents, children, spouses, teachers, mentors, and faculty—all so proud and so invested in making this day happen.

In the front row just to my left was Doug Taylor, dean of admissions, the man I credited for single-handedly convincing the admissions committee four years earlier that they should take a chance on me. Beside him was my Gross Anatomy professor, a teacher the likes of which I was sure I'd never meet again. Then there were my classmates, my family, and the stars of the show, my adorable children, as well as their aunt Gina and their dad—all witnesses to the day when the world stamped its approval on the collective skills and knowledge of my medical school class, the day we promised to make good on our vows to serve humankind.

Mama was there, the woman who had come every weekend when there were major exams to keep my laundry going and the meals made and the kids happy. She was proud to the point of tears every time my eyes caught hers. And sitting with my two babies between them were my father- and mother-in-law, two people who had been such loving supporters of my dreams in every way.

Conspicuously missing was Daddy.

The wound of losing him was too fresh for me to linger there very long. So I didn't. I couldn't have imagined him at the ceremony anyway, poking fun at how serious everybody was or trying to get some free diagnostic work done. I told myself it was just as well. I was determined to enjoy my dream-come-true day.

The dean of the school stepped to the podium and made some opening remarks about what a milestone we were reaching and how honored he was to be at a school that was leading the country in training doctors to serve in rural Appalachia. Then there was the speaker, a physician named Abraham Verghese, who would later write a bestselling novel titled *Cutting for Stone*. The only thing I remember about what he said was that we often enter the healing profession at some level believing that ministering to others will heal our own woundedness.

I thought of his words, and my mind telescoped out to a broader view, where I had a pinch-me moment at the thought that someone who came from where I came from was now sitting here about to be called *doctor* for the first time. Verghese's words rang true and stung at the same time.

This and so many things were going through my mind when we stood with our right hands held high and swore to uphold the Hippocratic oath. My favorite line was the last: "May I always act so as to preserve the finest traditions of my calling and may I long experience the joy of helping to heal those who seek my help."

As we lined up to walk across the stage for the conferring of the degrees, I knew that something would forever be changed when they called my name.

"Dr. Edie . . ." is all I heard, walking across the stage to receive my degree. After I shook hands with the dean, he finished, ". . . graduating with honors and accepted to our very own family medicine program here in Johnson City, Tennessee."

And just like that, I was a doctor.

I wanted to heave my diploma up in the air with a big, "Yeehaw, look who made doctor!"

Yes, Daddy, I finally did it.

But the truth was that I didn't feel like a doctor or look like what I thought doctors should look like or even act like a proper doctor should act, whatever that meant to me at the time. I had always been good in school and had never questioned whether or not I'd go to college, which is miracle enough, but people who came from the side of the tracks I came from didn't put "doctor" on their list of possible life goals. We just didn't. We put things like "Don't smoke dope" and "Don't get pregnant in high school" and "Don't get put in jail." Doctoring felt way out of my league.

And yet here I stood, holding a piece of paper calling me just that.

I was also thinking back to how I'd gotten here in the first place—those long hours working as a CNA in the nursing home, thinking I'd like to be a nurse someday and only considering medical school after the doctor told me that I sure did ask a lot of questions and maybe I should consider going further in my education.

Ever since I can remember I've been insatiably curious, and when I worked at the nursing home, I would often find myself reading about whatever ailments my patients happened to have and then bombarding the physician with questions when he'd make rounds the next day. That's how I ended up in a counselor's office changing my major less than a month later, which led to an endless application process calling for essays and references and MCATs and prep courses and hospital volunteer work and lab research. It was the proverbial "if you give a mouse a cookie" scenario. The nursing home doctor's offhand comment to me set off a crazy series of events—events that finally led to an acceptance letter from the Quillen College of Medicine at East Tennessee State University.

Then there was the process of actually moving to a new town and going to medical school, followed by the tests and the studying and more tests and more endless studying—four of the hardest and most satisfying years of my life.

Now all finished.

Every last requirement done.

Every last *T* crossed.

Everything should have been perfect, but everything felt wrong.

I got a lump in my throat with thoughts of it all—the emptiness I couldn't seem to fill. If this didn't make it all better, then maybe nothing could.

I was crumbling right along with my marriage, perhaps even causing it to crumble. It had been falling apart for years—for complicated reasons that are beyond the scope of this book and difficult to articulate at best. Growing up as I did, often in chaos and ruin, I knew so little about how to make a family work. I was as broken as broken could be and seemed helpless to fix myself, much less this tenuous marriage. In some ways, I think my drive for accomplishment was a subconscious striving to prove that despite what might happen in my personal life, I was lovable, or at least hardworking and talented. I see now how that never satisfies and how our personal lives are the things that matter. The MD behind my name was a poor cushion when the bottom fell out of everything.

As I walked outside after the ceremony to pose for pictures with Caiti and Taylor, then six and eight years old, the fracture between their dad and me felt like a chasm that would swallow me up. I knew it would all implode, and it felt impossible to stop. I already felt sick about how it would affect the two most precious people in the world to me. My most vivid memory of graduation day is the nausea that wouldn't leave.

The sun was beaming so bright that we sought out the shade of an oak tree for pictures. The wind was picking up, and I could see clouds gathering in the east, so we scurried off to the car, the kids and I hand in hand, holding on to each other tightly. I wanted to remember this day as the light at the end of the long tunnel, but all I could hear were the words to "Folsom Prison Blues" that Daddy had taught me when I was little, playing over and over in my head.

HE STOPPED LOVING HER TODAY

THE ONE-YEAR ANNIVERSARY OF Daddy's death was approaching, and my marriage was all but gone. I had braved some pretty intense childhood trauma, but my first year of residency was the hardest year of my life. With workdays that never ended, chronic lack of sleep, and the self-doubt that crept in when a patient needed an intravenous central line in the middle of the night and I was the intern on call made me lose a lot of weight and cry almost every day. I hung onto sanity by a very thin thread.

I was assigned to the most demanding attending (shorthand for the attending physician overseeing my work) on the surgical staff, which meant I lived at the hospital, for fear that I might miss a lab result or an X-ray or a good case from the ER. The bright spot came the morning I met Coach Thomas Allen Taylor. I was a brand-new doctor and he was a brand-new patient—my first one, in fact. Coach was an older version of my daddy, except he had all his teeth and was retired from a real job. He had been a high school science teacher and baseball coach, and he was still hand-some and Johnny Carson–funny despite jaundice and weight loss. A widower for two years whose only daughter lived in California, he spent most of his days alone.

We met when he was leaning over the side of his bed—retch-ing and writhing in pain, his morning newspaper unread and his clear-liquid diet untouched. When I introduced myself, he said, "It's nice to meet you, Doc, but I sure would like to go home."

To be perfectly honest, I knew close to nothing about medicine at that point, but according to the rumblings of my superiors, it would be a miracle if Coach ever went home, and he surely wasn't going today. On day six of his stay, we diagnosed him with adeno-carcinoma in the head of the pancreas with metastases to the liver. My attending informed me that I had the awful job of bearing the bad news. Coach took it like Daddy would've downed an ounce of whiskey, swallowing hard like it was nothing but a little sour wine to be gulped down like a man. Without any trace of fear or pity in his voice, he said, "Well, I guess there's nothing to do but fight. I'm ready if you are."

"I'm ready," I said, while a single tear from the corner of my eye said otherwise. As soon as we finished talking, I hurried out of the room before I had a complete meltdown in front of him.

A new slew of residents on surgical rotation walked by just about the time I was coming apart. One of them was joking around with the guy mopping the floor, but when he saw me, he stopped and put his hand on my shoulder. "Are you okay? Do you need any help?"

I was surprised by what appeared to be genuine concern, espe-cially in a place where coworkers were often more like enemies.

"Thank you—I'm okay. I just had to tell Coach Taylor he has pancreatic cancer. Every time I see him, I think of my dad, who died last year from lung cancer. It's been a rough year."

"Sorry to hear it. I'm Steve Wadsworth, and I just started my surgery rotation too. I've been working here at the VA for a year, though, so if you need some survival tips, just let me know. From what I hear, it's pretty tough on this wing."

"Yes, so far I have found that to be true. Thank you again, so much. Hope to see you around," I said as I slowly turned around and walked away.

Maybe it was just the intense emotions I was feeling for Coach Taylor and Daddy, but it felt like a weird collision of worlds. I met new people in the hospital all the time, and rarely did they pique my interest or make an impression. But someone who was friendly to the housekeeping staff and kind enough to check on my over-flowing emotions? It stayed with me for weeks. There was something about him. Something different.

Talk began stirring among the medical staff of a possible Whipple procedure for Coach, a grueling surgery with a high mortality rate and a long and protracted hospital stay—*if* he survived the surgery. This was the kind of diagnosis and care plan that young, eager doctors and surgeons loved to be part of, and since I was Coach's primary physician, I worked hard so that I'd be allowed in the operating room during the procedure. As we tested and prepped and tested some more, Coach and I became buddies.

He was an expert card player, so I bought a deck of cards in the gift shop, and he kept them in the top drawer of his night table. On the nights he felt well enough, we played gin rummy like two Vegas gamblers, using packets of alcohol wipes for chips. He always won, but we both knew that the talking was the thing that mattered. He wasn't afraid of dying. He told me about his faith in God and that he'd never really felt normal again after his wife died. He hated living alone.

He asked me all about my kids, my life, my dreams. Little by little, we shared our stories with each other. I ran into his room the first time I closed an appendectomy on my own, and he celebrated with me by killing me in rummy.

"Doc, I hope you sew people up better than you play gin

rummy," he teased, his face looking more hollowed out with each passing day.

"Don't you worry. I'll practice up so I'm ready when it's your turn," I said.

"Well, I tell you what—I'm proud of you, Edie. You're gonna make a fine doctor one day."

He said it like a dad would. He said it like he meant it, and so I believed him.

Despite the push from the team of doctors, he wasn't sure he even wanted the surgery. He finally agreed to it so that we "kids would get more practice at helping sick people." I'm pretty sure he still didn't include himself in that sick-people list.

He begged me to bring him a real breakfast before we got too close to "doomsday"—his last real meal before the biggest surgery of either of our lives. He liked Hardee's sausage biscuits, so I violated his dietary restrictions the week before he would go under the knife and fulfilled his request. We shared the tray table, some biscuits, and one large black coffee, and talked about everything but what was really on both our minds.

He laughed about my recent debacle in the OR where I showed up for surgery on an empty stomach and passed out at the patient's feet twenty seconds after the surgeon made the incision. We talked smack about our beloved college football team, the UT Volunteers, and how we might fare in our first season without Peyton Manning. We talked about Coach's daughter, who was pregnant with her third child and in her last trimester, which made flying out of the question.

I would be his doctor and his surrogate daughter for the worst week of his life, and it both honored me and scared me to death. I knew if the procedure wasn't successful it would feel a little like losing Daddy all over again, and I wasn't ready to face either of those things. We prayed together on the morning of his surgery, and when I bent over to give him a hug, he wouldn't let go.

Sometimes words aren't necessary. I knew everything he couldn't say, and I told him not to worry, that this was all in God's hands and we'd get through it together.

"I promise you that I won't leave your side until you wake up. I'll be the first and last face you see, like it or not."

We pinkie swore and I ran to the OR suite, already worried I'd be late to scrub in.

When I got to the scrub room, my chief resident was already gloved and gowned and in the operating room checking the instrument set.

The second-year resident and I were elbow deep in suds and hot water, both cautiously optimistic that Coach would pull through.

I bumped open the door of the OR, waiting my turn to be gowned and gloved for my first pancreatic resection. I'd be lucky to touch the hem of Coach's garment during that surgical marathon, a procedure that was estimated to take six to eight hours. The chief resident was the primary surgeon, and my favorite third-year resident was first assist. I expected I would probably be somewhere down by the foot of the bed after all the scrub nurses and other residents took their places, but I knew this patient better than anyone in the room so I wanted to be as close to him as possible.

I had spent countless hours with him—measuring his urine, holding cool cloths to his head after he vomited, and studying his lab work and body scans. I was the one who told him about his cancer, the one who sat for hours helping him process whether or not he should have surgery, and the one who knew every last thing about his favorite baseball team.

Before the anesthesiologist gave him the happy juice, I approached him.

"Coach, you're ready for this, and we're going to fight together. I'll see you in a few hours. Don't you worry—this is all going to be okay," I said, squeezing his hand between mine.

One thing I hadn't yet learned was how to have boundaries as a doctor, and sometimes I think it's best that way. Everybody knew I was too close to Coach. They tried to protect me from the attending physician, but when he came into the operating room, he addressed me first.

"You've got potential as a surgeon, but I'm going to tell you right now, you get too attached to the patients. We're not here to make friends and play cards. We're here to cut out the bad stuff, that's all. They've got family doctors and psychiatrists to deal with all the other problems. Here, we do the job we've been trained to do. You could be spending all those extra hours in the suture lab practicing tying knots and closing wounds. People don't need a nice surgeon—they need a skilled one. You've got a lot to learn, I'm afraid."

My face went hot, and I wanted to crawl under the table. Most of the feedback I had ever gotten in my life was positive, and I didn't know how to respond to the criticism.

I simply said, "Yes, sir," and hoped he would forget about me altogether. I wasn't embarrassed that I was close to Coach; I was proud of that fact. What bothered me so much about the dressing down was that it was true. I just didn't know how to reconcile that in a way that was true to my own personality and gifts.

Part of what I wrote in my journal that night said, *"I don't think I'm cut out to be a surgeon. I don't think I can ever just do my job. I'm hopelessly attached to people, especially the dying ones. This is true."*

Coach Taylor died on the table.

I was the last person to leave the operating room that night, the last person with him, just like I promised. I sat in the cold room by his side and then followed his stretcher down to the morgue, where the pathology staff told me they'd take it from there.

I went back to his empty room, the moonlight streaking in through the slatted blinds, and fell asleep in his hospital bed, like a little girl crawling into bed with her parents during a storm.

The sound of rolling carts moving toward me the next morning startled me awake. Housekeeping had arrived to clean.

Oh my word, I must have slept here all night, I thought. Groggy and disoriented, I put the playing cards and the memories in my white lab coat and left a piece of my heart in room 216.

It was such a difficult good-bye. Everybody tiptoed around me for days. They didn't know whether to comfort me or just leave me alone. I tried to avoid that room at all costs, but the next patient I took care of in room 216 had a routine appendectomy and went home.

Watching Coach suffer and die reminded me how human we all are, that sickness and death and pain are universal, whether your life seems charmed or cursed. I emptied my heart onto the messy notebook pages of my journal and kept doing my best to take care of sick people, praying no more of them would die on my watch.

Ever since I could remember, I'd seemed to feel the grief and pain of others intensely, as if another person's emotional distress was as evident to me as the color of their eyes. My attending was right about one thing—I would have made a terrible surgeon. Instead, I was heading into family practice.

The instrument of healing for me has never been a scalpel. It's always been the things I most undervalued—mostly, my own suffering and heartache, which became a portal of sorts that helped me enter into someone else's skin.

The very thing I would have counted as the unfortunate by-product of my upbringing was becoming the one thing that made me of service to my patients. But it was also becoming the one thing that made it hard to be a doctor. Bearing other people's burdens was now my job, and I sometimes doubted if I was strong enough for the task. How could I really help anyone else when I was so messed up myself?

29

WHISKEY LULLABY

Six months later I was leaning on a concrete wall in the maternity ward outside a patient's room, trying to decide whether anyone would notice if I curled up into a ball on the floor and shut my eyes. Just the act of stopping all movement for a brief minute had made my eyelids feel like somebody was standing on them and wouldn't get off.

It was at times like this, when I was too exhausted to keep my guard up, that the fault lines in my life seemed to be widening. It felt like it was only a matter of time before I wouldn't be able to straddle the gap. On one side of the chasm were all the positives— I had two amazing children who filled my life with joy, and I had an incredible job where people called me *Doctor* and paid me to learn how to take care of the sick.

With all my heart, I loved medicine, and learning something new every day felt like an adrenaline rush. For all my flaws and shortcomings, I was teachable and compassionate, and this served me well in my training, making it easy for me to excel—as if the unfortunate circumstances of my early life had equipped me to do this exact work. I felt more at home in my own skin at work than anywhere else. This place needed me, and it didn't matter how broken I was on the inside.

Then there was the part of me that felt like I was disappearing, maybe dying. Every day, I seemed to be failing at the one thing I claimed to want—a strong and vibrant family. If I let it, a deep, aching loneliness could consume me at any time and I didn't know how to handle it; I did not feel loved and seen and known, and I craved that approval like a drug.

What Daddy looked for in the bottom of the bottle, I looked for on the faces of every person I met. I guess we weren't that different after all.

The wall I was leaning against felt like the most dependable thing in my life. Snapping back to reality, I looked down at the blue scrubs I had worn every day for months and wondered how long it had been since I'd changed them. Grabbing the edge of my shirt collar and sniffing it, I decided that whatever mix of Betadine and antiseptic vapors had settled into the fibers of my scrubs wasn't offensive enough to mandate a fresh pair. Given my time constraints and the choice of either changing scrubs or eating breakfast, I chose food.

It was week four of my OB rotation. Exhausted from delivering two babies in the wee hours of the morning and sleeping only around forty-five minutes total for the night, I pried myself off the wall and went to check the clock. David, the second-year resident and my boss for the month, was at the nurses' station with his head resting on his arms, his breathing beginning to crescendo into a snore. I wouldn't have nudged him awake except I thought I should see if he wanted to eat.

"Morning rounds are in twelve minutes," I said, tapping his shoulder. "That's exactly enough time to run to the cafeteria and eat on the way back."

"I'd rather sleep twelve minutes than eat. You go on," he said, switching his head to the other side.

"Should I bring you something?"

"No, I'm so sleepy I'm nauseated. I just want to go to bed, and I plan to, as soon as rounds are over," he said, eyes promptly shutting, discussion over.

I ran to the cafeteria to grab some toast and oatmeal, which I ate on the way back. I passed one of my fellow classmates, who looked like he had had just about as much sleep as I'd had. We raised our mobile breakfasts toward each other and pretended to clink them like champagne flutes, in solidarity for the misery of all interns everywhere.

Back at the nurses' station, I printed out my patient list, noticing three new admits. So after rounds I set about doing their histories and physicals, trying to predict how my day might unfold with the possibility of three new births. I hoped against all hope that I could find a few minutes to sneak off to the call room and crash. The last of the three had a note on the chart that said, "Please see Dr. Smith before entering the patient's room. No students or interns allowed without express permission."

I asked Cindy, the charge nurse, about it, and she said that the patient was here for a termination and didn't want any students or extra people around. I was reading the chart so I'd at least be familiar with the case when the attending physician whirled around the corner and grabbed it from my hands.

"You obviously can't read. This chart says no interns. No interns means NO INTERNS," he said.

"Oh, sorry. I thought I should still be prepared to talk about her case even if I couldn't examine her."

"No, I'm taking care of this case, and I don't want any students or residents near her room or her chart. I hope that's clear," he said, nearly spilling his coffee on us as he wheeled around the corner.

His harshness probably wouldn't have bothered me so much if I hadn't been awake for two days, but I was beat so his words stung. Having come from such a tough background, it always surprised me how fragile I really was on the inside—so sensitive to even a perceived criticism. He wasn't usually a jerk, so maybe he hadn't gotten enough sleep either. Too dazed to think much about it, I went on with my day, racing through the hospital to and fro, doing all the regular stuff interns do—running down lab work and X-ray results, checking on ER patients with gynecological complaints, and assisting the second-year resident with deliveries.

I thought about my kids a lot while I was working, but honestly, the busyness kept me from thinking about my marriage. I was married to work and clung to the hope it gave me of a better life.

At 6:45 p.m., I walked through the nursery doors one last time to check on one of my babies born late that afternoon. The frenzy I walked in on stopped me in my tracks.

The charge nurse was trying to organize the chaos as murmurings of a terminated baby filled the room. Everybody's voices were hushed and strained, and nobody knew exactly what they were supposed to be doing.

"Get the protocol sheets out so we'll know what we're supposed to do with the baby," she said to one of the other nurses, both of them exchanging worried looks.

"Will the baby still be alive?" I heard the nurse intern ask.

"I'm not sure. I think they're supposed to inject something in utero, but I've seen that not work before."

Then they all scattered, trying to find protocol sheets, finish feedings, and get ready for shift change, which is when I realized I was still standing in a daze, not having moved. Before the dust settled, a delivery-room nurse pushed through the door, gowned and gloved, holding the little purple baby.

"This is the termination," she said, quickly laying the baby in an empty incubator by the utility closet. "Twenty-one-week-old boy, terminated for genetic abnormalities, only a few shallow attempts at respiration, no cry at birth, should be gone any time." Then she skittered out of the room, saying something about the mom hemorrhaging and the staff needing help in the delivery room.

Less than ten feet from the baby, I stood terrified, moving only my eyes enough to see the outline of his almost lifeless form, fearing that if I turned my head to look, I would be somehow complicit. I turned my eyes toward the door that hadn't fully closed, and the thought crossed my mind to shimmy through the door and pretend that whatever was happening in front of me was none of my business. That might have worked except my eyes had already betrayed me and there was no unseeing this. Nothing stood between me and the tiny baby but my paralyzing fear. Then I thought I saw movement.

This was like nothing I had ever experienced. What was I supposed to do? The nurse intern in the room kept glancing over toward the incubator, but the nurses' protocol sheets had made it hard for them to do anything but just wait for the time of disposal. Though my attendance at church had been spotty of late, Psalm 139:13 suddenly came to my mind: "You formed my inward parts; you knitted me together in my mother's womb" (ESV).

Then I remembered the vow we'd all made the day we graduated from medical school about doing no harm. I glanced over toward the closet again and noticed that the tiny little thing was not even swaddled up properly. I had to do something. I wasn't bound by their protocols so I picked up the baby and wrapped him tight in his nursery blanket, in a state of disbelief that this was happening right before my very eyes, in a place where we prided ourselves on preserving life.

In a dark corner there was a rocking chair, so I sat alone, holding the baby as close to my heart as I could, rocking gently and straining to listen for sounds of life.

Was it my own heart I felt throbbing? *I should talk to him— he can probably hear me*, I thought. I tucked the blue-and-pink-striped nursery blanket in closer to his neck to cover the mottled skin as I whispered, "Jesus be with you, little one. He is your Father, and He loves you."

His chest heaved up against the blankets, mimicking a heavy sigh, trailing off into his last shallow breaths. The distinctive shape of his eyes and nose reminded me of my brother Jim Bob when he was born. Down syndrome. *The "genetic abnormality,"* I deduced. My mind was reeling and the little one was fading.

I whispered a prayer and began to sing "Amazing Grace" as I watched his tiny lip quiver into a long stillness. It felt like time was locked and here we were, our souls somehow intertwined in the most inconceivable way—bound together beyond time and space by nothing but a hymn and a prayer, on the fragile threshold that exists between life and death.

I couldn't take my eyes off his button nose, and I couldn't stop thinking about what a privilege and responsibility it is when we bear witness to the suffering of someone else, whether that someone is a father or brother or the ones who are helpless. The thought of what would happen to this baby's body next kept me in that rocker for longer than I anticipated, but finally I laid him gently in the incubator and left as quickly as I could. Dusk was turning to night as I headed home, the first chill of spring making me clutch my white coat to my chest, the smell of both life and death lingering for days to come.

All the way home, I thought about his perfect little face, almost like looking into the face of God. In retrospect, the heartbreak of that moment might have shaken me awake to what I was about to do to my own children, but it didn't.

Maybe the best of me was already too far gone, drifting away like the last breath of hope. Or maybe I was doing to my life what Daddy would have done—burning it all to the ground.

30

I FALL TO PIECES

IT WAS THE DAY MY DIVORCE was being finalized, and Mama and I were walking toward the courthouse, the November air and my own sober thoughts chilling me to the bone. She put her arm around me and pulled my collar up, perhaps sensing that I didn't have enough life left in me to keep myself warm.

"Honey, I know how awful this feels, but we're going to get through it, I promise," she said, pausing long enough to dab at the tears forming at the corners of my eyes.

Coming from a long line of DUI offenders and drug users, my family was no stranger to courthouses, but I had never been summoned there myself. A large clan of folks were gathered by a nearby tree, smoking and complaining about how long they had waited already. From what we overheard, an embittered custody case was brewing among their family. One of the men had the same thin frame and weathered skin as Daddy, and his profile made me pause.

Since Daddy's death two years earlier, I saw him everywhere, but when the man turned to look at me, puffing out the smoke from his cigarette, his face was hardened and missing that old familiar smile. It felt like a sucker punch, to be forced to go through the hardest day of my life without Daddy here to say something completely inappropriate or to make me laugh when all I wanted to do was cry. The world felt heavy and wrong and dark without him in it, and I was making it heavier and darker by the day with my string of bad decisions.

I looked back toward the man who was now stomping out his cigarette on the ground with his boot, hopeful that maybe he'd smile or give me some kind of sign of support. But he didn't. It seemed that even Daddy's shadow couldn't bear to be with me today.

The trees were nearly bare along the sidewalk, stripped of all their golden glory, the wind blowing the leaves into oblivion. I was unrecognizable to myself, on a strange and lonely path that I had willfully and dangerously chosen. Having been caught in an affair, I had made my bed and now I had to lie in it, as the saying went, or more accurately, I had torched my bed. In mediation, we had come up with a parenting plan that we both could live with, although I could hardly imagine not having my kids on certain weekends or on holidays. This ache for my kids felt worse than anything I had experienced in childhood, and knowing that it was my fault made the anguish almost unbearable.

The nights leading up to the court date felt like a countdown to death. We were still in the same house, though we were sleeping in separate rooms. I rarely slept and hardly ate, so mad at myself for having let the bottom fall out of everything. And when nearly starving myself didn't provide enough numbing, I began to drink.

Within two months, I lost twenty pounds and drank more than I ever had in my life, hoping to find something to stop the searing pain. Despite my overwhelming guilt and the despair that was eating at me, I didn't have the willpower to completely quit the affair, so I snuck around and lied and cheated—things I would never have imagined having the capacity to do. And now here I was, about to face my crimes against my family. The reality of what was unraveling began to take hold, and I wished for all the world that I could just disappear from life.

We entered the building and made our way down the long, sterile hall to the courtroom. Inside, it felt like a trauma room at the hospital, with the worst of hurting humanity on display for all to see. And I was among them, my life bleeding out all around me while I stood cold and pale and helpless to save myself.

This is what I deserve, I thought. I knew that was true, but the part I couldn't live with was what it was going to do to my children. I looked back on the string of events that exploded my life, and I was the one who lit the fuse. Everything I held dear lay in ashes all around me. Looking back, I realized my marriage didn't stand a chance, but I hated myself for not having the courage to face it. I was a coward and I was a cheat, and I was on a merry-go-round that was making my soul sicker by the day.

We eased into a seat beside my attorney, and I immediately got queasy. How in the world could this ever be made right with my kids? How in the world would I get through it?

The judge called our names and commended us for having worked out a parenting plan. She said that she could tell how much we both loved our kids by how willingly we had compromised, despite our own differences. A few words and signatures and then, just like that, it was over.

Except nothing was over. It was just the excruciating beginning of the hardest road I've ever walked down, a road I had chosen in broad daylight, and worse than a death in many ways. Our kids would have to learn to navigate between parents, always without someone they loved.

We met back at the house to tell Taylor and Caiti, to begin severing everything they had come to know and trust. The pain of that day and those surrounding days can't be put into words. Some things are only for the heart to hold, too fragile and too private to share on paper—groanings too deep and painful to be uttered. Every time I looked at them that day, my breath got shallow and my throat tightened, their silent hurt so clear on their faces.

Days later, we all moved out of our home. He rented a house nearby, and I moved into a hotel room until I closed on a little house I'd bought by the hospital. It was his Wednesday with the kids, so Mama and I headed back to my hotel room, my belongings filling up both our cars. Over dinner that night she tried to cheer me up by telling me stories about Daddy, but somehow we ended up on one I'd never heard, about how she had jabbed through Daddy's flesh with the butcher knife after he'd thrown hot tomato soup at the wall in a whiskey fit. Perhaps it shouldn't have been funny or comforting, but it was both, because it felt like somehow all wasn't lost, that if she could recover from life with Daddy, I could recover too.

Mama left before it got too late to make the drive back to Knoxville, and I climbed the stairs to the hotel that would be my home for the next two weeks. I sat in the room alone with my own guilt and shame—shocked at what one woman could tear down in a matter of a few months.

Seeing the gilded edges of a hotel Bible sitting on my nightstand, I wasn't even sure I believed its words anymore or that they could possibly help someone like me. I had quit going to church months before, partly because it was easy to justify with my schedule and partly because I didn't want to feel any worse.

Maybe the blind faith I had found as a child was wrong and these pages were for people who had their lives in order. Was there any real comfort here for those of us who had seen too much and known too much and done too much? The words in that book felt so far away from me, here alone in a hotel room without a family, without my children, without anything that really mattered.

Before one more thought passed through my mind, I heard the words of Psalm 51 being recited in an almost audible voice, as if someone kind and gentle were standing over me and saying them for me like they would for a child. I had memorized these words for Bible drill so many years before. I couldn't stop them— so seared and exact were they in my memory. They dripped like water into my consciousness, though I didn't have the courage to mouth the words myself:

Have mercy upon me, O God, according to thy lovingkindness: according unto the multitude of thy tender mercies blot out my transgressions.

Wash me thoroughly from mine iniquity, and cleanse me from my sin.

For I acknowledge my transgressions: and my sin is ever before me.

Against thee, thee only, have I sinned, and done this evil in thy sight: that thou mightest be justified when thou speakest, and be clear when thou judgest.

Behold, I was shapen in iniquity; and in sin did my mother conceive me.

Behold, thou desirest truth in the inward parts: and in the hidden part thou shalt make me to know wisdom.

Purge me with hyssop, and I shall be clean: wash me, and I shall be whiter than snow.

Make me to hear joy and gladness; that the bones which thou hast broken may rejoice.

Hide thy face from my sins, and blot out all mine iniquities.

Create in me a clean heart, O God; and renew a right spirit within me.

Cast me not away from thy presence; and take not thy holy spirit from me.

PSALM 51:1-11

I knew those words like I knew my own name. Every single one. Those words were the first ray of hope I had had in months, maybe years. They felt like they were written just for me, maybe even the words I'd tried to find earlier but were too painful to utter. My hands were shaking as I opened the Bible to the psalm. I wanted to read it out loud but I couldn't. I couldn't pray or speak at all. I repeated the words in my mind over and over and over.

I cradled the Bible in my arms and finally drifted off to sleep, tears wetting the pillow under me.

I woke up the next morning with sunlight coming through the blinds. With the tiniest inkling of faith, I told God I was so, so sorry. I told Him I was sure He couldn't forgive me just yet, but that I wanted to find Him again, if He would have me. I thanked Him for the psalm and for King David and even for Bathsheba. I asked Him to help my kids get through the day. I asked Him to please not leave us.

As I closed the Bible and laid it back on the nightstand, it occurred to me that I had been the one who had left, not God. He had been there all along, and those verses that King David spoke had always been available to me.

I asked Him to send help. I needed people who would help me figure out why I was so messed up, people who would help me stop turning everything that mattered in my life to ashes.

I was surprised when He did.

31

ALL GOD'S CHILDREN AIN'T FREE

I STOOD AT THE FRONT DESK OF the psychiatrist's office filling out a stack of paperwork a mile high, already red in the face from trying to answer the questions on the second page.

"Are you having trouble sleeping?" Yes.

"Do you feel anxious?" Yes.

"Are you engaging in foolish, risky behavior?" Yes.

"Do you feel hopeless or helpless in your current situation?" Yes.

"Do you have a poor appetite?" Yes.

"Do you feel excessive shame?" Yes.

"Have you thought about hurting yourself?" Pause.

Hmmm. *No, I don't think I would ever do that.* I started to wonder if these admissions would affect me keeping my job as a resident, but I answered them as honestly as I could, figuring this was my chance to figure out why I was burning down my life.

Steve had been the one to insist I get some help. We had made stabs at trying to stop or pause our relationship, mostly to assuage the guilt we both felt for what we had done to our families, but we always ended up together again. By now we were both divorced, navigating the murky waters of single parenthood. We talked about marriage, but I harbored secret fears that it would be doomed from the beginning. I was barely functioning, always on the verge of tears and neck-deep in shame. After talking me down off the ledge for the hundredth time, Steve insisted I see a counselor.

I finally finished the paperwork and handed it to the receptionist, wondering whether or not this day would confirm what everyone thought: Something was wrong with me—and not just wrong, but wrong beyond repair.

I sat and waited for my name to be called, thinking about those questions I'd been mulling over. I was sure mental illness ran in my family, but the only thing I could remember ever being talked about was how so-and-so's "nerves was shot." Occasionally, one of my aunts would have a nervous breakdown and have to be hospitalized. And though that was rare, the threat of it was always looming around the edges of everything, like an afternoon storm that might pop up out of nowhere.

We had a mental hospital nearby that was officially called East Tennessee Hospital for the Insane, but which my people called "the Eastern State." "They'll have to put me in the Eastern State" was a comment that didn't even garner my attention, it was said so often by Mamaw, by Aunt Johnny, even by Daddy. Naturally, I constructed my own idea of what the Eastern State must have been like—with tranquilizers and straitjackets and other less-than-desirable treatment plans. Although as an adult, I would come to sympathize with those on the verge of losing their sanity, as a child, I remember hoping I'd never end up there.

I guess that's why it made my skin crawl to be sitting in a psychiatrist's office. Whatever he found out about me was probably not going to be good. Maybe I was a head case, as I'd heard Daddy call some of his enemies, or maybe I was bipolar or just plain crazy. But as afraid as I was to be trying to find out what was wrong with me, I was more afraid to go back to the way I'd been living.

Sweat was rolling down the front of my abdomen, my heart-beat visible through my silk shirt, when the nurse called my name. Suddenly I felt a wave of nausea, and my hands became clammy. I stood up and walked toward her, trying to smile. She patted me on the back and asked me if I was okay.

"I'll get you some water as soon as you are situated in Dr. Dresden's office, darlin'. You aren't looking very well," she said as she smiled sympathetically, leading me down a long hallway toward his office.

The kindness in her voice was the reason I hadn't turned and run to my car, despite my worries over how this confession of my less-than-stellar mental state might affect my job and the stability it would take to raise my kids. So far, those were the only two things I hadn't managed to torch.

The nurse showed me into the office where Dresden, as the psych residents called him, was waiting for me. His warm and welcoming personality put me at ease right away, his voice and cardigan reminding me of a sturdier version of Mr. Rogers. It wouldn't be long before his stoic side took over.

"I see you're a family practice resident here in Johnson City," he commented, looking at me over his reading glasses. "So what brings you in today?"

All I got out was, "My daddy's been gone . . ."

Then I cried for ten straight minutes, trying between breaths to gather myself into someone more respectable and professional. But this wasn't Dresden's first rodeo, and I soon got the feeling that my version of crazy was not all that shocking to him. He sat there through the whole spell and didn't move. Finally, he leaned in toward me, and handing me a tissue, said, "Take your time. We're in no hurry here. Tell me more about your father." He settled into his chair and folded his hands, his index fingers resting on his top lip.

"Everything feels wrong since Daddy left," I said. "I'm so lost and so confused and so . . . sad," I managed to squeak out before I tasted the salt from my tears rolling down my cheeks again.

"Your father must have been pretty special to you," he said.

"Daddy was an alcoholic my whole life, but he was also my hero. I'm pretty sure I'm screwed up from it. When he wasn't drinking, he was the funniest, kindest, most generous man I've ever known. He died when I was a third-year resident, and now my life is falling apart. I think the two may be related."

I managed to get most of that out without taking a breath. I was starting to feel the color come back to my face and my heartbeat leave my throat. From there, I eased into our story, taking long drinks from the glass of water the nurse had set on the table beside me. I told Dresden how I was missing Daddy so much since he died, and how his death was upending every part of my life.

"I went to Al-Anon a few times and have read their Big Book from cover to cover. Most of what I've read makes me think I have some kind of hero complex and feel responsible for Daddy. I spent most of my life enabling him. I'm pretty sure I'm crazy," I said, smiling and trying to make eye contact. I felt like I was rambling now, but Dresden nodded me onward, so I just kept stumbling through my words.

"I got married when I was nineteen to someone much older than me, probably wanting a father figure at the time. Now my divorce is final and I hate myself for fracturing my kids' lives. I starting drinking and had an affair, and it just feels like I'm on some sort of self-destructive bent that seems to have no bottom. The only thing I haven't detonated yet is being a doctor."

Dresden's demeanor was emotionless and intimidating.

Nervously, I kept talking. "The thing that scares me most is that for the first time in my life, I feel angry. I don't ever really recall being angry," I said, fighting a quivering lip.

Finally Dresden interjected. "Why do you suppose you're angry?"

"I don't know. I'm just so . . . I just am." I couldn't even finish my thought. I sat there staring into my hands, the skin on the sides of my fingers raw from my constant picking and biting. I gnawed on them as I waited to see if he was going to say anything else. He didn't.

"I guess I'm angry at Daddy, at God, at myself. I'm tired of trying so hard to fix everything. I couldn't fix Daddy. I can't fix me. I can't fix anything. I'm just so tired of everything around me and in me being broken. Nothing has ever been easy in my life. And it just seems to get harder."

You could have heard a pin drop in that room. Dresden sat quietly, just looking at me, waiting for me to say something else, studying me for clues—to what, I didn't know. Wasn't he supposed to be the one doing most of the talking by now, telling me how to fix this mess I was in? Wasn't that why I was here?

But he didn't. He just sat there quietly, waiting for me to incriminate myself, which didn't take me long to do.

Finally, he asked me more about my childhood, which led to me talking for at least twenty minutes nonstop. Some of the stories that came out of my mouth made the hairs on the back of *my* neck stand up. For some reason, talking about prison visits out loud made it seem like they were probably not all that good for a child. Then there were all the times at the trailer with Daddy mostly drunk and us mostly hungry; the violence, the loneliness of never having a stable father, the insecurities that came with always seeking love; and the nights at Genie's Bar when Daddy would be too drunk to drive home. By the way Dresden's eyes seemed to bore through me, I was sure he thought I was making up most of it. But he didn't flinch.

I told him I was worried I'd end up like my family, addicted to something or in jail or worse. Then I told him the thing that I was most afraid to say out loud.

"I'm supposed to be a Christian but I have gone against everything I say I believe. Maybe I don't really believe it or maybe I'm just a fraud. Maybe I always have been. Sometimes I feel the worst guilt, but mostly I'm numb. I'm not sure where that leaves me, but it feels like I've never been more alone."

He did not respond to that at all, just looked at his watch and said our session was over.

It was one of the most grueling hours of my life. I walked out of the office feeling like somebody had just beat me with a billy club, my neck and back aching with pain. Judging by the number of follow-up sessions Dresden scheduled, I was pretty sure he thought I was unfixable. Honestly, seeing a shrink was nothing like I thought it would be, and I wasn't sure I liked him at all. He didn't seem too fond of me, either. He was nothing like the Southern men I had grown up around, and in my opinion, didn't have much of a bedside manner.

Two days later, I wanted to cancel my first follow-up appointment, but Steve made me go. This time I was much more at ease and glad I hadn't flaked out. For thirty minutes, I went on about all the injustices of my life and how angry I was that Daddy left me—angry for all the things he was unable to give; angry that he showed up drunk more often than sober; angry for all the missed birthdays and sad Christmases; angry at the insecurities that came with his perennial absence; angry that he would never know that I managed to become a doctor; and angry that even if he had known, it probably wouldn't have mattered much anyway.

I told Dresden how I was barely sleeping, continuing to lose weight, and crying all the time, and how I was in a hole so deep that I wasn't sure I even wanted out anymore. Numb and alone, I sat in his office week after week, devastated with the weight of grief bearing down on my already lonely world. I was worried that I had lost faith in God or that He was too angry with me to hear my prayers.

For so many months, I wondered when Dresden was going to give me the answers I was seeking. He was unraveling a thread that seemed to have no end, and I was growing impatient with all the rehashing. I was tired of crying my mascara off every day, tired of not sleeping, tired of hating myself, tired of doubting God.

We had talked about every incident with Daddy I could remember. Mostly about the times he wasn't there—the rejection, the loneliness, the feeling of being unhinged in the world and unspoken for, the shame of looking for nurture in every man's face for as long as I could remember. Honestly, there was some relief, but I see now that the heart doesn't settle easily for blame—it longs to be redeemed.

For months on end I sat in the same chair, staring at the file folder that I worried held a psychiatric diagnosis that would be a life sentence. Most days, I felt worse when I left, more and more exposed and vulnerable with every awkward admission. Daddy was gone, I was a mess, my children were hurting, and my psychiatrist didn't seem to have any easy fixes or answers.

It would be nearly a year before I would dismantle the heavy load of emotional scarring that was uprooting me. In his own quiet way, Dresden was my safe house, providing the patience and kindness it would take for me to share some of the worst details of my life. After months and months of listening, he began to slowly drop in little nuggets of wisdom to help me learn better life skills. He had managed to pry open the closet filled with all my scary demons, and once they were exposed to the light, they slowly began to lose their power.

One early summer morning, I sat down in that familiar chair and noticed that my heart felt lighter. Before I left that day, Dresden said, "I think this will be our last visit, Edie. It has been a privilege to meet you and hear your story. You have remarkable resilience and compassion, and I can't wait to see the path your life takes. Trust yourself. Forgive yourself. And never lose your vulnerability. You were a wonderful daughter to your father, and you will make an excellent physician."

I sat there, stunned at his words. I'd had no idea that he thought me anything but crazy. Over the next few months, those words would repeat in my mind like a refrain, bringing me untold comfort and healing. Just a few words, just a cup of cold water to someone dying of thirst.

I slowly started sleeping and eating again. I learned to hold my *compassion for* Daddy and my *wounds from* him in the same heart. I learned that I was seeking approval and love in every man I met, and I slowly began to teach myself a better way. I learned that we all have wounds, and we can either open them up to the light of day so they can heal or we can keep them buried, where they will fester and one day wreak havoc on us.

As it turned out, forgiving Daddy and the others from my past was the easy part. Forgiving myself would be a process that would take years. But at least I was finally on the right road.

32

BLESS THE BROKEN ROAD

THAT AFTERNOON WHEN I walked out of the psychiatrist's office for the last time, I noticed the dogwood trees all around the medical complex. Had they been there all along? I paused to take in their collective outline against the cloudless sky—dozens of them in pink and white, declaring that spring had officially begun. Had I been so mired in my own self-loathing that I was oblivious to the fragrant beauty that was evident in front of me? I stood there for the longest time, taking slow, deep breaths. The world had shifted. My chest felt lighter, as if the air itself went in and out of my lungs more easily. I got into my car and rested my head on the steering wheel, warmed by the sun's heat. I began thinking back on my time with Dresden.

The therapy had given me an aerial view of my ground zero, which was now much more solid. Relieved that he thought I was ready to move on (as opposed to needing some sort of inpatient treatment, which is what I had feared at first), I was also disoriented and scared. It was like being dropped off on some

Appalachian mountain road that was beautiful and wild but full of potholes and nauseating switchbacks. It had all looked much easier to navigate when we'd laid out the steps from the comfort of his office. My task was to find my way back home—whatever or wherever that was; I still wasn't exactly sure.

Nothing looked the same now—not the outside world and not the world I lived on the inside. That inner world had to be the most brutal of all, as I was trying to live a better story. I thought about something Dresden had said: "Most people are just doing the best they can with what they've been given. You never know what someone's struggles are." We were talking about Daddy at the time, but I knew that I would need a dose of that grace for myself before too long.

I headed over to the historic part of town, where my friend Susan was probably feeding my kids their afternoon snack after overseeing a wild game of capture the flag. Old dogwoods and redbud trees were blooming on every corner, and so were churches. I hadn't been to church in almost a year, probably the longest stretch of time in twenty years that I had missed. At one point I was sure I'd never go back—too mixed up inside, too full of shame to put myself in such a vulnerable place. Still at a loss for how to go back and what kind of church to even look for, I decided I didn't have the courage to do it just yet. But for the first time in a long while, there was a part of me that wanted to go back, and I was hopeful.

Rounding the corner to Susan's house, I saw the kids running through the yard, spraying each other with the water hose, the sun filtering through the tall oaks that surrounded the house. Her husband, Johnny, was an internist at the hospital where I worked, and our kids attended a small private school together. Every time I walked into her kitchen, the scene felt the same—chocolate-chip cookies cooling on the counter, the spiral steno pad with her handwritten to-do list on her countertop desk, her Bible open on her dining room table, and the smell of supper already starting to make my mouth water.

Seventy-hour workweeks and emotional upheaval had left me so bankrupt that coming to Susan's house was like stepping into an oasis. Her soothing Mississippi accent could disarm even the most calloused and overworked soul, but what always caught me off guard was how welcomed and loved I felt in her home, as if she was just waiting for me to show up, hoping I'd drag in tired and hungry, in need of a kind word and some warm bread.

"Hey, sweet girl," she said as I hugged her and quickly found a seat at her dining room table. "Oh honey, you look so tired; let me get you some iced tea and a cookie."

Susan was probably ten years older than me, but she mentored me in a way that I found both foreign and irresistible. While she poured my tea, I noticed that her Bible was open to Isaiah, the margins full of notes.

"You don't know how thankful I am for you getting the kids for me in the afternoons. Thank you so, so much," I said, reading snatches of her notes as she heaped cookies on a plate.

"Listen, I adore those kids and I adore you, and I'm just so thankful God brought us together. I really am. And that Caiti-bug is mine; I'm just going to keep her here with all my boys. We need a girl around this house," she said, patting my back and sitting down right beside me.

It's hard to describe what her friendship meant to me. She was a Christian but she lived her faith unlike anyone I'd ever known. There was a seamlessness about her life that I couldn't quite put my finger on, as if her faith were like yeast in a loaf of bread, permeating every part of her life.

"I know that I don't know everything that's going on or what this is like for y'all, but I do know this—God is faithful when we're not and strong when we're weak, and the faith life is about holding on to Him, not looking at ourselves for what we are or aren't bringing to the table. I was reading this in Isaiah today," she said, picking up her reading glasses and holding on to my hand as she began.

The Spirit of the Lord God is upon me,
    because the Lord has anointed me
to bring good news to the poor;
    he has sent me to bind up the brokenhearted,
to proclaim liberty to the captives,
    and the opening of the prison to those who are bound;
to proclaim the year of the Lord's favor,
    and the day of vengeance of our God;
    to comfort all who mourn;

That's as far as she made it before she was weeping. Soon we were both crying, but she kept going . . .

to grant to those who mourn in Zion—
    to give them a beautiful headdress instead of ashes,
the oil of gladness instead of mourning,
    the garment of praise instead of a faint spirit;
that they may be called oaks of righteousness,
    the planting of the Lord, that he may be glorified.
They shall build up the ancient ruins;
    they shall raise up the former devastations;
they shall repair the ruined cities,
    the devastations of many generations.

ISAIAH 61:1-4, ESV

I would hear Scripture like this in church growing up and think it was for other people—the ones with normal lives, without my kind of past. After all I'd done in the last two years, it felt more for other people than ever. But something about Susan's belief in those words combined with her love for me shook me to the core. She believed them not just for her, but for me, too.

"Oh no, the bread!" she said, jumping up and laughing. She and the Lord would be enjoying each other's company so much, she admitted, that inevitably no one would pay attention to the bread in the oven. Her infectious laugh made me miss Daddy. Soon we were setting the table and feeding the kids homemade tomato soup and ever-so-slightly burned bread.

As soon as I smelled the soup, I realized how hungry I was, maybe how hungry I'd been for a long time. It was a simple meal—a warm bowl of soup and some bread—but it was everything I didn't know I needed. Enough to sustain me for another day. Enough to show me the transforming power of one woman's kindness. Enough to keep me moving ahead, one day at a time.

Susan loved me with food and words and child care and with an indescribable hope that this way of life—this way of love—was possible for me, too. Her Jesus way of hospitality changed everything for me, giving me the hope and the courage to keep walking until I saw light.

Susan and Johnny and their boys joined us a few months later when Steve and I got married in a backyard ceremony on the edge of a new little town where we'd moved to begin our new jobs. Getting married felt like a risk, given my past, but I loved him and was desperate for another chance at having a family. With daisies in my hair and a bluegrass band playing on the porch, I took my brother Todd's arm as he escorted me around the side yard, both of us joking about what Daddy would be saying if he were here. Probably something like "Nise, what in the world have you got a bo-kay of flowers comin' out of your head for?" Or "You reckon there'll be anythang good to eat at this shindig?" I stopped momentarily to let Mama and Sister adjust my daisy bouquet and kiss me on the cheek. Mama asked me if I was ever going to start wearing eye makeup again, and I told her I would if I ever learned to make it through a whole day without crying.

Todd walked me up to Steve, who was waiting with our collective six kids and our closest friends and family. He took my hands and steadied me as I cried through the whole ceremony—tears of gratitude and hope mingled with sadness and loss, forging ahead through pain and love and the incredible resilience of our kids.

After we said our vows, we walked around the side of our house, just the two of us. His eyes were full of tears. He bear-hugged me and told me I was everything his heart wanted and needed. He kissed the tears off my cheeks, and I knew I was loved. He promised to do whatever it took to patch our families back together. We danced on our back porch to Bob Dylan while the kids blew bubbles under the canopy of bright July stars.

From those rough and humble beginnings, what would follow would be both a road of unspeakable joy and a trial by fire neither of us could have imagined. What we didn't know was that God's forgiveness and unconditional love were waiting for us there.

33

MAMA, HE'S CRAZY

I DIDN'T HEAR WHAT STEVE SAID, if in fact he said anything, but I did follow his head nod as he walked out the back door—the door that led us out into the very same backyard where a year earlier we had said our homemade vows over banjo music. The August air was stifling, and as I followed Steve to a row of white pines, I must have asked three times where we were going. He didn't say a word but pointed to a whole cluster of wild grapevines he'd told me about earlier. I could see the woody vines as clear as day, tangled up in the tops of the evergreens, hundreds of clusters draping from the branches, their fruit the deepest shade of purple I had ever seen. But I had never noticed them until he pointed them out.

It was the third season the wild grapes had flowered, but only the first time there had been any fruit. I loved that the lobes of the grapes were heart-shaped, the fruit smaller than blueberries.

Steve was my botany teacher, who gently pointed out that the copper-colored foliage I had harvested from the yard last fall to display in a blue willow vase on the kitchen table in all its autumn glory was actually poison ivy. My itchy, oozy arms were a constant reminder the next week that it pays to have an eye for such things, but I had not been trained to observe trees and flowers and weather patterns. The only plant I had ever paid attention to was the daisy I'd watched grow on Mamaw's porch as a child, and that didn't end well. Besides, with four kids, including adorable six-month-old Eleanor and her precious but stubborn two-year-old sister, Emaleigh Mae, I had enough to keep an eye on. They were napping and I was anxious to get back to the stack of books that occupied my weekend free time, especially *Mere Christianity*.

Still looking up at the trees, Steve said, "We should make jelly."

I followed his gaze and wondered how in the world we would do that—and why. I wanted to get back to devouring Lewis's profound words for a second time since we'd returned from vacation.

But Steve was determined, so I agreed to be his sous-chef. He hauled a ladder home from Lowe's that was tall enough to reach the bounty, and I assembled the rest of the accoutrements for our adventure, including a homemade cheesecloth contraption that we hung from the knobs on a kitchen cabinet. He assured me they were grapes, but after seeing them close up, lying on my table, I thought they looked more like poisonous berries than any grapes I'd ever eaten.

We were trying to make our way through the sometimes thorny minefields of blended families, including the two youngest girls we'd had together, and we were both feeling the pressure of working stressful jobs. After exhausting myself pulling the weekend night shift as an emergency room physician, I had joined the multispecialty group that Steve was in, hoping to be able to build a sustainable practice working part time. Some would say there's no such thing as a part-time physician, and there's some truth to that.

We were sitting at the kitchen table, looking at our jelly operation, when Steve offhandedly said, "At the board meeting the other night, a few people mentioned that you might need to start taking calls on weekends."

"Yes, I heard murmurings from someone else. I also heard they want me to start working full time, which I obviously don't want to do with the girls still so little," I said, watching Steve put the first batch of boiled berries in the cheesecloth, dripping juice into the bowl below it on the counter. Even without the news, I had already been struggling with being away from my kids.

The jelly-making process was long, and I felt like a pioneer. When we finally finished on Sunday night, I mentally high-fived Daddy, who would have approved of that day's work, given all the jars of chowchow he'd proudly made.

At times like this, it dawned on me how far out of my league I was with Steve. He was a study in paradox—gentle yet fierce; tender but never weak; smart but down to earth; rugged but refined; a bird watcher extraordinaire and a self-educated botanist; a lover of Bach, Pearl Jam, and Johnny Cash; as apt to tear up over a toddler as he was to lose his temper over an uncooperative lawn mower. Being married to him was an education in all things normal—all the things I had missed growing up in survival mode.

We collapsed into bed that night exhausted. I picked up my already tattered copy of *Mere Christianity* to read the last pages for the umpteenth time.

"That book has you in its grasp, doesn't it? You haven't put it down since we got home," he said.

"Yeah, it has pretty much destroyed me. In a good way, I think," I said, opening up to the last two pages.

I had made the mistake of taking the book with me to the Bahamas, and the last pages of that book nearly ruined our trip. As I read the words, my legs felt like they had been cut out from under me, and I came back reeling with doubts and questions and a longing to find a more meaningful life, one that included God again.

Here's the truth of the matter: I don't remember that much about that trip of a lifetime. I'm sure the sunsets were amazing and the sand was crystal white. I'm sure the food was divine. I'm sure that on the day we took a trip into the town market, I bought some cute souvenirs for my kids, but I don't remember for the life of me what I bought. What I remember are the words of Lewis, words I kept coming back to over and over.

> Your real, new self (which is Christ's and also yours, and yours just because it is His) will not come as long as you are looking for it. It will come when you are looking for Him. Does that sound strange? The same principle holds, you know, for more everyday matters. Even in social life, you will never make a good impression on other people until you stop thinking about what sort of impression you are making. Even in literature and art, no man who bothers about originality will ever be original: whereas if you simply try to tell the truth (without caring twopence how often it has been told before) you will, nine times out of ten, become original without ever having noticed it. The principle runs through all life from top to bottom. Give up yourself, and you will find your real self. Lose your life and you will save it. Submit to death, death of your ambitions and favourite wishes every day and death of your whole body in the end: submit with every fibre of your being, and you will find eternal life. Keep back nothing. Nothing that you have not given away will ever be really yours. Nothing in you that has not died will ever be raised from the dead. Look for yourself, and you will find in the long run only hatred, loneliness, despair, rage, ruin, and decay. But look for Christ, and you will find Him, and with Him everything else thrown in.[1]

By now, I had read that passage so many times I could almost say it by heart.

Lewis became my tutor in the faith. I read all of his books and letters. I read nearly every book and author he mentioned in his writings. I read his book on the Psalms and then reread the Psalms through his eyes. He taught me everything a fledgling, doubting, struggling believer should know about love and forgiveness and hope.

Sometimes, during the day at work, I would hear his words in my head: "Give up yourself, and you will find your real self. Lose your life and you will save it."

What did that even mean, and how would I ever manage to do it? I knew I didn't want the version of faith I had known as a child, but I also knew down deep that I'd never be happy outside the church.

> Keep back nothing. Nothing that you have not given away
> will ever be really yours. . . . Look for yourself, and you
> will find in the long run only hatred, loneliness, despair,
> rage, ruin, and decay. But look for Christ, and you will find
> Him, and with Him everything else thrown in.

I needed to talk to Steve about all this, but I was scared because I didn't really know what it would mean for any of us. When we got home from work that night, I told him I wanted to take the kids to church on Sunday.

"Hmmm, not sure if I'll be joining you or not, but I can see why you want to do it," he said, flipping through the channels to find the baseball game.

I didn't say anything else. I was relieved that he didn't seem to disapprove and took that as a sign that maybe he'd reconsider and go with me.

With this newfound sense of purpose, everything we had built our lives on up to that point began to lose its luster. Then, with pressure mounting at work, I quit my job—the one I had trained for the past decade to do, the one that had defined everything about me, the one that meant I was needed and productive in the world.

I didn't anticipate the loss I would feel in coming home.

34

EVERYTHING'S GONNA BE ALRIGHT

I STOOD IN A CLOUD OF white all-purpose flour, brushing a fleck of it off my eyelash with my wrist and then blinking profusely to keep it out of my eye. Despite the fact that I was wearing an apron, I was covered in white dust and so was every inch of my kitchen. It had been two weeks since I'd quit my job as a family doctor, and I had no idea how to fill in the gap of daytime hours that were free to me now that I wasn't working. So I decided to teach myself how to bake bread.

I bought a book, watched some videos, asked random ladies at the grocery store lots of questions, and then took my new knowledge to the kitchen to begin experimenting. I found myself wrestling not only with the directions in front of me but also with the heavy uncertainties in my life. Mixing the ingredients, kneading the dough, rolling it out, punching it down, watching it rise (or wondering why it didn't), all were steps to the thing that always catches me off guard—the absolute joy and delight of the bread's warm and yeasty smell taking my house hostage for an afternoon.

I learned so much about bread and even more about myself that year, as the contentment I'd felt at Susan's began to inch its way into my home and life. I first mastered focaccia bread, and then boule, and then, months later, slender loaves of French bread. Working with my hands in the dough made me slow down long enough to realize that it was the simplest things that often brought the greatest pleasure and that feeding someone was just as important as prescribing their blood pressure medication. I began to read M. F. K. Fisher, who explains the experience well in *The Art of Eating*.

> It does not cost much. . . . It is pleasant: one of those almost hypnotic businesses, like a dance from some ancient ceremony. It leaves you filled with peace, and the house filled with one of the world's sweetest smells. But it takes a lot of time. If you can find that, the rest is easy. And if you cannot rightly find it, make it, for probably there is no chiropractic treatment, no Yoga exercise, no hour of meditation in a music-throbbing chapel, that will leave you emptier of bad thoughts than this homely ceremony of making bread.[2]

She was so right. That day was the first of a string of days in which all of the bad thoughts about the horrible mistake I was surely making with my life by leaving my job and staying at home slowly dissipated. Day after day, month after month, the bread-making grounded me, keeping my hands from being idle and my heart from growing discontent.

After my confidence grew, I began to hone my culinary skills out of sheer desperation. There was nothing more frightening to me than the paws of eight hungry cubs pulling at my shirt at five o'clock. Steve had grown up with regular family dinners and a mom who was an excellent cook. But my story was different. Having grown up with a single mom who worked nights and then spending most of my twenties working crazy hours, I had never really learned to cook, and this regular responsibility now felt overwhelming. I couldn't use the excuse that I was working to justify ordering out or throwing in a tray of fish sticks at the last minute. I figured I was an educated woman—how hard could it be to feed people?

Really hard is how hard. Just ask any mama who is trying to feed her troops with her own hands from stuff found in her own pantry.

I fumbled around in my kitchen for months, watching the Food Network, purchasing a slew of Rachael Ray videos that I bought online one night in a fit of meal-planning mania, and laughing hysterically over Julia Child's old videos on YouTube. I was trying to face the supper hour without so much angst and bitterness. Wasn't I a highly trained physician who should be doing more important things than stirring a pot of soup? My arrogance faded over time as I began to realize what a gift it was to have so much food available at my disposal, and as I saw the satisfaction that came from nourishing my people with my own two hands.

Slowly, meal preparations became less intimidating and more pleasurable. I realized that feeding my people is part of God's work for me. It's ordinary and necessary, yes. And at times it drives me completely crazy—thinking of new things to make, trying recipes that turn out to be complete failures, dealing with the mess afterward. But it's also life giving and humbling and rewarding.

For months, I worked on a beef stew recipe, trying to figure out how to make it better—adding mushrooms, wine, and then finally what would become the crowning glory of all my recipes— heavy cream. One night as I served up dinner, Steve said, "This is absolutely the best beef stew I've ever eaten." *My work here is done*, I thought to myself, patting my proverbial back, knowing full well that wasn't true. They'd all be hungry again by morning. But it was all the encouragement I needed to keep at it, to keep learning, to keep serving the people right in front of me.

Once I learned how to feed my family, I began to grow hungry for the spiritual things that had once been so important to me. It was easy to justify not going to church when Steve and I were both busy physicians. Honestly, during those years, our superficial lifestyle became our substitute for deeper things. We had it all and didn't need anything else. But something about the tangible, ordinary realness of everyday life at home and the humility it required exposed the void in me. I missed God. I missed the Scriptures. I missed church.

C. S. Lewis's writings were my constant companions, but feasting on them wasn't the same as putting myself under the teaching of a pastor.

Steve and I finally decided to try to find a church together. Baptized as an infant and raised in a conservative Lutheran church, he was way more knowledgeable about the Christian faith than he had ever let on, so he grew impatient very quickly when I began to drag him around to every last church in town.

He said that he'd only keep humoring me with this "church thing" if I would agree to try a liturgical church. I didn't even know what that meant—I imagined icons and candles and incense and robes and mostly deadness. But when Steve talked about the seasons of the church, the centrality of the gospel, and Martin Luther's teachings, I was intrigued.

We decided to try a conservative Lutheran church like the one he'd grown up in. Our youngest daughter, Eleanor, was five when we walked through the doors of the church for the first time.

The architecture itself was fascinating. Not since Daddy took me to the charismatic church in the backwoods of East Tennessee had I so taken to anything.

Everything about the colors and textures and dappled light through the stained-glass windows drew me in. There were symbols and crosses and candles. It had the ambiance and smell I imagined I'd find in an old English library. Everywhere I turned, I was puzzled and inspired by what I saw.

We nestled into a pew on the left side of the church, midway in the sanctuary. I couldn't take my eyes off the stained glass. There were twelve huge windows that depicted the life of Jesus. My senses were beckoned from every side by something beautiful. There was a holy reverence within the church that was palpable.

Steve handed me a hymnal, and everything in him relaxed. He was home.

We stood up and sat down and read prayers and sang hymns, some of them dating from the eighth century. We stood some more, we knelt, we chanted, we sang, we recited the Nicene Creed, we stood up again, we prayed the Lord's Prayer. At first, the formality felt awkward to me. But there was also something mysterious about this place that I couldn't quite figure out yet yearned for.

The main objective of my faith growing up was to be sure that Jesus was in my heart. Everything here pointed to Christ—everything taught the gospel story. There was a fullness and celebration here that was foreign to me. I had never known this kind of abundance. I had always set out to make my heart pure and devout, as if my heart were the only place to find spiritual life.

This place wrecked all that. It seemed to be celebrating the mysteries of Creation; or as if at any point, there might be a wedding where Christ would turn water into wine.

A few months later, I took my first Communion. I remember it like it was yesterday. I listened closely to the pastor's words.

"Our Lord Jesus Christ, on the night when He was betrayed, took bread, and when He had given thanks, He broke it and gave it to his disciples saying, 'Take, eat. This is My body, which is given for you. This do in remembrance of Me.'

"In the same manner also, He took the cup after supper. And when He had given thanks, He gave it to them saying, 'Drink of it, all of you; this cup is the new testament in My blood, which is shed for you for the forgiveness of sins. This do as often as you drink it, in remembrance of Me.'"[3]

I walked slowly to the rail for the first time behind a woman with pancreatic cancer, whose skin was tight and shiny and the color of pumpkin. She had been teaching our girls Sunday school when she was diagnosed, and now the cancer was ravaging her body. My eyes were overflowing by the time I reached the front—thinking of her, thinking of Daddy's cancer, thinking of the ways we were all dying, and how this meal was a promise of life.

I knelt and held my hands out like a beggar, waiting for the bread. I glanced over at Steve and was overcome with gratitude.

By the time the pastor reached me and placed the bread in my cupped hands, tears were streaming down my cheeks as he said, "Take, eat, this is the body of Christ, given unto you for the forgiveness of all your sins."

I couldn't stop crying. He brought the cup next and said, "Take, drink. This is the blood of Christ, shed for you for the forgiveness of all your sins. Depart in peace."

I drank the wine and ate the bread. It seemed so very earthy and small. But what happened in my actual body that day confounds me still. I knew I would never be the same. The Bread of heaven joined with my own body, my own flesh, making me whole and giving me tangible assurance that He is always with me. It seemed impossible. I believed it, but I doubted it too.

The woman with cancer was crying, too, as she hobbled back to her seat and bowed her head in thanks. I'll never forget the ray of sunshine that streamed just past the reds and ambers of the stained glass beside us.

This Bread was for everyone, including me.

I never knew the depth of my own yearning and hungering until then. The Bread of heaven fills the parts you didn't know were hungry.

It took years of coming to the table of the Lord before I realized what it truly meant. It is where we glimpse wholeness. It is not the altar where we surrender all; it is the altar where *Christ has surrendered all*—where He has given everything in preparation for this meal. Here we know that Christ has come to save sinners. All the anger, the months and years of bitterness and imperfect relationships, the miscommunications, the feeling of being abandoned and unspoken for, my own paralyzing sin—all of it was answered here in this most sacred bread-breaking.

All that was only the beginning of how Christ found me and began to nourish me at His table. It felt strangely like coming home, or like heaven, or like something so otherworldly that it could only be grasped by faith and humility.

The table of the Lord changed everything.

And that's when all hell broke loose.

35

WHEN THE WORLD STOPPED TURNING

THE AIR WAS THICK WITH the smell of sulfur when I woke. The clock glowed through a fog, reading 4:30 a.m. I blinked repeatedly and realized the fog was actually smoke.

I leaped from bed and flipped on the light while black smoke drifted under the bottom of the door. I heard a roar on the other side of the bedroom door that made it all feel like a dream.

Nothing was right, and for a moment, I thought of closing my eyes to escape the nightmare. I felt a weight of doom tied to my chest that could have pulled me to the bottom of the ocean.

"Steve! Get up! There's a fire!" I screamed as I touched the bedroom wall, jerking my hand away from the heat.

He jumped awake. A man of few words, even in a crisis, he raced to our bedroom door and ripped it open. An angry mix of black smoke and flames tumbled in like an avalanche. We coughed and beat at the rushing inferno knowing that upstairs, beyond that wall of smoke, the girls were asleep in their beds while flames consumed the house beneath them.

Our eyes met, and I knew what Steve was thinking: *Let's get the front door open so the girls can escape down the stairs.*

Dressed in nothing but his boxers, Steve covered his nose and mouth with the crook of his elbow and without another word or thought for his own safety disappeared into the smoke.

He expected me to follow him. I took a step out, then retreated from the smoke rolling in. Through the acrid haze outside the door, I glimpsed flames consuming the dining room—the beautiful table I loved, set with Christmas dishes, the gingerbread houses, the Advent wreath—our beautiful Christmas becoming soot and ash.

I mumbled a broken prayer and raced for my phone on the nightstand.

As the 911 operator answered, I became hysterical.

"Our house . . . fire . . . hurry," I managed between broken sobs and a fit of coughing.

"Ma'am, please try to calm down. I can't understand you. What did you say?"

"Our house is on fire. My children are on the second floor. I don't think they can get out. Please hurry."

"Ma'am, are you safe?"

I wiped my eyes and felt the sting from the smoke. The roar of the flames had grown in the seconds since Steve disappeared, and smoke was hovering over every square inch of the room. I couldn't see six inches in front of my face.

"I'm okay, just hurry! Please, God, help us."

I gave our address and hung up, then ran to the window. Though our room was on the main floor, the house was built on a hill that dropped off toward the lake. I saw nothing but hard frozen earth that seemed to slope into dark oblivion.

I pushed the window up and smoke poured into the numbing December air. The reflection from the flames danced off the lake, but it was the nothingness that scared me—no fire trucks, no neighbors, nothing but the eerie rumble and crackle of what felt like my world coming to an end.

Without another thought, I pushed out the screen and jumped, my knee jamming like a counterpunch into my right eye. My bare feet hit the frozen earth and I rolled down the hill until I hit a tree, leaving me stunned.

I scrambled up in my pajamas and ran around the side of the house toward the front door. When I got there, out of breath and frantic, I saw Steve facedown on the steps, heaving and wheezing, desperate for air. My split second of relief turned to horror as I realized he was alone.

He had opened the door, but he hadn't been able to get the girls out.

With the front door now open, smoke poured out, billowing and tumbling like a waterfall. I couldn't make out the stairwell less than ten feet in front of me.

My children were at the top of those stairs, probably sweetly sleeping and dreaming of the Harry Potter chapter I had read aloud just a few hours before. Little Emme and Elea had shared the same blankets after begging me to push their matching twin beds together.

Just around the corner in the next room, Caiti, now eighteen, had come home from school and was staying overnight, a last-minute decision to continue our Christmas baking festivities into the next day. We had invited her boyfriend, Cody, to stay with us, too, since we had plenty of room and sleeping quarters in the basement.

Taylor was away at college, the only child of mine who was safe right now. The girls were just a few dozen feet away, but it felt like the space between us was an endless ocean.

I barely heard Steve pant, "Get the girls. Hurry. Go now, hurry."

"Emme! Elea! Caiti!" I screamed into the sky and the smoke. Covering my nose and mouth with my shirttail, I broke into the dark and smoke and reached the staircase, tripping over the first step. The smoke felt like a hot iron searing my lungs and blinding me. I managed to get halfway up the stairs before I collapsed against the carpet. My hands dug into the rug as I slid down and crawled out to the air outside.

I coughed uncontrollably beside Steve. After a few deep breaths I faced the thick, toxic smoke again.

"Emme! Elea! Caiti! Come down the stairs!" I screamed between coughing.

Steve was still unable to stand, gasping for breath. I had never seen him this helpless and knew he needed emergency care. He could die from smoke inhalation, but even with my thirteen years of medical training, there I stood, wanting to help him but wishing he could help me get up the stairs to the girls.

I yelled to the girls again.

I pulled my shirt up as a makeshift mask and tried for the stairs again, but immediately the fumes smothered me. I couldn't breathe and nearly blacked out, then somehow managed to crawl headfirst back down the stairs.

I collapsed next to Steve, who was still choking and gasping for breath. "Do something!" I begged him, my panic pushing me beyond all reason. "Please! We can't just stay here and watch them die!"

Steve tried to claw his way along the sidewalk into the house, but his arms crumpled. He tried to stand but fell into the doorway. I sobbed and screamed for God to help us.

As much as I screamed, I couldn't match the roar of the fire, drowning out everything in its wake. I made up my mind to crawl back up those stairs as far as I could and die with them, the thought of losing our girls too unbearable for words. One last time, I got ready to launch onto the stairs.

A large crack sounded above us like a wall starting to cave in, the sound of it so loud and apocalyptic that I covered my ears.

Maybe this is how the story ends for people with a past like mine, I thought. *Maybe this is what I deserve.*

One thing I knew for sure was that if my girls were going

to heaven early on this December morning, they weren't going without me.

As soon as I approached the stairway, another terrifying cracking sound stopped me in my tracks. Then I heard what sounded like a whole glass wall shatter, with heavy shards hitting the ground. Were the floor-to-ceiling windows in the bedroom caving in? Maybe the back wall? The sliding glass door?

Oh dear Lord, please protect my girls. Please let them live.

We were running out of time.

And then, like a Christmas miracle, Caiti broke through the black smoke with her two sisters on either side, the three of them with their faces buried in their pillows, the outlines of their head and shoulders lit up like angel halos.

"Oh, thank God, thank God, you're safe. Thank you, thank you, thank you, Jesus," I said. I couldn't stop hugging them and kissing their faces, all three of them stunned and pale from shock.

"Caiti, you are our guardian angel; you saved your sisters. We will never be able to repay you for what you've done. You saved their lives. All my girls are safe." I clung to her so tight, wrapping the little girls up in our hug, our tears mingling together. Steve had managed to stand up, and as he reached for the girls, I saw thankful tears streaming down his cold cheeks.

"I could hear you screaming," Caiti said, almost out of breath herself. "So I ran to the girls' room, but there were already flames below their windows and that's when I heard you scream that the stairs were clear. I woke up the girls and told them to grab their pillows. I'm glad I didn't know how bad it was." Her voice quivered as she wiped her face with the sleeve of her sweatshirt.

"Oh no! I need to go get Cody—he's still asleep in the basement. It looks like that side of the house is okay right now, but I'd better hurry," she said as she took off around the other side of the house.

I followed her to make sure the fire hadn't spread that far; it hadn't. Soon, she and Cody and the dogs joined us in the front of the house, every one of us stunned at what was happening right before our eyes.

The weight of the world melted away around me. I didn't care about anything else anymore. My babies were safe—Emme with her slept-on curls clinging to her cheek and Elea clutching her blue blanket, tears wetting her pillowcase. They stood in front of me, not one hair on their heads singed, and I couldn't let go of them— I just kept hugging and kissing them. We cried, we shouted in disbelief, we hugged and cried some more, unable to let go of each other. I cupped their precious faces in my hands and kissed them over and over.

Steve moved his car out of harm's way and left it running so we could warm up. While Caiti and Cody took the girls and ran to the neighbors' house for help and blankets, Steve sat in the front seat of his car, shivering and trying to regulate his breathing. Following his lead, I moved my car away from the house into the grass, thankful that I also had left my keys in the ignition.

Walking back toward the house, I folded my arms tight around my chest as a shield against the cold. I noticed the neighbors' lights go on so I stood waiting for the kids to return, watching in horror as the first side wall gave way. It crashed like thunder toward the lake in what sounded like an avalanche of bricks and glass and heavy debris. I wondered if the whole house would just tumble down the steep bank into the water. Tears, relief, and horror all melted into numbness as I watched everything we'd worked for slip away. "Where are all the fire trucks?" I said to myself as I stood in disbelief that this was happening. I called 911 again.

"I know I called you before, but it's been at least fifteen minutes and no one is here yet. Please hurry. We'll all out and safe but everything we have will be gone if you don't hurry." My voice trailed off into tears as the wind picked up and scattered embers onto the white frost. I shivered, standing there still holding the phone to my ear, lost for a moment as I watched the blurry orange glow of the tiny coals slowly fade to black.

"Ma'am, I understand how upset you are, but we are doing everything we can. You live in a rural area, so it will take more time than normal. I promise someone will be there soon. Is there a neighbor or somewhere safe you can stay while you wait?"

"Yes, we are all okay. Just hurry," I said, kneeling down to avoid the wind. Next I tried to call my mom and sister.

Caiti and Cody came running back with robes and blankets, and Caiti draped a thick robe over my shoulders. Steve was still in his car trying to get a cell signal to call his mom. The only thing I heard him say was, "Edie and the girls are all safe. I'm just sitting here watching it all go up in flames." He coughed every few seconds as he tried to talk.

When Sister returned my call a few seconds later, I managed to say, "Our house is burning down," followed quickly by, "we're all okay," before I lost it.

"I'm on my way," she said.

She was the one person in the world who I needed most—the person most like me, most able to comfort my kids, most equipped to handle everything that a tragedy like this would bring. She and I had always been close, but the years with her had only gotten sweeter, it seemed, as our kids were aging and our marriages maturing. Jamie and I had always joked that if we were stranded on a desert island, we'd take Sister over anyone else. There had always been something special about her, but our secret sister language had always shown best on the hardest days. We knew how to make everything okay for each other.

After getting blankets for Steve and me, Caiti went back to check on the girls, now snuggled up and watching cartoons at the neighbors' house. I found a place on the cold ground where I could sit by myself, waiting for Steve to get off the phone with his family in Minnesota and waiting for my family to arrive.

Pools of orange flames danced in my eyes as I huddled in my neighbor's robe on the frosty grass, watching my house burn to the ground. It reminded me of an old movie, slightly out of focus, the edges of light blurred soft in front of me against the charcoal sky. Tiny snowflakes (or were they ashes?) whirled and flittered in the early morning air, pausing as if to comfort me—twirling right in front of my eyes in slow motion, their outlines visible against the red flames. I heard echoes of my pastor's voice from two days before, summing up our eight-month study on the book of Job, "The Lord gives, and the Lord takes away. Blessed be the name of the Lord."[4]

So there I sat, numb and cold, watching all the pretty things turn black.

How ironic that after all those years of hearing crazy stories of Daddy burning things down, fire was now my legacy too. Sister found me on the frozen ground when she drove up with Mama. I rose to greet them and then fell into their arms, letting the heartache of forty years have its way.

36

IF WE MAKE IT THROUGH DECEMBER

IN THE BITTER COLD of early morning, just as light began to peek over the hills behind us, we watched the remaining walls of our home crack and fall. I knew that nothing would ever be the same, that this day would overshadow every other day, that we would always see life through the filter of this horrific loss. The euphoria of our family's miraculous survival was slowly giving way to the reality of what we had lost.

I spent most of the day on my neighbor's sofa surrounded by my mom, Sister, Todd, and a host of family and friends who came by to show their love and support. Steve had been checked out by a physician friend of ours and, after a clear chest X-ray, was given some inhalers to help his breathing. It was only three days until Christmas, so Sister sat beside me with her computer, ordering Christmas gifts for our kids and having them overnighted. When she asked which American Girl dolls our girls wanted, I said without thinking, "Don't get Kit; we already have her and her bed."

"No, you don't, Sissy," Sister replied gently. "The girls don't have any dolls anymore." That slap of reality went on for months, when I would inadvertently be looking for something, only to realize it was gone.

By late afternoon, when I felt like I was suffocating from it all, I walked outside to see the house. I wanted to see it, but I was afraid to look, so I kept my eyes averted until I got right in front of it. My knees nearly buckled when I saw the chimney swaying in the wind over the charred patio stairs that were partially dangling in the air. Nearly everything else had caved in on itself, the top floors now lying in an ash heap in what once was the basement.

For more than twelve hours, the firefighters had tried to contain the damage, but it was for naught. Only a couple of partial outer walls and the chimney were still standing. My sister braced me against the cold wind as we stood there looking at what surely was a bad dream. Both of us were devastated.

Why? Why us? Why now? kept running through my mind.

But today wasn't the day when answers would come. It was a day for doubt and despair and constant nagging questions of how to reconcile the evidence we saw in front of us with what we believed to be true about God—that He loved us with an everlasting love despite everything else and that the evidence of that love was Christ's death on the cross, not the amount of money in our bank account or the beauty and comfort of our former home. I kept reminding myself of that when my face would go hot and I would wonder if somehow this was all my fault, my punishment for so many awful decisions.

I woke up the next morning disoriented in a strange bed and felt like my insides were on fire. The room looked cloudy, as if it was filled with smoke, and I felt like I couldn't breathe. I kept blinking my eyes over and over again to clear the haze. My heart raced. Sitting on the side of the bed in panic, I shook Steve awake.

"The room looks cloudy. Do you smell smoke?" I said, still straining to clear my eyes.

He sat up and looked around. "No, I don't see smoke. I think you may be dreaming," he said, now too startled and awake to try to go back to sleep again.

Yesterday's crying had taken its toll, and my eyes were so puffy I could barely open them. There was no smoke, no fire—only the most hollow feeling I'd ever had, like waking up at Mamaw's after the trailer fire, but worse this time. Because now I was an adult and was responsible for trying to make this okay somehow for my kids.

Everything we loved was gone. The Christmas gifts we'd bought the kids, their toys and artwork, the sweater I'd spent two years knitting for Caiti, the handmade scrapbooks, my grandmother's ring, thousands of photographs, thousands of words filling the pages of journals, every last handmade quilt, all the diplomas, all the art, my brand-new kitchen—all gone.

"The Lord gives, and the Lord takes away. Blessed be the name of the Lord," kept running through my mind, words that might at one time have brought me comfort. In fact, when our pastor had said them three days ago, I wholeheartedly believed them and nodded my head in agreement. Yes, God was trustworthy and good and always had our best interests at heart. Those words had seemed fine until now.

The rest of that day is a blur to me. Steve went to work because that's what he knew how to do. My family stayed to help me and the kids settle into a nearby summer house offered by a good friend. They told us to stay as long as we needed. The house happened to be right across the cove from where ours still smoldered.

The second morning after the fire, I woke up feeling physically ill. I stood for the longest time looking out the window across the lake, wondering how all this would ever be okay again. It felt strange to see the world from that perspective, to realize that the way we saw things was only the way they looked to us. How different this must all have looked to God. If Daddy could look down on us from heaven, how would he see it?

Smoke was still rising from the ruins, coming mostly from the chimney side of the house and mixing with the frigid air into a thick white cloud. Steve's clinic was closed, so we loaded the girls up and drove over to see the remains, finding a swath of yellow caution tape outlining the perimeter. The girls walked gingerly around the tape, peeking into the hole where our house once stood. I kept watching them for signs of distress, but they looked more shocked than anything. It reminded me of when Aunt Glenda took Jamie and me to dig through the ruins of the trailer fire.

"Where was our room, Mommy?" Emme asked, trying to get her bearings, her long braided ponytail whipping in the wind.

"It was just above where that turquoise chair is sitting," I said, pulling her hood up over her ears and patting her back.

I was fine until I saw the garage. It looked like the house was vomiting out of the garage door, the metal skeletons of the stove and the washing machine visible in the ash heap, the stove turned on its side from falling through the floor. Then I saw a Land's End bag, fully preserved, the orange W monogram on the outside not even blackened.

But it was the way the sun illuminated the turquoise Adirondack chair that stopped me in my tracks. It was made of wood. How had it not been burned? It was still sitting right side up, its bright color such a stark contrast to the sea of charcoal gray that lay before us. That chair became a sign to me—the color of hope and life, a reminder of the promise that all is not lost; redemption will have its say.

For the next few days, we were flooded with love. My mom and sister stayed by my side nearly every hour. My friend Jeannie brought a fully decorated Christmas tree and a carload of gifts; my book club friends completely replenished my C. S. Lewis collection. My friend Patti coordinated meals and showed up every day with more cards and gifts that she had collected from people who loved us but didn't want to be a burden. My friend

Myquillyn sent me a bust of David, my favorite Bible hero, to decorate our temporary home, knowing what comfort it would bring to the long days ahead.

I walked around mostly like a zombie. It looked like I was functioning on the outside, but I was an empty shell. I was eating but not tasting. I was breathing but not living. I did the bare necessities. But every time I closed my eyes, I went to a lonely, helpless place.

Christmas Day came, and I was as broken as I'd ever been. Sister and Mama had gone back home for their own Christmas celebrations. I snuck off to my borrowed bedroom to call Sister, and when I heard her voice, I knelt in the corner of the room, feeling like the blood was draining from my body as I collapsed onto the floor, leaning hard into Sister's hope and strength. She tried her best to comfort me, but I wondered, *How can Christmas come to us now? How can it come when we're so far from hope? What does it mean for the incarnate God to become one of us? And why does He feel so very far from us?*

Constant prayer was the only way I stayed upright most days. I knew it would take time to recover. And in my best moments, I trusted in God's provision. Steve and I frequently gathered around the neighbors' fireplace after dinner, talking about how all of life could be distilled to two things—trusting that we are loved by God and finding tangible ways to give that love away to others. Too often we had complicated His simple plan when our hearts had fallen for anything else but Him. The clarity that tragedy brings is a gift—a gift that comes alongside the despair to enlighten and teach us. Some days we truly believed all those things. And some days we chose to wallow in the confusion that was always quick to settle over us.

In those first weeks, everything felt heavy. I didn't want to be alone, but I didn't want to be in a crowd. It was the most helpless few months I've ever experienced, and I was able to live through it only by regular Communion, regularly hearing the gospel, and the love of our family and friends, who became the hands and feet of Christ for us.

The only thing worse than the fire was the lingering whisper that this was the punishment I deserved. The accusation came when I was at my lowest, but I had learned not to argue with the Accuser, only to confess and cling to the forgiveness of Christ, which was the only defense I had.

I was learning to live in the open. I had to refuse to hide or to harden my heart just to keep my secrets safe. The fire stripped me of the need to protect myself—leaving everything raw and exposed. The only thing left standing in my life was love. I had to trust that it was enough. The angel God sent to remind me of that was Sister.

She would get me through the coming weeks and months. She would hold me and tell me it was going to be okay. She cried as much as I did, but she knew what needed to be done next. She would comfort my children through their night terrors and sit in silence with us when nothing else could be said. She would walk with us every step of the way.

I held on to her like a lifeline. Those months following the fire, I would fight for my life, struggling through anxiety and depression, trying to stay above what felt like quicksand, and she was just as steady as a rock. Sister braced me against her own body and walked through hell with me until one day, without much fanfare, we finally walked out into the light.

Life would never be the same, but I began to see with new eyes. My children were safe; I still had everything that mattered. I prayed that this gift of seeing the world differently would stay. That I would trust that Christmas had come, that Love incarnate, come in the flesh *for me*, was the gift that could never be taken away.

We walked into our church exactly eight days after the fire, the aisles flickering with a thousand tiny flames, candles everywhere lighting the way to God's Son and His humble birth. I remember the Scripture that was read that night, its comfort steeling me against despair.

For I consider that the sufferings of this present time
are not worth comparing with the glory that is to be
revealed to us. For the creation waits with eager longing
for the revealing of the sons of God. For the creation was
subjected to futility, not willingly, but because of him
who subjected it, in hope that the creation itself will be
set free from its bondage to corruption and obtain the
freedom of the glory of the children of God. For we know
that the whole creation has been groaning together in the
pains of childbirth until now. And not only the creation,
but we ourselves, who have the firstfruits of the Spirit,
groan inwardly as we wait eagerly for adoption as sons,
the redemption of our bodies. For in this hope we were
saved. Now hope that is seen is not hope. For who hopes
for what he sees? But if we hope for what we do not see,
we wait for it with patience.

Likewise the Spirit helps us in our weakness. For we
do not know what to pray for as we ought, but the Spirit
himself intercedes for us with groanings too deep for
words. And he who searches hearts knows what is the
mind of the Spirit, because the Spirit intercedes for the
saints according to the will of God. *And we know that
for those who love God all things work together for good,
for those who are called according to his purpose.*
ROMANS 8:18-28, ESV (EMPHASIS ADDED)

That final verse. I couldn't believe it was being read. Years earlier I had adopted that same verse as my own, the year I began giving my testimony at church. It was a verse I would take in like air.

The first miracle was the day food started to taste good again.
I made my infamous beef stew recipe in my brand-new soup pot,
and something about its familiar taste gave me hope.

And then Steve laughed for the first time. And then Elea finally slept through the night. Life slowly began to feel bearable. Hope sparked in the corner of my heart and slowly inched back into my life. We lived for Sunday morning Communion, and we held on to our faith like it was all we had—because it was.

It would be a long nine months of rebuilding. On October 7, Todd's birthday, we moved into our new house, rebuilt on the same spot. Steve and I stood together on the back deck beneath the orange maple tree, noticing how charred and bare some of its outer branches were, the fire having left its mark on everything in sight. We prayed that God would use this house to bless and nourish those He would bring our way. Maybe we'd even pursue adoption, as we'd talked about so many times before.

The house fire was part of God's plan to show me how much He loved me, if by no other means than by how desperately I loved my own kids.

How much more fiercely and purely He fights for my rescue; how bravely He runs to find His sheep; how completely His love and His death on the cross have transformed my suffering into hope.

This is a God who loves me with a love that I can't even fathom.

This is a God who humbled Himself and became a man, suffering all in order that I might live.

This is Christmas. This is what it means to be tethered and cherished and watched over and cared for.

This is what it means to be loved by Someone who will never, ever let go.

This is what it means to have a good, good Father.

37

WE'RE GONNA HOLD ON

FOUR YEARS AFTER the house burned down, Taylor came home from medical school to celebrate his sisters' September birthdays. Caiti would be twenty-two and Emme was turning fourteen. We'd always been a family large on birthdays and football, so it was the perfect Saturday celebration, with our Vols about to take the field against Oklahoma. Taylor came through the door bright eyed, wearing his equally bright Volunteer-orange pants.

"The team does better when I wear my orange pants," he said, grinning.

"Mom, before I get all caught up in the game and the birthday celebration, I'd like to tip my hat to you for making it through medical school with two kids. I have no idea how in the world you did that, because I am studying like crazy and always feel behind," he said, grazing on the tailgating food arrayed on the kitchen island and patting me on the back as I stirred more hot sauce into the chili.

"I don't think *anybody* can believe how much work and study it takes to get through med school," I replied. "But I do know this. You're smarter than me and less distracted, I'm certain. You're going to do great."

With that, Taylor found Steve, and the two of them got lost in a deep conversation about the Vols' offensive line and our less-than-stellar quarterback situation, while Caiti, Elea, Emme, and I put the finishing touches on the cake with our signature buttercream icing. When Sister and her daughters, Hope and Marlea, got there, we headed downstairs for a loud round of karaoke. I made them back me up on my all-time favorites—"Coal Miner's Daughter," "Mama Tried," and "Stand By Your Man." They rolled their eyes but then laughed at Sister and me making fools of ourselves.

The next weekend, the girls and I headed to Lincoln Memorial University, tucked on the edge of the Cumberland Gap, where Taylor's medical school class was having their white coat ceremony. The natural beauty of Appalachia never ceases to amaze me— I find those mountains and valleys so comforting, set against the backdrop of everything I've come to love and cherish.

We found our seats in the auditorium, trying to spot Taylor in the sea of white coats. A few weeks before, when Taylor had said to me, "I don't think the ceremony is that big of a deal, and y'all don't need to drive up here just for that," I promptly scolded him.

"Being accepted to medical school and being presented with a white coat is a very big deal. We are most certainly coming, and you are most certainly attending," I told him firmly. He was easy to convince. And now as we looked around at this early Saturday crowd, I was glad I'd forced the issue.

The white coat—or the cloak of compassion, as it is called— was the symbol of the promise he was about to make to his future patients and colleagues. A promise that he would esteem others with the highest regard, treating them with the utmost care and compassion. It was important to remember that wearing that coat actually meant something, and that wearing it was a privilege.

The families and friends of the future physicians were dressed in their Sunday finest, proud to be bearing witness to this rite of passage. Emme and Elea were sitting beside me, and Elea spotted Taylor first, the three of us tracking him by his scruffy goatee and big, bright smile. I couldn't have been prouder of him. Caiti would have loved to be there, too, but as a junior in nursing school with an exam on Monday, she had to take a pass.

The ceremony felt a little like a graduation, so it wasn't until nearly the end that we got to see him walk across the stage for his robing. I suppose I've always seen the resemblance between Daddy and Taylor, but as I watched him make his way to the front of the stage, I couldn't help but experience a full-circle moment. Taylor looked like his dad and paternal grandpa for sure, but there was something of me and Daddy in him that couldn't be denied.

He was following in my footsteps, taking his first vows as a medical student.

He was a typical firstborn—obedient, eager to please, and a pleasure to be around. I remembered those days when he went with me to class. Who could have known that twenty years later, he'd be sitting in Gross Anatomy lectures without me, with a tamed cowlick and the same wide smile, awaiting the day he'd be getting his own white coat? His charming personality was exactly like Daddy's, itself a healing balm to all who meet him.

My heart was full of love for this boy of mine whose guitar strumming and songwriting had soothed me and ministered life to me, this boy whose laugh would spread in a room like wildfire and whose love for others was inspiring. He had been God's grace to me, this child—a reminder that nothing is lost in God's economy.

Like me, he was a child who suffered through a divorce, and who, if I'm honest, still suffers for my sins. I've wrestled with guilt—so much angst about how things might have been different if I hadn't had such a stressful life when he was younger. If only I had done things differently. If only I hadn't been so young and inexperienced. If only, if only, if only.

I've ached for a second chance, for a way to be more present, more available, and more full of wisdom. I've regretted so many things and prayed that the years the locusts have eaten would be restored.

But as I sat in that crowded arena and watched Taylor receive his white coat, I couldn't help but be humbled by the fact that so much of this is out of our control. Whether we work or don't, whether we homeschool or not, whether we've had nurturing marriages or not, we walk in humility—knowing that we are dependent on God to use mostly our failures to teach us something of what it means to be a parent, to be a human being.

We fumble around in the dark, begging for wisdom, praying that our children know how much they're loved, trying to be willing to admit when we're wrong—because we so often are. Parenting and living require more faith than knowledge, more grace than rules, more trust than answers.

I found myself so proud of the man Taylor was becoming, in spite of all the things I got wrong.

All the years I spent ashamed of my past, ashamed of myself, scared to death that I was destined to repeat some cobbled-together version of my family's collective story, running to escape something that even to this day I can't rightly name, were finally coming to a close. In my heroic efforts to save myself from the likes of my people, I turned into something much worse—a woman who had forgotten that we're here to fight for others, to see our people and begin to meet their needs, leaving our own messes and failures to the only One who can answer them, namely Christ.

Taylor found us after the ceremony, laughing with two of his buddies as he made his way through the crowd.

"Hey Mom, hey girls, thank y'all for coming. This was actually pretty cool; I'm glad you made me do it," he said, smiling and leaning in to accept our smooches.

"We wouldn't have missed it for the world," I said, hugging

him and admiring his name embroidered in navy blue on his white coat. "I'm so very proud of you, Tay. You are going to make a fine doctor one day. Maybe I'll start doing to you what Papaw Jim used to do to me, and ask every time I see you whether you've made doctor yet."

"Yeah, right now that feels like forever away," he said, not knowing what I knew—that the years would come and go before he could blink his eyes and that he would wish he could freeze time and somehow make these moments stand still.

I looked at Taylor and I saw Daddy, evidence to me of how God is always redeeming every little thing.

38

FIRE AWAY

SIX MONTHS LATER, when the buds on the maple trees were just beginning to form, I left the house with several errands to do. The list I was holding reminded me that I needed to make stops at Sam's Club, Target, and Trader Joe's to get things like tomatoes and limes and butter—all good things to be buying on an ordinary weekday. An hour later, the only things I was gathering were deep breaths and enough strength to keep driving. My car felt like it was steering itself.

It must have been the music I was listening to that stripped away the layers of my respectable suburban life, making me a girl who desperately needed only one thing—her daddy. In the time it took for me to reach the interstate from my lake house, I lost hold of the thing that kept me buoyed up most days. Every time I so much as tilted my head downward to get a clear view of the blurring yellow line on the road, tears ran down my cheeks. I took mad swipes at them to try to catch them before they fell.

I drove with what felt like a fist to my throat, and forty-five minutes later, before I knew how to stop myself, I was kneeling at Mount Olive Cemetery, brushing leaves off Daddy's marker so the full inscription could be read—*James Hugh Rudder (Jim), Beloved Brother and Daddy*. The word *Daddy* was always littered with dirt and pine needles. There I sat, alone in a graveyard in the middle of an already colorless day, bewildered by how quickly the bottom falls out of everything when I become lonesome for him. I always try to remind myself that it isn't necessary anymore.

There's no sense in this. You are not the little girl from the trailer waiting on her daddy to get sober anymore. It's over. Move on. Let go. Enjoy your life with your healthy, wonderful children and your hardworking, supportive husband who loves you. You have everything. You're safe now. Everything is finally okay. Why do you always end up here?

But no amount of self-talk about my socioeconomic status or my apparent health and vitality or even my stout faith could shut the door to the ghosts in my head that were always tearing through the thin veil of my arguably charmed life. Kneeling by Daddy's grave, I could almost feel his five o'clock shadow tickling the edge of my face. Or maybe it was just the wind. I turned around to make sure.

Of course, he wasn't there. I knew that, but this place was where I held his memory closest. The cemetery was less than a mile from nearly every place he had taken me as a child and only a few minutes from Mamaw's trailer. The memory of that place was always catching up with me, no matter how far I had come in life. The grave hadn't been able to right everything, but in our family's economy I was Daddy's person and he was mine, and seventeen years of separation by death hadn't really changed that.

I guess it was only fitting that I'd be the one to keep him company here, too, although I suspect he'd been just as lonely in life. What a burden he must have carried in his last days—sober yet dying from the worst kind of cancer, slowly smothering to death as his lungs filled with fluid and his heart (I could only guess) with regret. It seemed to me that our relationships with those gone on before us don't really end; they just change over the years. Apparently I had decided it was still my job to make sure Daddy was okay, to ease the hurt for him, to tell him that despite everything, he gave me the one thing I needed—a father who loved me and who wanted me by his side.

Since his death, I've seen him a thousand times—in the disheveled Cajun selling spicy barbecue out of a school bus lit up like a Christmas tree, telling jokes while he sloshes his wares into Styrofoam containers; or in eyes of the mechanic changing the tire on my car, cigarette hanging from his lips, razzing me about my bad curb checking habit; or in the raspy voice of the toothless farmer demonstrating with great care how to pick the juiciest Grainger County tomatoes out of his worn-out bushel basket; or nearest, in the faces and laughter of all my children.

The sun peeked out and warmed my face, and I lay prone on the dry grass. Maybe fathers are that thing that you're floating on through life, providing a safe place for you, but not all that noticeable until they aren't there. Daddy was always more like a piece of driftwood—endlessly interesting but not very dependable, which may have been why it seemed like I was always treading water.

That is, except for that one night so many years ago, still so fresh in my memory.

When I closed my eyes, I was seventeen years old again, waiting to find out who'd be chosen homecoming queen, but more importantly, waiting for Daddy to show up. I could almost feel the October chill from 1987 on my neck . . .

"This year's homecoming queen is . . . Edie Rudder!"

I was shocked when they called my name.

But that wasn't what mattered the most to me that night.

Daddy showed up, teeth in, monkey suit, and all.

I recalled his words to me, and they made me laugh all over again.

"Aw, they was runnin' a special—buy a set o' teeth and get a monkey suit free."

My daddy showed up because he loved me.

I knew it then, and I realized I had always known it.

I wish he was here now, I thought. But all I had of him was this gravestone.

The wind picked up, swirling last fall's leaves in a frenzy across the cemetery. My eyes followed their dance until the steeple of Mount Olive Church came in full view. Mount Olive—no doubt named after the Mount of Olives in Jerusalem. I zipped up my jacket, cinching it close to my neck, my mind turning that name over and over until it came back to me. The Mount of Olives was the hill where Jesus was both betrayed and transfigured according to a podcast I heard a few months before, and I immediately thought of Daddy.

Everywhere I turned in that cemetery, I saw nothing but dull, grayish-brown hues. Spring was still a lifetime away, the dogwood branches bare and swaying in angry fits—their tightfisted buds not yet giving way to hope. Maybe Christ could turn this betrayal, this winter I felt inside, into some sort of transfiguration.

I prayed and begged God for mercy, for forgiveness, for a hinging and a tethering that would join me forever to something strong and sure—the things He has so freely given at His table, in His Word, and in the cleansing waters of baptism.

I looked down at my phone and realized two hours had passed. The wind was finally settling into a warm breeze, the sun staking its claim even over the dead. Gathering my things, I made the sign of the cross over my heart and walked back to my car, more sure than ever before that I was Daddy's beloved daughter and a recipient of my Father's grand and gracious redemption.

I was finally the girl whose Daddy had come for her.

AFTERWORD

My NEXT VISIT to Mount Olive Cemetery would be in early December of 2014 for the burial of my cousin Sonny. The northwest winds were blowing a hard rain onto the tent sheltering the grave site. None of us had expected Sonny to live as long as he did, given the fact that not long after he was released from prison, he was diagnosed HIV positive. He'd never managed to wrestle his demons to the ground, so I could only imagine that as hard as it was to lose their brother, my cousins who'd cared for him and worried over him all those years surely felt a little relief, knowing that his battles were finally over.

Straining to see through the sheets of water pouring onto my windshield, I made the slow and stressful drive to Knoxville to pick up Uncle George, Aunt Glenda, and Aunt Darlene for the graveside service. Once we arrived at the hillside where the family was gathered, I heaved Aunt Darlene's wheelchair from the back of my SUV, helped her into it, and sludged it up a steep incline toward the casket. The flimsy umbrella that Uncle George was trying to hold over us did nothing to keep us from getting drenched. I saw Jim Bob and Shirley huddled under the tent with my cousins Tim and Sis, Jim Bob's grin a mile wide when he saw us.

"Hello, Sister! I love you, you know it?" he said, patting me on the back and helping me get Darlene situated. "Where's Gina Hope?"

"She's in Haiti this week on a missions trip, visiting the orphanage her church sponsors," I said, hugging him tight and telling him how much I'd missed him.

Shirley came and hugged me too and filled me in on how all her kids were doing, and then I saw Jeff, Jamie's brother. He was a sight for sore eyes in a group of people that felt almost more like strangers than family. I had tried so hard to escape the family curse, but seeing these cousins reminded me that deep down, I was still the same Rudder girl I had always been.

It was a small group that had gathered, and without Sister or Jamie there, I felt a little lost. Tim, Sonny's brother, had elected not to have a preacher at the graveside, instead asking Jim Bob to say a few words and sing. There was no funeral service, no fanfare, and no family potluck. Just pure love that emanated from Daddy's only son as he proclaimed, "Jesus loves Sonny and He loves us all."

As I left, I made brief eye contact with the man who had stolen my innocence so many years ago, and I felt pity for him more than anything else, my shame and guilt all but gone. Making our way down the hill, Jim Bob and I paused at Daddy's gravestone, tears mingling with the rain on both of our faces. Daddy's legacy endured stronger than ever in the hearts of his children—one off in Haiti serving fatherless children and the other two of us here, mourning with those who mourned. It seemed we'd all somehow managed, despite our own demons, to choose love above all else.

Time marched on and life returned to normal at home. I was in the kitchen one day when Steve called to ask if we could help out Addie, one of his elderly patients, by taking care of her two-year-old great-grandson for the weekend. Even though it was the first time I had met him, I knew Thomas well because Steve had been texting me photos of him ever since Thomas was six weeks old. His parents had both been incarcerated for drugs, and there was no one else in the family who could take care of him except Addie. She had been doing that since he was a few days old. But her health was beginning to fail, and she loved Thomas too much to imagine him going back into the state's custody, so Steve and I agreed to take him for the weekend.

I had kept his photos on my phone since I'd received the first one two years earlier. Steve and I talked about him all the time. I remember the day Steve told me Thomas was sitting up, then walking, then starting to talk. I felt like I was watching him grow up before my very eyes. There had always been something so special about him for us, in ways that are hard to explain.

When Addie asked for our help, it was an easy yes.

This is what has always been so incredible about the man I share my life with. This is what he says yes to—not golfing at the country club on a Saturday afternoon or taking long lunches with pharmaceutical reps at work or even seeking out extravagant vacations in the Caribbean, not that there's anything wrong with any of those choices. But his yes to Thomas was immediate and complete. And I knew it.

The next day I went to Knoxville and got everything I thought we'd need to take care of a two-year-old for the weekend. Toy trucks, diapers, footed pajamas, a few clothes, sippy cups, and books. Lots of books. What else was I missing? It'd been so long, I wasn't even sure.

All day I worried. I was so scared. Scared he would miss his surrogate mama, scared he wouldn't sleep, scared we wouldn't bond or that we'd bond too much, making the Sunday separation a heartbreak. I was right about one thing—a year together hasn't made the Sunday separation any easier.

Over these past months, God has increased our love for the rambunctious little gift from heaven named Thomas. A few months after we started taking him on weekends, Addie made us joint legal guardians with her and has arranged for us to be his parents when she's no longer able to care for him.

Thomas is my weekend warrior. He jumps on the couch, pees in my shower, announces his arrival every Friday by throwing all the fresh fruit out of the basket on the kitchen island, and makes me walk up and down the stairs 10,000 times—and I wouldn't have it any other way.

That little boy is as much ours as any person can be. He has a room in our house and free rein of everything. When he refers to the dogs, he calls them *his dogs* and he does the same with the boat, the four wheeler, all Steve's tools, and everything else in our house. It's all his. Rightfully so.

He sits on my lap every Sunday at church, wallering (Appalachian for wallowing) me plumb to death and slowly learning what it means to be loved by such a good Father.

Thomas came into our lives when I was rewriting this book for the third time—my book about fatherlessness. God's timing was not lost on me, and I marvel at how gracious He is when He brings into our lives people He knows we need.

Every time I see Thomas's face, a quote from Frederick Buechner goes through my mind: "Compassion is the sometimes fatal capacity for feeling what it is like to live inside somebody else's skin. It's the knowledge that there can never really be any peace and joy for me until there is peace and joy finally for you too."[5]

Maybe that's it.

Maybe that's why the ache won't stop.

Maybe it was never supposed to.

Maybe it wrings us out and wears us down until we finally see the point of it all—that we have been snatched out of the fire of our brokenness in order to serve and love and bless the dear ones God has placed right in front of our eyes, the ones who need our very meager gifts and offerings the most—the fatherless, the misfits, the prostitutes, the jailbirds, and all those whose despair has rendered them hopeless.

May the Friend of sinners, the Father to the fatherless, the Fourth Man in the fire, and the Finder of lost sons and daughters be our constant joy and peace. He who became one of us to experience the depth of our struggle is right there in the dirty midst of it all—making all things new and raising what's dead to new life.

ACKNOWLEDGMENTS

For my husband, Stevie—the one my soul loves, the one who rescued me from myself, and most importantly, the one who brought me to the table for my first Communion. It will always be my favorite place to go with you. Thank you for the years of faithful and tireless provision for our family, and for bringing us Thomas. I've never met anyone like you. You are my King David—a lover, a fighter, a protector of the weak, a father to the fatherless, a man after God's own heart.

For Mama—For giving birth to me in the January cold and bundling me up on a Friday night for my first homecoming; for carrying me through hell and back; for working all the jobs; for sacrificing everything a woman can; for never complaining; for loving me, believing in me, and for working harder than anyone I've ever known—I can never repay you. You laid down your life with quiet courage so that I might someday stand tall and find my voice. This is how I learned to be a woman. This is how I learned what it means to empty myself. You were first light for me. You made my every homecoming possible. Your love plays a melody in my heart.

For my sister, Gina—Nobody has walked with me through this fire like you have. Nobody else knows what our hearts know and nobody shares the same broken heart. Nobody else could have been my soul sister but you, and I thank God every day that He gave you to me. You have been the one constant in the chaos, the anchor in the storm, the fierce protector of my always-bleeding heart. You have guarded this family with your life and fought hard to see every silver lining. You are pure light, a dazzling reflection of our Father's love.

For my sister-cousin, Jamie—You're definitely the smartest one of us all, and the funniest, which seems slightly unfair, if you ask me. Thank you for making me laugh more than any other person in my life—a much-needed ministry of healing to those of us who know what it's like to live with darkness. Thank you for enduring hours upon endless hours of questions about this book—about who was there and who was drunk and who went to jail and who cussed out who, and what we were wearing, all with savant-like clarity. Thank you for remembering every good song title and every perfect one-liner and for pointing out all the inappropriate times I broke into sobs. You have been my best friend, my therapist, my sister, my karaoke partner, my pop culture teacher, and my personal stylist. It still burns me up that you got the skinny genes and Mamaw's thick head of hair. But I forgive you because you told me about Sugarlips tank tops and the George Jones memoir. I can't imagine life without you. You have been such a gift.

For Taylor, Caiti, Emme, and Elea—I couldn't have known at the start how being your mama would wreck me and change me and give me life. You are the reason for everything good that God has done in me. Your kindness and grace to me have steadied me in ways you'll never know. You are everything I could have asked for and beyond my wildest dreams. I am so very blessed by your love.

For Aunt Glenda—You were Daddy's best friend and always like a second mama to me. I can hardly stand it when you tear up talking about him. I can tell you miss him as much as I do. You are more precious than you know and one of the funniest people I've ever known. I pray you'll see beyond the hard parts here and find that this book comes from a heart of love—the one thing you and Daddy gave me in spades. There will never be anyone like you, and I'll never tire of listening to your stories or hearing you say that I'm just like my daddy. Thank you for carrying the family through the hardest times and especially for being by Daddy's side as he crossed over Jordan. You're an icon to me—the last remnant of an age gone by. I love you forever.

For Jessica, Sarah, Bonne, and Cindy—If there ever was a difficult job in publishing, you had it. Thank you for helping me finally tell this story—for all the hours of tender guidance and patient listening, for wiping the tears and putting the chapters in order and asking the hard questions and reminding me that I could do this thing, which always seemed impossible to me at the time. I'll never be able to repay you for this gift. This writing has birthed so many good things in my heart and has changed me forever, thanks to you. You've been my sisters, my midwives—cheering and coaching and cleaning up all the messes so that I could make this offering to the world. I'm so indebted to you for that, and I hold you close to my heart.

For my sister friends—the women who gave me courage to share my story by going first, by offering advice, help, love, the occasional kick in the pants along the way. You've written and spoken some of the most challenging and comforting words I've ever read or heard, and I love you and thank you for shining His light—Ruth Soukup, Myquillyn Smith, Melanie Shankle, Sophie Hudson, Denise Voccola, Emily Freeman, Amy Greene, Paige Knudsen, Jeannie Jett, Susan Ward, and the women of my hometown bookclub.

For the men in my life—Steve Wadsworth, Todd Cook, Mark Williams, Jeff Finley, Gary Woodby, Steve Moser, David Cross, Eddie Wadsworth, Bill Riden, Jim Bob Rudder, and all the men who stood in for Daddy when he wasn't able to be there for us. You can't know the gratitude I hold in my heart for you. You have been a father to the fatherless, a rare and precious gift. May God bless you richly.

For my Life{in}grace family—I thought of you the whole time I wrote this book. I pray it gives you a deep and abiding peace in a Savior that never fails. Thank you for eight of the best years of my life, for helping me find my voice, for thousands of life-giving messages, and for getting me through some of the hardest seasons. I love you and can't imagine trying to do this without you. You're like sisters to me.

DISCUSSION GUIDE

1. The pages of *All the Pretty Things* are filled, mainly, with the complicated story of Edie and her daddy. What does it mean to be a father? Who has fathered you most throughout your life?

2. Edie's childhood home in Appalachia plays a key role in her life, almost as if it is another character in her story. Where do you feel deeply rooted? Are there ways that you have been shaped by where you were raised?

3. Edie treasures good memories—though few and far between—of growing up with her daddy, "dancing one off" on the side of the road and making him bologna sandwiches served with a glass of buttermilk. What are some of your favorite childhood moments with your parents?

4. When Edie cut her foot and went to the emergency room, it was quite a dramatic experience for a little girl. But later it became one of her favorite memories and even impacted what she would choose to do when she grew up. In your own life, what experiences have impacted the purpose God has called you to?

5. Hearing someone criticize us, whether a teacher or peer or even a parent, can cause different reactions. Edie used these comments to fuel her quest to prove her family and friends wrong. Has someone ever made comments about you and

your abilities that deeply impacted you? How did you react and what did you do?

6. When Daddy met Shirley, Edie witnessed a glimpse of the amazing transformation that faith can have on a person. Where have you seen this redemptive power in your own life?

7. Though Daddy's faith transformation ended up impacting his life only temporarily, it planted a permanent seed in Edie's life—one that would take root and guide her through her future. What are some ways we can plant seeds of faith in the people around us?

8. Against all odds, Edie finds Jesus, escapes her Appalachian childhood, and "makes doctor." She excels in her career, gets married, and has two beautiful children—but then she burns it all down, destroying everything she has gained. If you feel comfortable doing so, share an experience in which you finally achieved all your greatest dreams . . . then self-destructed. What did God teach you in this season?

9. For Edie, Daddy was "her person"—it was her responsibility to take care of him, making sure he was looked after. Yet, the relationship feels uneven, and Edie struggles to make sense of the way Daddy abandons her and fails to show up when she needs him. What is your relationship with your parents? How has it shaped the way you interact with your loved ones?

10. Tragically, Edie's home as an adult burns down, echoing the trauma of her past. How do we reconcile God's goodness and the tragedies of our life? In what ways do you see beauty in the ashes of your experiences?

11. Edie describes *All the Pretty Things* as "the story of my homecoming . . . my cliff jump." How can we use our past—the dark and lonely parts as well as the joyous and courageous—to bring glory to our true Father?

NOTES

1. C. S. Lewis, *Mere Christianity* (New York: Macmillan Publishing Company, 1952), 190.
2. M. F. K. Fisher, *The Art of Eating* (Hoboken, New Jersey: Wiley Publishing, 1937, 2004), 247.
3. See 1 Corinthians 11:23-25.
4. See Job 1:21.
5. Frederick Buechner, "Spelling Out the Truth," *Third Way* 17, no. 5 (June 1994): 21.

ABOUT THE AUTHOR

EDIE WADSWORTH is a speaker, writer, and blogger who has been featured in various print and online media (including *Better Homes and Gardens* in 2013 on the topic of her family's home rebuild after a fire). After overcoming her difficult upbringing to become a successful medical doctor, Edie left her practice to raise her family and pursue her love for writing. Her passion is to love her people well and to see women embrace the full measure of their life's passion and purpose. She has shared her story at conferences and churches around the country. Edie is a Compassion International blogger who traveled to Nicaragua in 2013. She blogs at lifeingraceblog.com on a variety of topics that center themselves on home—including vocation, hospitality, faith, parenting, cooking, and life in the Appalachian South.